THE MYSTERIES OF

AN INVESTIGATION OF THE MOST FASCINATING BOOK IN HISTORY

THE APOCALYPSE

A BOOK BY JEAN-MARC THOBOIS AND CHRISTOPHE HANAUER

Forefront
BOOKS

The Mysteries of the Apocalypse
An Investigation of the Most Fascinating Book in History

© 2022 Jean-Marc Thobois and Christophe Hanauer

Previously published by EMETH-Editions (2020) as *Les Mysteres de L'Apocalypse: Une Enquete Sur le Plus Fascinant de L'Histoire.*

Published by Forefront Books.

ISBN: 978-163763-051-8
ISBN: 978-163763-052-5 (e-Book)

CONTENTS

Authors' Notes 6

Notice to the Reader 11

Foreword 12

GENERAL COMMENTARY
ON THE END TIMES

Genesis: The Book of Last Things 15

Between Heaven and Earth 19

The Struggle between the Messiah and the Serpent 29

The Apocalypses 31

Evidence of Borrowing 37

Interpretive Approaches to the Book of Revelation 41

The Book of Daniel 43

The Four Empires of Daniel's Visions 47

The Kingdom of God 57

Babylon and Jerusalem 63

The Sign of the End of Time 69

The Great Apostasy 75

The Antichrist 81

The Mystery of the Two Beasts 87

The Heavenly Tribunal 95

The Synagogue and the Cult of Heaven 97

The Second Exodus 101

September 11, 2001 107

The Son of Man 111

The Final War of Gog and Magog 113

The Resurrection of the Dead 121

The Rapture of the Church 129

From Big Data to Big Brother 135

The Millennium 141

From the Millennium to the Eternal State 147

The Eternal State 151

A New Creation 155

COMMENTARY ON PATMOS
AND THE SEVEN CHURCHES OF REVELATION

Patmos 161
   Geography 161
   History 163
   Archaeology and John's Sojourn on Patmos 164

Ephesus 169
   Geography 169
   History 170
   Archaeology 171
   Commentary on the Biblical Text 176

Smyrna 181
   Geography 181
   History 181
   Commentary on the Biblical Text 184

Pergamon......................................193

    Geography....................................194

    History......................................196

    Commentary on the Biblical Text...............198

Thyatira......................................209

    Geography and History........................209

    Archaeology..................................210

    Commentary on the Biblical Text...............210

Sardis..217

    Geography and History........................217

    Commentary on the Biblical Text...............220

Philadelphia..................................227

    History......................................228

    Commentary on the Biblical Text...............229

Ladoicea......................................235

    History......................................235

    Commentary on the Biblical Text...............237

Conclusion....................................247

Images..257

Bibliography..................................263

Notes...267

AUTHORS' NOTES

I had already been cultivating an interest in theological and spiritual matters for some time when in 2011, I happened to purchase several recordings by a lecturer who was described as an Hebraist of rare quality. As I listened to the first talk about the theme of the end times, I immediately knew I had stumbled onto a work of exceptional importance for the comprehension of Christianity and its founding texts. The approach of Jean-Marc Thobois, the speaker, was quite original, even unique.

Although spiritual revelation can never be more than partial due to our limited perception of heavenly realities, I had just come face-to-face with a system of thought that, in its universality, would challenge my vision of the world. For the first time in my life, I contemplated with wonder a clearly described and comprehensive presentation of the deepest mysteries that inhabit the hearts of men. The classic foundations of theology, far from being undermined, were boldly and precisely illuminated to highlight and give color to these spiritual depths. It would take several years of studying the work—masterful in vastness and complexity—for me to grasp its great coherence and incomparable value. (Many of these lectures are available from the association Keren Israël.)

The theological approach it proposes is, in my view, truly revolutionary in several respects and offers a coherent vision of all Scripture, Old and New Testament alike. Its great originality lies in enriching "classic" theology with the original contribution of Jewish thought. For us in the West, it can be difficult to appreciate what Christianity is—namely, a Jewish religion—and that Hebraic thought is therefore its very soul and essence. The Bible is a Jewish book. The text was written by Jews and principally for Jews.

Over the years, however, the culture of our pagan-European civilization has mixed with the Christian tradition. The biblical message has thus reached our generations in a somewhat modified form, filtered and de-Judaized by 2,000 years of church history and cultural adaptation. We discover Christianity *a posteriori*, downstream from history. The names of figures in the New Testament are a perfect illustration: the apostle Yochanan has become John, Ya'akov has been turned into James, Kefa Bar-Jonah has been renamed Peter, and so forth.

Jean-Marc Thobois was one of the Francophone pioneers who, thanks to his erudition, had the ability to place the Bible back in its original archaeological, cultural, historical, and linguistic context. This man who, even at the end of his life, never ceased asking his fellow human beings, "What time is it on God's clock?" suddenly passed through death's door in March 2020 in the midst of a host of projects and the outset of the global COVID-19 pandemic. His final series of lectures dealt with "New Prophecies on the End Times in the Book of Genesis," a subject we discuss in the opening chapters of this book.

The loss of such a distinguished exegete is immeasurable and also raises the question of the role of this pandemic in the eschatological process. Some, indeed, have described this epidemic as "apocalyptic."

Jean-Marc Thobois dedicated his life to rediscovering the Jewish roots of the Christian faith, enabling us to recover the Bible's message in its original Hebrew, increasing the precision of its revelation and the quality of its original flavor, smell, and color. As in the restoration of an Old Master painting, the image that emerges is refreshed, and we can better appreciate what its creator desired to communicate.

The fact is that the New Testament is built entirely on Hebrew scriptural foundations, and this is particularly true for the exceedingly mysterious and fascinating book that concludes the Bible—the book of Revelation. Indeed, the church fathers thought it so markedly Jewish that they nearly excluded it from the biblical canon! It contains the visions revealed to the apostle John by the resurrected, glorified Messiah, who announces the events of the end times to warn humanity of the dangers to come and to prepare themselves by changing their ways by repenting.

This text contains more than five hundred citations of or allusions to the Jewish Bible, or Tanakh, and is perfectly consistent with the pronouncements of the Jewish prophets Ezekiel, Isaiah, Daniel, and even Zechariah.

The study of this enigmatic and captivating text convinced us of the merits of creating a documentary series on the theme: *Les 7 Églises de l'Apocalypse*, produced by Millenium-Production with Ze Watchers and directed by Seven Production's Étienne Magnin.

This thrilling film project led our investigation to Greece, Turkey, and around Western Europe, often in the company of Irène and Jean-Marc Thobois or the American professor Mark Wilson, our technical experts for the film's theological and archaeological questions. This book is largely a reflection of Jean-Marc Thobois's lectures and a slight reworking of the preparatory notes for the documentary.

This work is designed to flesh out the topics dealt with in the documentary, which could only present its subject matter in summary fashion. The documentary and this book are therefore complementary. The second part of the book, more specifically, is dedicated to a commentary on the seven letters to the seven churches of chapters 1–3 of Revelation and owes a great deal to the reflections of Swiss theologian Philippe Decorvet in *Reprocher pour rapprocher*, published by Emmaüs.

Our aim is to share with you this extraordinary investigation of over three years that ultimately became a genuine quest for meaning, leading us to reflect on our time in this twenty-first century, its profound and sometimes disturbing transformations, the geopolitical scenario, and the prophecies of the end times.

In essence, we concluded that the end times described in the Bible not only point to a crisis but, above all, to a God attempting to reveal himself by his Word and his Spirit in the reality of men, in anticipation of a cosmic, eternal goal to which man is urged. And so we travel in equilibrium on the river of time, flowing through human history between the "past" and the "still to come" of God's biblical promises. We hope that what little we have glimpsed of these vast mysteries encourages you to take an interest in the message of he who promised:

I am coming soon *(Revelation 3:11; 22:7; 12; 20)*

and

I am making all things new! *(Revelation 21:5)*

Not only tomorrow, but today as well.

CHRISTOPHE HANAUER

The book of Revelation is a circular letter sent by the apostle John to the seven churches of Asia for which he was responsible. Asia here refers to Asia Minor, or roughly modern Turkey. During our journey to that country in 2017, our hosts made it clear that Turkey really is the second "Holy Land" after Israel. It was the crucial terrain for the apostolate of Paul and his missionary team, as we read in the book of Acts. In this vast country Paul founded numerous churches, which quickly flourished, and Asia Minor, which the Romans had divided into several provinces, became a bastion of early Christianity.

But when we read the letters to the seven churches, we realize that the age of spiritual splendor of these communities was already on the wane, and with the exception of Smyrna and Philadelphia, they are all rebuked by the Lord.

Must we believe these churches paid no heed to these divine warnings? All that remains of these once-flourishing churches are ruins. Turkey has become a bastion of an aggressive, hegemonic Islamism, as demonstrated by the emergence of numerous mosques in even the smallest villages.

The seven churches were certainly each distinctive communities, with their particular joys, sorrows, challenges, and problems, to which the apostle alludes but with which we are not entirely familiar. In these churches it is not possible, therefore, to see this period of ecclesiastical history as certain people would like to. Nevertheless, the number seven is a number of plenitude, which in the coded language of Revelation, means that in addition to these seven communities, the letter is in fact addressed to the church of all times and all places, and particularly to the church of the end.

In our view, the near-total disappearance of these churches in Asia (Turkey) is a warning of what could happen to the church if it succumbs to the same errors and compromises, just as the communities to which the letter was originally addressed did.

The Apocalypse of John is an obscure book. Its very name says as much: *Apocalupsis* means "unveiling." It belongs to a particular type of Jewish literature: Sod ("mystery, secret"). The book reveals itself little by little, as evidenced by the breaking of the seals beginning in chapter 5. The full extent of the mystery of the Messiah will not be completely revealed until the very last moments. It is futile, therefore, to try to plumb all its mysteries. God's secret must be respected, as specified in the other canonical Apocalypse, the book of Daniel. Only at the end of time will knowledge grow and wise men understand.

Nevertheless, because we are now in the end times, God raises a part of the veil, and we can achieve a degree of insight into this mysterious book.

Bringing this understanding to light is the aim of this work, though its authors do not claim to offer a final, complete explanation of such a difficult text. But if this book can contribute to heightening the zeal of some of its readers, leading them to a renewed vigilance in the wait for the last things, it will have fully achieved its goal.

JEAN-MARC THOBOIS
1944–2020

NOTICE TO THE READER

It is important to clarify that this book does not claim to impose a definitive doctrine. Instead, it presents reflections and points of view that to us seem worthy of interest, given the state of our understanding of things in the twenty-first century. We strongly encourage readers to conduct their own research and form their own opinions on the topics discussed here. It should also be said that we feel it is impossible to establish a precise chronology, much less a detailed calendar, of the end times. Due to an excessively rigid interpretation of biblical prophecies, after all, certain orthodox Jews during the Second World War are said to have refused to believe in the coming drama of the Holocaust that would unfold in Europe in the 1930s and 1940s.

It behooves us, therefore, to be quite flexible vis-à-vis the prophetic interpretation of historical events. Up to the present, after all, all attempts to predict the date of the end of the world have systematically failed. We also ask for the gentleness of readers with different theological viewpoints, just as we respect those that differ from our own. These differences are a source of richness that is far more important than the futile reasons for disagreement. We judge neither the deeds of the great historical churches presented in this book, nor the people of the Muslim faith whom we love and call to dialogue, though we do denounce the politicization and, even more so, the belligerence of a certain type of Islam.

No Christian denomination is perfect or devoid of error, as the history of Christianity demonstrates. Let us recall Paul's warning to the Romans:

> Therefore you are without excuse, whoever you are, when you judge someone else. For on whatever grounds you judge another, you condemn yourself, because you who judge practice the same things. *(Romans 2:1)*

Lucidity does not prevent love. To the contrary, it demands that we find the courage to love. So it is important, for those who take the words,

> I am coming soon

seriously, to be vigilant and ready, for there is no precise scenario for the end times, as Jesus himself desired it. We must therefore "be prepared at all times," because according to the Bible,

> [He] will come in the same way as a thief in the night. *(1 Thessalonians 5:2)*

FOREWORD

In the language of the Bible, a mystery is a truth contained in Scripture that man, due to his limited intelligence, is incapable of discovering on his own. It is a supernatural revelation that only God can grant.

The biblical texts also tell us that there is a hidden design to human history, albeit one that is destined to be only partially communicated, as the prophet Amos states:

> Certainly the sovereign Lord does nothing without first revealing his plan to his servants the prophets. *(Amos 3:7)*

Michel Renevier, whose influence in Swiss Romandie had such an impact on his generation, told me once that new understandings of the book of Revelation appear every ten or fifteen years, and hence the discovery of its meaning is continually evolving. The Apocalypse and eschatology (the study of the end times of man and the world) are subjects so complex that new, additional insights continue to shed light on this profound mystery. But the key verse in the book of Revelation can be found in chapter 21, verse 5:

> I am making all things new.

More than any other book in the New Testament, the Apocalypse of John contains a host of references to our "Old Testament," meaning Scripture and, more precisely, the Jewish Tanakh. Revelation is certainly the most Jewish book in the New Testament, so much so that Christianity nearly excluded the text from the biblical canon due to the many Hebraic references that were quite familiar to the church fathers. Today these references have been smoothed over by time, culture, and translations to the point that the text's Hebraic heritage passes almost unobserved for a Christianity severed from its Jewish roots.

The first key to understanding the New Testament is to refer continuously back to the Old Testament—to the Scriptures that were the Bible for Jesus, Paul, and John. To understand the New Testament, we must ask ourselves how the people of ancient Israel would have understood and interpreted the teachings of Jesus and the apostles in their own time. Otherwise we are limited by our own uncertain interpretations—those of modern-day Westerners estranged from their own roots and, consequently, forced to reinvent in a profoundly different cultural framework. This interpretive key is crucial to deciphering the text's meaning and grasping its allusions and symbolism.

The second key to a more precise comprehension of the text is taking into account the historical and political context of the age in which the author lived. In the first century AD, the Roman Empire was predominant and, at times, persecuted the disciples of Jesus Christ with extreme violence.

Finally, the third key is to view the entire book of Revelation as a sort of synthesis, a summary of the eschatological prophecies present throughout the Bible—to the point of sometimes nearly paraphrasing previous scriptural passages.

Neglecting these three main interpretive keys increases the risk of losing an overall vision of the text, of getting lost in the maze of symbolic images or, worse still, of settling for a numerological interpretation and a series of proclamations of the date of the end of the world, which only harm the book's true message when the announced events do not occur.

A final risk lies in contentious and sterile theological debates which, as history shows, can lead to sectarian doctrines and divisions and conflict among the communities of the faithful, with each group convinced that it alone is the bearer of truth. Such interpretations produce the opposite effect of the goal the author envisioned: to inspire joy and unity in the faith among believers by announcing good tidings.

One is naturally inclined to approach this subject with great respect and humility; few texts, indeed, have had a greater impact on human history. The peculiarity of our Cartesian West is precisely the desire to understand and explain all things, but the author of Revelation intentionally left ample room for hidden mystery.

Consequently, questions such as the chronology of the final events, dates, the exact duration of time, the identity of the Antichrist, and the interpretation of numbers—such as the famous 666—are shrouded in mystery, destined to remain concealed until their fulfillment in history.

The author did not attempt to write a book of predictions, but rather, a sermon that, like a personal and civilizational mirror, invites us to examine ourselves bravely in the face of the absolute gaze of God, who knows all his creatures and calls upon them, for their own good, to change their lives before it's too late. This same God tells man to purify and sanctify himself in anticipation of a personal encounter of which he is forewarned:

> … prepare to meet your God. *(Amos 4:12)*

Heeding this call and readying ourselves transforms the cataclysmic perception of God's wrathful judgment into good news: that of a people who have been singled out, called to make ready, like a loving bride-to-be who rejoices at the idea of meeting her beloved and longingly awaits the liberation this encounter promises.

Although our image of the Apocalypse is often "popular for the wrong reasons," in the Bible it is a piece of good news comparable to a letter of love and great hope for the faithful Church, a bride-to-be sighing with the Spirit of the Living God, saying:

> Come! *(Revelation 22:17)*

The Messiah, the text's protagonist, is simultaneously God, priest, and a warrior lord who will come to save his bride-to-be and destroy the wicked.

How, then, do we position ourselves in the face of such irrevocable proclamations? Believers who take this text seriously can ultimately do only one of two things: try to escape history or try to change history—our collective history, certainly, but above all, our own personal history.

CHRISTOPHE HANAUER

General Commentary on the End Times

GENESIS: THE BOOK OF LAST THINGS

We read in the first chapter of Genesis:

> In the beginning God created the heavens and the earth. *(Genesis 1:1)*

One of the greatest biblical scholars, Professor Israel Eldad, argues that this is the most important verse in the whole Bible because it contains the entire essence of divine revelation. We should also clarify that in Hebrew the Bible begins with the letter Bet, the second letter of the alphabet that corresponds to the numerical value "two" (according to Jewish numerology).

This poses a question that, to us in the West, might appear incongruous: "Why is the first letter of the Torah the second letter of the alphabet, rather than the first?" The letter Bet provides a clue.

In the beginning, God created two realities: heaven and earth, two different and complementary worlds. Bet, the second letter of the Hebrew alphabet, is designed like a square open on its left side, in the direction of Hebrew writing, symbolizing the impossibility of turning back time that flows like a river in just one direction, from the past toward the future.

According to the Bible, there is a purpose to the history of man. The word *bereshit* also means "for a goal, for a purpose." There is thus a divine goal for humanity. Paul sums up this aim when he states:

> . . . for all things in heaven and on earth were created by him—all things, whether visible or invisible . . . were created through him and for him. *(Colossians 1:16)*

Jesus Christ, the Messiah, is the aim of the Torah, this Torah that is like a teacher leading humankind toward this goal, this purpose, and allowing us to discover it.

> This is the record of the family line of Adam. *(Genesis 5:1)*

The book of Genesis is the book of the history of humanity. The Bible teaches us that the choices we make impact our future beyond our own existence and for all eternity, for when

the silver cord is removed *(Ecclesiastes 12:6)*

then

the life's breath returns to God who gave it. *(Ecclesiastes 12.7)*

Each man is thus the author of a unique personal history, and the sum of these individual histories becomes the history of humanity.

It's no secret that the book of Genesis is the book of beginnings. But according to an ancient rabbinical tradition, it is also the book of last things. The postulate of this rabbinical exegesis is the following: the book of Genesis is a prophetic book for the history of the patriarchs and constitutes a prophecy for their descendants and for the end times.

The first chapter of Genesis contains an important passage that, according to the rabbis, holds a prophecy concerning the entire history of humanity:

Now the earth was without shape [*tohou*] and empty [*bohou*], and darkness [*hosher*] was over the surface of the watery deep [*té'om*], but the spirit of God was moving over the surface of the water. *(Genesis 1:2)*

According to this interpretation, the four empires composing the four great human civilizations are already prophetically evoked here in the Bible's opening words! These four kingdoms, referred to by the terms *tohou, bohou, hosher,* and *té'om,* will be compared to the diabolical and terrifying beasts we also find in the vision of the book of Daniel. The last of these four satanic beasts will be a prominent figure in Revelation.

Adam, the first man, is meant to reign over the terrestrial creation by taking authority over the animals and dominating them. The Hebrew expression *tov vera,* "to name good and evil," means "take authority over" or "decide for oneself that which is good or evil." In the same way, the second Adam, the Messiah, is meant to take authority over the entire universe, then subjugate these four terrible, supernatural animals to institute his kingdom on earth and reign over a wholly pacified world.

The process of God's creation is undertaken by commandment. God says:

Let there be light. And there was light! *(Genesis 1:3)*

The process of creation contains ten words as does the Ten Commandments in the book of Exodus. While contemporary Western society tends to judge commandments negatively, it is nevertheless by commandments that God gives life and makes all things possible.

In the beginning, then, God created the world. Here the Bible uses a peculiar word, *bara*, translated as "to create." It is a quite special and rare word in the Bible that means "to create from nothing," "to create ex nihilo." In other words, prior to this original event, there was no material universe.

The Bible thus states that the physical universe has not always existed. In 1965, scientists made the surprising discovery of relic radiation generated by a gigantic explosion of light and heat, thanks to their measurements of the cosmic microwave background. The existence of this radiation supported the theory of the Big Bang, the initial explosion at the origin of the existing material universe.

In the beginning there was darkness over the deep, and light was created on the first day. Yet the sources of that light (the sun, moon, and stars) only came into existence on the fourth day. During creation, God separated the light from the darkness. He also separated the sea, an image of the darkness of death, chaos, and nations. By creating the world, God triumphed over his enemies: nothingness, death, darkness. From this struggle, he emerged victorious.

Heaven is the spiritual world, and in this particular act of creation, God made beings that are solely spiritual and do not possess physical bodies—the angels. They are pure spirits, though on certain special occasions they can materialize in the physical world to interact with our reality.

> Are they not all ministering spirits, sent out to serve those who will inherit salvation? *(Hebrews 1:14)*

Then God created the earth, the material, physical world that we know. The creation of the earth probably is subsequent to that of the heavens, for the book of Job relates that the angels acclaimed this creation:

> Where were you when I laid the foundation of the earth? Tell me, if you possess understanding . . . When the morning stars sang in chorus, and all the sons of God shouted for joy? *(Job 38:4–7)*

God began populating his earthly creation essentially with vegetal beings that have a physical body but also a sort of primitive consciousness. (Plants and trees perceive elements outside of themselves and react by communicating chemically through the air and soil.)

The animals, for their part, are made of flesh and blood; they are not moral beings but are programmed to act according to their instincts. Animals are purely material and terrestrial and thus, to a certain extent, the opposite of the purely celestial, immaterial angels.

Last, God introduced a wholly unique and peculiar being to his earthly creation—man.

God is a moral being. He makes a value judgment regarding his creation: "God saw that the light was good," implying that, to the contrary, darkness is evil. This also means that from the first moments of creation, good, as well as evil, have both existed.

The creator expects the creatures he made in his image to exercise the moral capabilities with which they are equipped. For a moral being is a free being:

> He has told you, O man, what is good, and what the LORD really wants from you: He wants you to promote justice, to be faithful, and to live obediently before your God. *(Micah 6:8)*

While animals are governed by their instincts, man possesses free will that gives him freedom but also gave him the responsibility of choosing between good and evil. This raises the fundamental question of how to define good and evil. Who, then, possesses the true authority to decide what is good and what is evil? Can man have a correct and absolute knowledge of these two domains?

In reality only God knows good and evil objectively; man has only a partial, sensory, and thus subjective representation of them and cannot function correctly if he is separated from God. God created the universe by and for the Messiah, with a design at whose center he placed man. It is a cosmic act of love.

The Creation of Light
Engraving by Gustave Doré

BETWEEN HEAVEN AND EARTH

In Genesis 1, we read:

> Let us make humankind in our image *(Genesis 1:26)*

The word *image* is only a vague approximation of the term *beitsalmenou* whose root *tselem* offers two translations. The first is "shadow." Man is thus the shadow of God, and even if a shadow is an image, it cannot exist without the object that creates it. The second translation is "side" or "rib." Man's vocation is to walk alongside God, with him, like the shadow that is always in our company. We will find the same word *tselem* at the moment of the creation of Eve, the woman made out of Adam. Jesus said:

> …you have no life in yourselves. *(John 6:53)*

Life is something external to man. Man cannot therefore exist on his own.

The man Adam came from the earth, but he possessed something more than the plants, the animals, and the angels. He received the breath, the *ruah*, the spirit of God within him. The human being is thus a creature of quite special value, for he carries within him the image and the mind of God. He is conceived to be part of a spiritual relationship with his creator and is designed to be able to connect with him. At man's creation, there were no obstacles to this face-to-face communion with God. If the spirit of God withdraws from him, man is no more.

The theory of evolution teaches us that man descended from the primates, that he is an evolved monkey. The Bible, on the contrary, states that man is a unique creature, that God created man as his shadow, in his likeness, and encouraged him to obey his Word as counsel for life, so that he might live happily in the marvelous earthly garden that has been entrusted to him.

The difference between the living God of the Bible and the pagan idols is that the latter are visible to man. They have a shape, a morphology, while the Lord, the God of the Bible, is a living but invisible God:

> God is spirit, and the people who worship him must worship in spirit and truth. *(John 4:24)*

Nevertheless, man can hear him because, unlike the mute idols, God speaks to his creature. In chapter 6 of Deuteronomy, we find one of Judaism's fundamental texts, the prayer Shema Yisrael:

Hear, O Israel *(Deuteronomy 6:4 KJV)*

God is he who calls to man and speaks with him. The entire story of the Bible is this voice of God trying to call to man to establish a relationship with him. After the fall of Adam and Eve, God called out to man in the Garden of Eden: "*Adam eichecha?*" meaning, "Man, where are you?" The Lord looked for man and called to him. The Scriptures, which are improperly referred to as the Old Testament, are texts in which God ceaselessly calls out for men to walk in his path, by his side, toward their true life and destiny in the footsteps of Enoch, who

walked with God *(Genesis 5:24)*

It is written in the opening lines of the gospel of John:

In the beginning was the Word, and the Word was with God, and the Word was fully God. The Word was with God in the beginning. *(John 1:1–2)*

God is thus Word; Jesus is presented as being the Word, the Word incarnate, made flesh. God is he with whom we can establish a relationship, communication. Man is made in the image of God because he speaks, unlike the animals. He is

lower than the angels for a little while. *(Hebrews 2:7)*

Man's mission is to unify the horizontal and vertical realities, heaven and earth. Through his verticality, man is a link between earth and heaven, between the celestial and terrestrial realities.

Further along in the creation story,

The LORD God took the man and placed him in the orchard in Eden to care for it and to maintain it. *(Genesis 2:15)*

After Adam called to and named the animals of the earth to take authority over them,

The LORD God said, "It is not good for the man to be alone. I will make a companion for him who corresponds to him." *(Genesis 2:18)*

…no companion who corresponded to him was found." *(Genesis 2:20)*

So God put Adam into a deep sleep and took one of the ribs from his *tsela* to create a marvelous, unique being, which in turn became the side and shadow of man—woman.

Man has a fundamental need for "this companion who corresponded to him" if we translate more precisely the terms *ezer kenegdo, kenegdo* meaning "facing him," "opposite him," and even "against him." Adam has the mission of taking care of creation:

> The LORD God took the man and placed him in the orchard in Eden to care for it and to maintain it. *(Genesis 2:15)*

and he needs help to do so. Now a hierarchy appeared: God, the Messiah, man, then woman. Until then man was an incomplete, partial image of the Creator. Only now will the plan be fully realized:

> Let us make humankind in our image. *(Genesis 1:26)*

Adam Contemplating the Sleeping Eve
Engraving by Gustave Doré from the work *La Sainte Bible selon la Vulgate* by Bourassé and Janvier, illustrated by Gustave Doré, 1874

From the moment that man could be physically united with his woman, they became a couple, one sole flesh. The word employed for "one" is the Hebrew word *ehrad*. The couple is "one." Once united, they, too, become creators in the image of the creator and have the power to give life.

Hebrew has two words to define unity: *ehrad* and *iarid*. *Iarid* is oneness, while *ehrad* contains the notion of unity, but it is a plural unity.

They are one, but with the conservation of their diversity and complementarity. When we consider the differences in the words *man*—ish—and *woman*—isha—we get the word *Ya*, which means "God." When man and woman combine what differentiates them, they produce the image of God. If we take away the differences in ish and isha, we get the word *esh*, which means "fire." Thus the absence of God in the couple leads to the destruction of its unity.

The biblical narrative opens with the union of Adam and Eve in Genesis and ends with a marriage between the Messiah and the church in Revelation during the wedding of the Lamb. This final meal is also the symbol of humanity's definitive reconciliation with God after a period of revolt and widespread chaos.

Man is the free being par excellence. In Eden, there are two trees, the tree of life, which reappears in Revelation and the eating of which grants eternal life, and the tree that leads to death, that of the knowledge of good and evil.

> Then the LORD God commanded the man, "You may freely eat fruit from every tree of the orchard, but you must not eat from the tree of the knowledge of good and evil, for when you eat from it you will surely die." *(Genesis 2:16–17)*

Then in the ideal setting of the garden where a perfect harmony reigned, a tempter appeared in the form of an earthly animal, the serpent, so terrestrial that it wallowed in the dust from which it was made. This animal is *aroum*, cunning. "The serpent was the cunningest of all the wild animals God had made." The serpent was initially a good creature, but it agreed to be possessed by Lucifer, the vanquished angel who had fallen to earth, also known as "Satan" (in Hebrew) or "Diabolos" (in Greek), meaning "he who divides." He tried to induce the man and woman into a revolt against God, to cause them to fall as he had and be separated from their Creator. To do so, Satan needed to be incarnated into a body. The serpent, intelligent by nature, accepted this role and thus became trickery and lying.

The drama of Eden thus takes the stage, the great drama of the human adventure. The serpent asked the woman:

> "Is it really true that God said, 'You must not eat from any tree of the orchard'?" *(Genesis 3:1)*

He introduced doubt:

> The serpent said to the woman, "Surely you will not die, for God knows that when you eat from it your eyes will open and you will be like God, knowing good and evil. *(Genesis 3:4–5)*

He lied by claiming that eating the fruit would be beneficial and that God didn't want the man and woman to achieve the same prerogatives as him, to be like him . . . but it was a lie because it is this couple's precise purpose to be in the image of God—for this they were created.

The serpent's ruse was insidious and subtle. There was some truth to his claim that, "you will be like God: you will know good and evil." God wanted to teach man to distinguish between good and evil, but through education, through teaching, and through submission to his commandments, as parents want for their children. And indeed, through disobedience, they would experience evil; they would have to explore it in its ultimate consequences: separation from God, illness, old age, and death.

Satan in the Garden of Eden
Engraving by Gustave Doré

By sinning, man alone would be responsible for his actions. He would be free, but responsible.

The serpent's lie can be summarized thus:

"Free yourself from God's authority! There is no good and evil intrinsically. You are free, and it's up to you to decide for yourself what you would like to call good and evil!"

This original lie is the lie of our own time as well. The tragedy of man and woman is in choosing to listen to the serpent. In the presentation of human history, the climax of this disobedience will be attained at the end of time by one man, the *anomos*, "the lawless man" of whom Paul speaks. He is the Antichrist, the great rebel who also chooses to be possessed by Satan to seduce humanity.

The quintessence of lying is not saying things that are completely false, but it is skillfully blending truth and falsehood. "Your eyes will open!" And their eyes were opened by the miserable reality of their fall, which they covered with fig leaves. Man, persuaded by the serpent, chose to be linked to the earth rather than to heaven. The experience of evil will be painful. Until that point, material creation had been in symbiosis, in harmony, a perfect whole. God is "one," *ehad*. The world that emerged from the creator's hands was perfect, united, harmonious. It was a world of beauty and moral purity governed by love, *a'hava*. Love is the fullness of communion and harmony.

When they sinned, man and woman hid themselves and revealed their fear. Fear is the consequence of distancing from God. God asked, "Where are you?" or "How did you get there?", "How did you fall so low?" They realized that they were naked, bare, without strength. Man became aware of his smallness. Humanity began to experience shame and confusion.

The fall has cosmic consequences because all creation is then subjected to vanity. Beast of the earth, you shall eat of the earth! And you, man who chose the earth, herein you shall return to the earth. By choosing revolt to gain autonomy and become like God, man gave free reign to his pride and sin. And the more his power to create increased, so did the dramatic consequences of his actions. From this moment on, we can pose the question of whether man can be a creator without being a destroyer.

The fall shattered the harmony that Jewish tradition calls shevirat ha-kelim. From the Creator's potter's wheel, the material world had come out perfect, like a magnificent vase, that broke into a thousand pieces after the fall, the fracturing of the world. This tragic event produced several consequences.

First, the relationship between God and man was broken; the latter was afraid and tried to hide himself. Then the communion between man and woman was broken, for she was considered to blame for the tragedy. Previously protective and benevolent, the authority of man over woman would change its nature: it became authoritarian, egotistical, dominating.

What's more, the harmony between man and animals was broken, and man became a frightening predator and destroyer of the land, of the plant and animal worlds.

Last, the harmony between man and nature was broken. The land produced thorns and thistles, and man would have to work hard to cultivate it.

Adam certainly wasn't meant to live forever, given that he was called upon to procreate, but he was certainly supposed to have a far longer life, similar to the first patriarchs such as Methuselah, who lived to be 969. Adam the "earth-bound," who chose to be of the earth, would return to the *adama*, the earth, the dust.

The story of Genesis teaches us that God's first attempt to repair this breaking of the world, this rupture in the harmony between heaven and earth, was to send certain angels to earth in bodily form. But they, too, succumbed to the power of satanic seduction: they copulated with the daughters of men and failed in their mission, further accentuating the consequences of this break:

> ... the sons of God saw that the daughters of humankind were beautiful. Thus they took wives for themselves from any they chose. *(Genesis 6:2)*

These unions produced the Nephilim, literally "the fallen beings," "the deposed beings," demiurgical creatures that are probably close to those described in Greek mythology.

Then God decided to intervene,

> But the LORD saw that the wickedness of humankind had become great on the earth. Every inclination of the thoughts of their minds was only evil all the time. The LORD regretted that he had made humankind on the earth, and he was highly offended. So the LORD said, "I will wipe humankind, whom I have created, from the face of the earth—everything from humankind to animals, including creatures that move on the ground and birds of the air, for I regret that I have made them." *(Genesis 6:5–7)*

So God sent a flood to eliminate all but a small number of this fallen humanity:

> So God said to Noah, "I have decided that all living creatures must die, for the earth is filled with violence because of them. Now I am about to destroy them and the earth." *(Genesis 6:13)*

After the flood, God made a new pact with the family of Noah:

But as for you, be fruitful and multiply; increase abundantly on the earth and multiply on it. *(Genesis 9:7)*

The sons of Noah who came out of the ark where Shem, Ham and Japeth. (Now Ham was the father of Canaan.) These were the three sons of Noah, and from them the whole earth was populated. *(Genesis 9:18–19)*

"The sons of Japheth; Gomer, and Magog, and Madai, and Javan, and Tubal, and Meshech, and Tiras. And the sons of Gomer; Ashkenaz, and Riphath, and Togarmah. And the sons of Javan; Elishah, and Tarshish, Kittim, and Dodanim. By these were the isles of the Gentiles divided in their lands; every one after his tongue, after their families, in their nations." *(Genesis 10:2–5 KJV)* [These are the fathers of Europeans and the West.]

The Fall of the Angels
Engraving by Gustave Doré,
from the work *La Sainte Bible selon la Vulgate* by Bourassé and Janvier.

Unto Shem also, the father of all the children of Eber, the brother of Japheth the elder ... And their dwelling was from Mesha, as thou goest unto Sephar a mount of the east. *(Genesis 10:21, 30 KJV)* [These are the fathers of the Semites and Asians.]

"And the sons of Ham; Cush, and Mizraim, and Phut, and Canaan ... And Cush begat Nimrod: he began to be a mighty one in the earth ..." *(Genesis 10:6, 8 KJV)* . [These are the descendants of Africans.]

But this primitive humanity came together and decided to build the city of Babel and, at its heart, a tower whose base touched the earth and whose summit reached heaven, to reunite the two symbolically and artificially. But buildings do not unite man and God. Only the Word unifies and binds the two realities. Babel shall fail.

A new attempt was then made to reestablish the original harmony: God called on Abraham, a man who rose from the abyss into which humanity had fallen, to establish with him a new divine covenant. He was the first to build not a pyramid of stone, but a spiritual pyramid. His grandson, the patriarch Jacob, also received a revelation of the unity between earth and heaven. He had a vision:

> ...a stairway erected on the earth with its top reaching to the heavens. The angels of God were going up and coming down it... *(Genesis 28:12)*

The people of Israel, who descend from Abraham, are those who are supposed to reconcile earth and heaven anew:

> ...because salvation is from the Jews. *(John 4:22)*

Thanks to the Torah—a collection of divine wisdom—God tried to reestablish the harmony of Eden. He will succeed at the end times through the Jewish people because God sent Jesus, son of David, to carry out this mission.

We often limit God's plan to the work of personal salvation, but his true aim is to reconcile all things, namely that which is under the earth, on earth, and in the sky. He has the goal of recreating the world and reestablishing the perfect harmony of the origins. The purpose of God's plan is to reestablish the glory that is his; it is a doxological plan.

The Jewish Yotzer prayer recites: "Each day, you renew the work of your Creation." Jesus, the second Adam, was the prototype of a new humanity. In his person heaven and earth are perfectly reconciled; he is meant to renew creation.

This is why the first Adam rejected the second. Natural man does not understand heavenly matters. As Jesus said,

> You people are from below; I am from above. *(John 8:23)*

Humanity is incapable of comprehending this divine perspective, this celestial reality. Yet in the process of the encounter, repentance, and personal pact with God, a process of reconstruction is implemented: by his Spirit, God remodels us according to his heart. Jesus said to Nicodemus:

> You must all be born from above *(John 3:7),*

meaning from on high. Not only again, but as though from a new source and origin of life, divine and heavenly.

He gives us the power to open our eyes to new heavenly priorities and to the things from above. Jesus did not say to leave the world, but to overcome it and to work within it to prepare his kingdom and to consider the importance of heavenly, eternal things as superior to terrestrial, transitory matters.

The seductive power of the serpent's lie—"Your eyes will be opened, and you will be as gods"—constitutes a quite serious danger for a generation such as ours, so avid for power and knowledge. Lucifer (the bearer of light) could easily be presented as a friend to humanity, one that desires to give us the light of esoteric knowledge that would allow man to rise to the higher level of superman, to a divine level. The God of the Bible could be presented as the enemy of man, attempting to keep humanity ignorant and far from the

Luciferian light, the only one capable of illuminating man's intelligence and freeing him to the fullness of his capabilities.

This pernicious lie could also originate gnostic occult religions that would present an immense danger for twenty-first-century humanity, should it be seduced, manipulated, and led to adore Satan, the mortal enemy of man, cunning enough to disguise himself as an "angel of light" and presenting himself as humanity's friend.

In the garden the serpent said: "Take and eat the fruit of death." On Easter, Jesus said: "Take and eat" the bread of eternal life. Being a disciple means learning. And learning also means "taking" from the Master, according to the words of Jesus:

> The one who eats my flesh and drinks my blood has eternal life, and I will raise him up on the last day. *(John 6:54)*

This reality is within everyone's reach:

> The word is near you, in your mouth and in your heart. *(Romans 10:8)*

On the last day, during the Son of Man's descent to the Mount of Olives in Jerusalem, heaven and earth will be fully reunited. With the fall, humanity, expelled from the Garden of Eden, condemns itself to cross through history in the course of a long exile on earth, separated from God, and become no *venad* (Genesis 4:12), a wandering nomad who knows not where he is going, in the quasi-diabolical hostility of a fragile life full of dangers.

Adam and Eve Cast Out of Eden
Engraving by
Gustave Doré, 1874

THE STRUGGLE BETWEEN THE MESSIAH AND THE SERPENT

With the fall of Adam and Eve, an animal, the serpent—actually Satan—received the worst of curses. Theologians have described this crucial proclamation as "proto-evangelical" because it is the first biblical text to announce the gospel:

> Because you have done this, cursed are you above all the wild beasts and all the living creatures of the field! . . . And I will put hostility between you and the woman. *(Genesis 3:14–15)*

But there is a serious translation problem in the classic versions of our bibles regarding "between your offspring and hers," because the word *zera*, "offspring," is masculine. So the text should read: "I will put enmity between you and the woman, and between your offspring and hers; he will strike your head, and you will strike his heel." This radically changes the meaning of this crucial prophecy. In the case of the usage of the feminine pronoun—"she will strike your head"—we might conclude that the woman's offspring—humanity or a fraction of humanity (the church)—will be sufficiently evolved to strike the head of the serpent and save itself, thus establishing the kingdom of God on earth on its own, without God. But if the subject is in the masculine singular—"he will strike your head"—this indicates that only a single individual in all human history will have the mandate to strike the enemy's head: it can be none other than the Messiah, conqueror of the serpent!

The gematria method of Jewish exegesis provides information that supplements the visible text by associating numerical values with the letters (so the first letter, Aleph, is worth 1, the second, Bet, 2, and so forth). By applying this method of interpretation, it's surprising to discover that the numerical value of the word "Messiah," *mashiah,* is 358, or exactly the same as the word *nahash,* translated as "serpent." Simply put, the entire story of the Bible is the clash between these two figures: the Messiah who is mandated by God to take on Satan and defeat him.

God made a promise: sin entered the world through a single man, and it will leave through a single man. The Messiah's role is to repair the world's rupture, to reestablish that original harmony, which Genesis described as coming out "very good" from the Creator's hands. In Hebrew, the process of repairing the breaking of the world is called Tikkun Olam, which literally means "repairing the world."

The Messiah, this perfect being, will be delivered to death in a struggle against the devil whose head will be struck, such that all humans may recover not just what they lost in the beginning, but above all a relationship of love with God based on justice. This victory will come at the cost of his own life. David could say with prophetic spirit:

> ...they pin my hands and feet. I can count all my bones. *(Psalm 22:17)*

It is remarkable to note that in 1970 an ossuary was found on the Mount of Olives that included the skeleton of a crucified man displaying an enormous nail through his heels, not his feet as Christian iconography most frequently represents it. This detail shows the extreme precision of the biblical prophecy.

The price the Messiah had to pay was immense; we know that the crucified could agonize for up to three days on the cross. During his suffering, one of the thieves insulted Jesus, while the other said:

> Jesus, remember me when you come in your kingdom. *(Luke 23:42)*

This unfortunate criminal was in search of compassion. The Lord replied:

> I tell you the truth, today you will be with me in paradise. *(Luke 23:43)*

We, too, can already receive a part of this glory to come. We all know that we have our faults and have made mistakes, but there is still both time and the means to be reconciled with the redeemer, the sole sovereign with the power to free us from the terrible power of the ancient serpent.

God Strikes Down the Leviathan
Engraving by Gustave Doré, 1874

THE APOCALYPSES

The Apocalypse of John, also called the book of Revelation or Christ's Revelation, is the final book in the biblical canon. It opens with a group of seven letters sent to the communities of the churches located in modern Turkey, in the region of Izmir. The author is quite likely the apostle John, "the disciple whom Jesus loved."

The Gospels do mention that John was gratified with a long life, and an archaeological detail substantiates this hypothesis. The church of the monastery of Chora, on the island of Patmos, contains a fresco of the apostle John dictating a text to his assistant Prochorus; this text is the first verse of the gospel of John. This means local tradition considered the book of Revelation and the gospel of John as issuing from the same author.

The Christian tradition also relates that the apostle John was responsible for the churches of Asia, whose center was located in Ephesus, the great ancient city across the water from Patmos. John's ministry at the end of the first century took place in a context of intense political persecution. The text is generally believed to have been written in the year 95 AD under the Emperor Domitian, Titus's brother, who held the title of Imperator Caesar Domitianus Augustus Germanicus and reigned from 81 AD to 96 AD, when he was assassinated by his own court.

But given that chapter 11 tells us that the temple of Herod in Jerusalem was still standing, we can conclude that the text was most certainly written earlier, prior to the destruction of the second temple in the year 70. Now the first persecution of Christians took place under Emperor Nero, who reigned from 54 to 68, the year of his suicide. Nero's reign was characterized by the worst debauchery and monstrous acts: to name a few, he had his mother, Agrippina, and wife, Poppaea, murdered; the latter, who was pregnant, was kicked to death in the stomach. Nero was suspected of being at the origin of the fire of Rome— some allegedly saw him playing his lyre before the spectacle of the city in flames. It was thus important for Nero to shift suspicion to others. He chose as his target a sect that had emerged from the Jewish people, the Christians, who lived well away from the ravaged part of the city and participated little in the Roman people's excesses. Nero ordered they be thrown to the lions in the arenas, while others were burned alive, and many were crucified.

According to the historian and Roman senator Tacitus (58–120 AD), "[Nothing] could stifle scandal or dispel the belief that the fire had taken place by order. Therefore, to scotch the rumor, Nero substituted as culprits and punished with the utmost refinements of cruelty a class of men loathed for their vices, whom the crowd styled Christians. Christus, the founder of the name, had undergone the death penalty in the reign of Tiberius by sentence of the procurator Pontius Pilate, and the pernicious superstition was checked for the moment, only to break out once more not merely in Judea, the home of the disease, but in the capital itself, where all things horrible or shameful in the world collected and found a vogue. First, then, the confessed members of the sect were arrested; next, on their disclosures, vast numbers were convicted, not so much on the count of arson as for hatred of the human race. And derision accompanied their end: they were covered with wild beasts' skins and torn to death by dogs, or they were fastened on crosses, and, when daylight failed, were burned to serve as lamps by night. Nero had offered his gardens for the spectacle, and gave an exhibition in his circus, mixing with the crowd in the habit of a charioteer or mounted on his car. Hence, despite a guilt that had earned the most exemplary punishment, there arose a sentiment of pity due to the impression that they were being sacrificed not for the welfare of the state but to the ferocity of a single man."

While always inhabited by a civilian population, Patmos was also used for punitive ends and still maintained the tradition during John's sojourn on the island. You can still visit the cave where John received the revelation and see the clefts in the rock that the old man could use to pull himself to his feet after praying.

Etymologically, the word *Apocalypse* is the transcription of a Greek term ἀποκάλυψις/*apokálupsis*, meaning "unveiling" or "revelation." The apocalyptic genre is a full-fledged Hebrew literary style dealing with eschatology, or last things. The word *Apocalypse* is troubling given its association with catastrophes, but the Hebrew word *itgalout* and Greek word *apocalypsis* lack this sense of impending doom. It is a revelation of hidden things, an unveiling that is an attribute of God's nature because:

> He reveals the deep things of darkness, and brings deep shadows into the light. *(Job 12:22)*

Over the centuries the term *Apocalypse* has acquired negative connotations distancing it from its original meaning, often evoking a massive, violent catastrophe. The word has "become popular for the wrong reasons." This perception is linked particularly with the difficulty of grasping a disconcerting literary genre that has no counterparts in contemporary literature.

Apocalyptic literature constitutes an ancient literary genre that probably appeared during the Babylonian exile—in the sixth century BC—with the texts of Ezekiel, Joel, and Zechariah. We could also cite the Greek and Syriac Apocalypse of Baruch, the Apocalypse of Abraham, the Apocalypse of Moses, the Apocalypse of Elias, the Apocalypse of Noah, or even the Apocalypse of Ezra. Numerous apocryphal texts also make claims to the genre or bear its name: the Apocalypse of Peter, of James, of Paul, of Stephen, and so on.

The genre blossomed with Daniel (toward 165 BC), whose book serves as a model for the Apocalypse of John, as well as the apocryphal Jewish and Christian Apocalypses, and even Paul's apocalyptic texts. In the New Testament, whole passages draw on this same literary genre: Jesus's eschatological discourse in Matthew (ch. 24–25), in Mark (ch. 13), and in Luke (ch. 21.5–36), certain passages in the letters of Paul (2 Thess. 1.6–12; 2,3–12) or Peter (2 Pet. 3.10). The Apocalypse of John, however, has had an immense, unparalleled influence on Christianity, the organization of Western society, and the history of the world.

In Jewish and Christian literature, the genre of these writings isn't testament to any specific theological current and can transmit the most disparate ideologies; if they display a great diversity, what they share is a pronounced taste for allegory and symbolism.

We can thus discern as common ground in this prophetic genre a narrative framework founded on a divine vision/revelation transmitted to a man, generally through the mediation of a supernatural being, such as an angel, in a representation of the world showing two facets of reality: the sensory human experience and a spiritual world invisible and inaccessible to life as we know it, but decisive for human destiny.

The demarcation line between the Old World at its end and the New World nearly come to fruition is marked by the divine intervention that judges the wicked and rewards the elect. Several features also characterize this genre of literature: first, the viewer of the Apocalypse was a writer who, unlike a prophet, commits his visions to writing; second, the author made use of cyphers, of symbolic objects and figures, without endeavoring to make this symbolism coherent.

There is, nonetheless, a fundamental difference between a prophecy and an Apocalypse. In the popular imagination, the prophet is a sort of seer, someone who reads the future, but the prophet is someone who is sent by God to the people so that the latter repent of their evil ways and who, substantially, says: "If you don't leave your wicked path, here is what will happen (for example, Jerusalem will be destroyed)." Finally, the prophet prophesizes so that what he announced does not occur, which at first glance might seem paradoxical.

The best example to illustrate this is the prophet Jonah in Assyria. At the conclusion of Jonah's preaching in Nineveh, the king proclaimed repentance and fasting. The key phrase of this biblical story is:

> Who knows? Perhaps God might be willing to change his mind and relent and turn from his fierce anger so that we might not die. *(Jonah 3:9).*

Ultimately the threat of the city's destruction by God didn't come to pass. Jonah's announcement was taken seriously by the Ninevites, the people repented, and God stayed his hand.

Upon seeing the grace that the Lord granted to this city, Jonah first became angry and then depressed, because now he was taken for a false prophet. But in the end, it was for this precise reason that he was sent to Nineveh: to provoke the Assyrians' repentance. The prophet's mission is to provoke in the people a radical change of course to modify God's judgments.

Another prophetic example is found in the book of Joel concerning the threat of the invasion of clouds of locusts:

> "Yet even now," the LORD says, "return to me with all your heart—with fasting, weeping, and mourning. Tear your hearts, not just your garments! Return to the LORD your God, for he is merciful and compassionate, slow to anger and boundless in loyal love—often relenting from calamitous punishment. Who knows? Perhaps he will be compassionate and grant a reprieve, and leave a blessing in his wake . . ." *(Joel 2:12–14)*

The case of Revelation is quite different: The announcements concern the end times, *acharit hayamim*, literally "the end of days." These days are established in the pain of a crisis that is going to strike the world, before finally leading creation back to the harmonious state of Eden. The image chosen is that of a woman who gives birth to a child after a period of painful labor.

The Apocalypse of John is the history of this final crisis that must lead to the repairing of the broken world. God will repair the damage that man has accumulated on earth through sin. Indeed, even if Jesus achieved this redemption on the cross, the consequences of his victory are not yet fully manifest in our world. Beforehand the just must receive their deliverance and the unjust their retribution, because for them, the end times will be a terrible period.

Prophecy is not something that is firm and definitive. In this case it is always still possible to change the course of history if you repent and listen to God. To the contrary, an Apocalypse is an irrevocable, unappealable decree, a declaration of the Almighty, and from that moment nothing can change the course of history according to the announcements made by God.

In the end times, the height of sinning and stubbornness will be such that man will no longer listen to the prophets and God himself will have to intervene directly in human history, which is extremely rare. In fact, men will create such a violent, dangerous, and unstable world that God himself will act to save his people and creation.

The prophecy is a spoken word, the Apocalypse is first written, decreed: "Write down what you see"; it is unappealable, irrevocable.

Ezekiel Prophesying
Engraving by Gustave Doré, 1874

EVIDENCE OF BORROWING

In *Les secrets de l'Apocalypse, mystique, ésotérisme et apocalypse*,[1] Professor Pierre Prigent demonstrates that Revelation makes extensive use of older biblical prophecies and predictions. So when the Apocalypse of John gives a detailed description of the fall of Babylon, everyone recognizes that, for Revelation, Babylon is a stand-in for first-century Rome. The image comes directly from the prophetic curses that Jeremiah pronounced against the capital of oppressive Babylonia. The parallel between the words employed in chapters 50 and 51 of Jeremiah and those of Revelation (chapters 17 and 18) are eerily similar.

JEREMIAH	REVELATION
…get out of Babylon quickly! *(50:8)*	Come out of [Babylon], my people *(18:4)*
Do to her as she has done! *(50:15)*	Repay her the same way she repaid others… *(18:6)*
Babylonia had been a gold cup… *(51:7)*	She held in her hand a golden cup… *(17:4)*
She had made the whole world drunk. The nations had drunk from the wine of her wrath, so they have all gone mad.*(51:7)*	…the earth's inhabitants got drunk with the wine of her immorality. *(17:2)*
But suddenly Babylon will fall… *(51:8)*	Fallen, fallen is Babylon the great! *(18:2)*
Cry out in mourning over it! *(51:8)*	…the kings of the earth…will weep and wail for her… *(18:9)*
For judgment on her…is piled up to heaven… *(51:9)*	…her sins have piled up all the way to heaven… *(18:5)*
…tie a stone to [this book] and throw it into the middle of the Euphrates River. Then say, "In the same way Babylon will sink…" *(51:63–64)*	…one powerful angel picked up a stone…threw it into the sea, and said, "With this…force Babylon the great city will be thrown down… *(18:21)*

Everything unfolds as though it were necessary to discern over time and human history the different incarnations of the powers of evil and various powers that arouse the great enemy against the people of God. According to

Pierre Prigent, this is the reason why in chapters 17 and 18 of Revelation the author doesn't just find his sources in the prophecy of Jeremiah against Babylon, but also borrows from the prophecy of Ezekiel against Tyre.

EZEKIEL	REVELATION
I will silence the noise of your songs; the sound of your harps will be heard no more (26:13)	And the sound of the harpists, musicians [...] will never be heard in you again (18.22)
...the princes [...] will [...] be shocked at what has happened to you. They will sing this lament over you: "How you have perished...O renowned city...!" (26:16–17)	...the kings of the earth [...] will weep and wail for her...and will say, "Woe, woe, O great city, Babylon...your doom has come!" (18:9–10)
...Tyre, who sits at the entrance of the sea... (27:3)	The great prostitute who sits on the waters (17:1)
...linen...blue and purple... (27:7)	...linen, purple cloth...scarlet cloth... (18:12)
...rowers...skilled men...mariners... (27:8–9)	...every ship's captain...seamen... (18:17)
...silver, iron, tin, and lead... (27:12)	...the kings of the earth...will weep and wail for her... (18:9)
...horses, chargers, and mules... (27:14)	...horses and four-wheeled carriages... (18:13)
...ivory... (27:15)	...ivory... (18:12)
...wheat...olive oil... (27:17)	...olive oil[...]wheat... (18:13)
...the sailors and all the sea captains...will throw dust on their heads... (27:29–30)	...all who make their living from the sea [...] threw dust on their heads... (18:17–19)
Who was like Tyre...? (27:32)	Who is like the great city? (18:18)
...you said, "I am a god; I sit in the seat of gods..." (28:2)	...she said to herself, 'I rule as queen...' (18:7)

The evidence of borrowing here is even more significant since, given that Rome wasn't a maritime port like Tyre, we cannot comprehend this description of the Revelation as stemming from an observation of reality, but, as being perfectly symbolic. If Tyre's characteristics are transposed onto Rome, it is to effectively underline the guilty impiety that the former announced for the latter and the inevitable coming of the divine judgment on Rome.

Revelation, and what's more, all the New Testament, is imbued with deeper meanings and nourished by the words of the Old Testament. What God does is and remains real throughout time; this is a central affirmation of the book of Revelation. To the new and faithful people who commune with God as during the exodus, there are now men who gain access to heaven and join the angels to receive and proclaim the mystery of all mysteries. The end is already there and, nevertheless, the history of man continues.

INTERPRETIVE APPROACHES TO
THE BOOK OF REVELATION

There are five possible interpretive approaches to the Apocalypse of John.

The first, Preterism, believes that the Bible's prophetic texts evoke events that have already happened in the past; they have thus returned.

The Futurist approach, for its part, describes the events of the end times in chapters 4 to 22.

The third approach is known as Idealist, and posits that Revelation describes the conflict between the church and evil and is an exclusively symbolic book. According to this approach, the apostle John uses images to express spiritual truths. The symbols have a universal scope and apply to the church of all times and not to a particular period.

The Chronological Historical approach is the fourth type of interpretation; it considers that the whole book presents panoramic, chronological visions of the history of the world and of the church from the apostolic age to today. According to this understanding, chapters 2 and 3 speak of the apostolic age; chapters 4 to 7, of the time of the martyrs from Nero to Domitian; chapters 8 to 11, of the church fathers; chapters 11 to 14, of the virgin saints whom the Saracens opposed; chapters 15 to 18, the struggle of the church against the degenerate Empire of Babylon; chapters 19 to 21, of the Antichrist and his defeat; chapter 20 of the millenniium and chapters 21 to 22, of the last judgment and the eternal state.

The fifth approach, the Prophetic Historical interpretation, considers that Revelation lays out the history of the world, but that the text is not chronological as in the case of certain Old Testament prophecies.

These different interpretive models, onto which is grafted the delicate nuance of the symbolic or real elements, make the analysis of Revelation quite a delicate matter indeed.

The chronological historical interpretation viewing the seven churches of the first chapters of Revelation as symbolizing the ages of Christianity is difficult to support. Each generation of believers tends to consider that the prophets have prophesied for their time and that we belong to the privileged generation par excellence. But the prophets prophesized firstly and above all for their own time and their contemporaries, hence the importance of rigorously framing the prophecies in their historical context. However, it is accepted by most commentators that the church that most corresponds to our own time is that of Laodicea; it is the sign of the church of the end times.

The number "seven" occurs numerous times in Revelation. There are seven shofars, seven stars, seven angels, seven spirits, seven churches, seven times three cataclysms, seven beatitudes ("fortunate is he who . . ."), seven seals, and seven cups. The book revolves around the number seven, which is the symbol of perfection, of the final conclusion, of the fullness of time.

With the group of seven letters, John—and the Holy Spirit that inspired him—is writing to the churches of all places and all times. It is a universal message that is still entirely relevant for our generation.

APPROACHES	PROPHECIES OF REVELATION 4 TO 19	EXPONENTS
Preterism	Already come to pass: fall of Roman Empire or destruction of Jerusalem.	Hugo Grotius, Henry Hammond
Historicism	Coming to pass: these prophecies describe the history of the Church.	Thomas Brightman, John Gill, John Wesley
Futurism	Will come to pass in the future: these prophecies describe the "end of time."	John N. Darby, C. Scofield

Major Trends in the Protestant Exegesis of Revelation
Summary by David Vincent, PhD student in Religious Science

THE BOOK OF DANIEL

The book of Daniel was written in Hebrew and, partially, in Aramaic. Its name, however, comes not from its author, who is unknown, but from its hero. It includes the stories of the trial of Daniel and his companions while they were serving at the court of the king as well as several visions concerning the future.

The book is thought to have been written during the Maccabean wars (from 167 to 164 BC), for the purpose of providing encouragement to the Jews in the face of religious persecution by the Hellenistic kingdom of the Seleucids and their Jewish sympathizers.

Daniel contains the only references to the resurrection of the body in the Old Testament. The name of the book's central character, Daniel, means "divine judgment" or "God is my judge." He was a young Jewish aristocratic exile who belonged to the elite of Israel. Nebuchadnezzar II, king of Babylonia between 605 to 562 BC, deported a part of the Jewish people to the capital of his empire, Babylon, an ancient Mesopotamian city located on the Euphrates in what is modern-day Iraq, roughly 100 km south of modern Baghdad. This Babylonian's first deportation of the Israelites took place in 586 BC, the second, ten years later.

The first six chapters of this book tell the personal story of Daniel and are set during the kingdoms of Babylon and then Persia. Chapters 7 to 12 present allegorical visions of historical events concerning distant times, from the beginning of the sixth century BC to the Seleucid era under Antiochus IV, between 175 and 163 BC, but the revelation also concerns the end times. Indeed, it will be said to Daniel:

Daniel in Babylon
Engraving by Gustave Doré

…seal up the vision, for it refers to a time many days from now. *(Daniel 8:26)*

In the Jewish tradition, Daniel is not considered a prophet, but more precisely a wise man to whom God illuminates hidden things. Even if the apocalyptic genre had developed significantly in the intertestamentary period, there are, in the strict sense of the term, only two Apocalypses in the biblical canon: the book of Daniel and the book of Revelation. One cannot be understood without the other; they function like two mirror-images, connected texts, the roots of the second sunk deeply in the first. Certain specialists, for that matter, think that the Apocalypse of John was written in Hebrew.

In this book, we find Gabriel, the same angel present at the time of Daniel and the same book, bound with seven seals. At the end of Daniel, it is said:

> Go, Daniel. For these matters are closed and sealed until the time of the end *(Daniel 12:9)*

that is, exactly the opposite of what is said in Revelation.

Revelation can be considered as the continuation of the book of Daniel in which we read:

> But you, Daniel, close up these words and seal the book until the time of the end. Many will dash about, and knowledge will increase. *(Daniel 12:4)*

for the wise will understand.

In his time, even Daniel was not capable of understanding the visions that were communicated to him, but he faithfully set these revelations down in a book whose meaning no one will be able to unveil. Now, in Revelation, the angel commands the apostle John:

> Do not seal up the words of the prophecy contained in this book, because the time is near. *(Revelation 22:10)*

> I saw [. . .] a scroll . . . sealed with seven seals [. . .] the Lion of the tribe of Judah, the root of David, has conquered; thus he can open the scroll and its seven seals. *(Revelation 5:1–5)*

The text of Daniel had remained incomprehensible because it was closed, sealed. The Messiah is the figure who is finally deemed worthy to break the seven seals, which provokes the unleashing of catastrophic events and cataclysms on the earth, but which also unveils the hidden meaning of the message of Daniel's visions. The Apocalypse is thus the revelation of Daniel's visions, which until then had remained incomprehensible. The secrets of God are revealed by the Lamb of God and the Apocalypse is an explanation of the book of Daniel.

In reality, these two books complete each other and come together to form a single book. The section of Daniel's "apocalyptic visions" includes three visions and a prophecy concerning the fate of Israel and of humanity.

Daniel announces the succession of four human, negative empires that are going to dominate the world, and which will be followed by a fifth empire, the kingdom of God, which will be positive. The prophet Isaiah as well, in his chapters 11, 25, and 65, announces a universal empire of harmony and peace whose advent is preceded by periods of grave troubles.

The book of Daniel is the Jewish Apocalypse of the Old Testament. It is the Jewish people's book of last things. In the Hebrew canon, it is categorized in the third part of the Bible, the *Ketouvim* or writings—the books of wisdom—also comprising the Psalms and the Proverbs. Daniel is a wise man in that he is comparable to Joseph. Just like the latter, he is capable of understanding dreams and hidden things. For in heaven there is a God who reveals secrets—even the secrets of the end of time.

For certain theologians, the entire New Testament can be considered as a commentary on chapter 7 of the book of Daniel. This shows the importance of this magisterial text, which is essential for revealing the meaning of the Apocalypse of John.

Daniel in the Lions' Den
Engraving by Gustave Doré

THE FOUR EMPIRES OF DANIEL'S VISIONS

We might sum up Daniel's visions in the following manner: human history is divided into four main eras governed by four empires, whose evolution is a process of gradual decay. According to this approach, our current civilization is less magnificent and less moral than those that preceded it. This appraisal is illustrated by the statue in Daniel's vision, the quality of whose materials progressively decays from a head made of gold to feet fashioned from a poor blend of iron and clay.

A rabbinical tradition reports that other prophecies evoke these four empires from the very first verses of the Bible:

> In the beginning God created the heavens and the earth. Now the earth was without shape and empty, and darkness was over the surface of the watery deep, but the Spirit of God was moving over the surface of the water. God said, "Let there be light." And there was light! God saw that the light was good, so God separated the light from the darkness. *(Genesis 1:1–4)*

Rabbinical exegesis gives us a fascinating interpretation of these texts. In Hebrew, we read:

> The earth was without form [*tohou*] and void [*bohou*]: and darkness [*hosher*] was upon the face of the deep [*té'om*] and the Spirit of God moved upon the face of the waters. *(Genesis 1:2)*

In this text that opens the Bible, the wise men of Israel saw the unveiling of the entire panorama of human history.

According to the visions given to Daniel, the first human empire is Babylonian. It is symbolized by a lion and by the statue's golden head. The word *tohu* characterizes this first Babylonian empire: *tohu* is "that which has no sense" or "that which is neither high nor low." In that it is synonymous with *babel*, "that which is confused."

In Genesis 10, we learn that the peoples descending from the survivors of the flood came together in Mesopotamia in the land of Shinar, a Hebrew word meaning "unsettled," "shaken," which is a mark of instability. The territory of Shinar is located in the Tigris and Euphrates basin, what is modern-day Iraq. These peoples were unified under the aegis of King Nimrod and formed the Akkadian kingdom, which is the first organized human society.

Nimrod is known in secular history by the name of Sargon of Akkad, who built the capital Babylon and its tower of Babel. Nimrod is the founder of a vast universal human empire composed of a single people, speaking a single language, united in a sort of great global village, a theme with which we have become familiar in this twenty-first century.

Expelled from the original paradise after the fall, man now lived on the earth in exile, wandering and fragile. So he tried to found a universal city where men could inhabit a place where peace, safety, and prosperity could be offered to all.

Nimrod descended from the line of Cain and Ham, the cursed. His name, Nimrod, comes from *mered,* which means "the revolt." He is a "skilled hunter," *gibor tsaïd, tsaïd* meaning "hunter." The name *Nimrod* is often connected to the Hebrew root *marad* meaning "to rebel." It can be interpreted as a first-person plural ("we will rebel"). This is how it has been understood in the Jewish tradition, which has made Nimrod into the prototype of pride and rebellion against God.

This man was animated by a totalitarian, dominating spirit in which all things were assumed by man. He attempted to drive God out of his creation by drawing humanity into a revolt against the Creator and defied him with a city driven by sin and revolt. The sin of the men of Babel was not building a tower but trying to make a name for themselves:

> Then they said, "Come, let's build ourselves a city and a tower with its top in the heavens so that we may make a name for ourselves. Otherwise we will be scattered across the face of the entire earth." *(Genesis 11:4)*

In the language of the Bible, making oneself a name amounts to wanting to be one's own master, for to name is to take power and authority over someone or something. In response to the commandment to take control over creation, Adam calls to and names the animals to establish authority over them.

In the language of the Bible, naming oneself amounts to refusing God's sovereignty and essentially proclaiming: "Let us be our own masters, we have neither God nor master."

Flavius Josephus wrote in his regard: ". . . little by little, [Nimrod] transforms the state of things into a tyranny. He deemed that the only means of removing men from the fear of God was that they always trust in his own power. He promises to defend them against a secund punishment from God who wants to flood the earth: he will build a tower so high that the waters are unable to reach it and he will even avenge the death of their fathers. The people were well disposed to follow the view of [Nimrod], as they considered obedience to God as servitude; they set about building the tower [. . .]; it rose faster than one might have thought.[2]

The men of Babel tried to form a single people, a single nation under the scepter of a single man, and the eternal one saw that they would not achieve happiness, but that they would work to create a totalitarian dictatorship, a hell on earth.

So God intervened directly in the course of human history to stop this project by sewing confusion in the language of men. He said:

> Come, let's go down and confuse their language so they won't be able to understand each other

and

> they stopped building the city. (Genesis 11:7–8)

This dream of the men of Babel to create for themselves a paradise on earth and an ideal city has never ceased to haunt humanity, but God has always made sure that this dream does not come to pass. In his visions, however, the apostle John discovered a mystery: The city of Babylon has finally been resuscitated and even brought to completion for a short period in the end times by a new Nimrod, the Antichrist, an absolute dictator. This, it seems, is permitted so that humanity can experience and assess the folly of this project.

The second empire of Daniel's visions was also clearly named in the text and leaves no doubt as to its identity. It is that of the Medes and Persians and was represented by a bear and the silver belly of the statue of Daniel. This empire was located in modern-day Iran and had its capital at Persepolis. The apogee of ancient Persia was represented by the Achaemenid dynasty, whose conquerors Darius I and Xerxes I extended the territory all the way to India.

This second empire was designated in the first chapter of Genesis by the term *vavohu,* which means "that which is empty, without firmness." The Persian Empire truly was wholly based on appearance, as we see in the book of Esther where King Ahasuerus indulged in his wedding for months on end. The empire possessed immense material riches but was spiritually empty and collapsed like a house of cards.

The third empire of Daniel's visions was also clearly named in the book of Daniel: It is the empire of Javan, in ancient Greece, illustrated by a leopard with four wings that symbolizes the speed and agility of action of its founder, Alexander the Great (356–323 BC) who became one of history's greatest conquerors by taking possession of the immense Persian Empire and advancing to the banks of the Indus.

In 331 BC, Alexander the Great attacked the Median king Darius III, who was defeated during the Battle of Gaugamela. In this confrontation, considered to be one of the most important in antiquity given the size of the armies, the Greek kingdom of Macedonia definitively vanquished the Achaemenid Persian Empire, and Alexander, in turn, made Babylon the capital of his quasi-universal empire.

The Greek Empire was also symbolized by the bronze on the belly of the statue seen by Daniel.

This third empire is described by the Hebrew word *hosher*, which means "darkness." Some commentators have concluded that this third empire would spread the darkness of the so-called light of its wisdom and knowledge throughout the known world.

It is interesting to note that, in the constituent act of the European

Daniel Interpreting the Inscription on the Wall of the Banquet Hall
Engraving by Gustave Doré

Union, the politicians purposely stated that Europe is founded on the basis of the heritage of the Enlightenment in the eighteenth century, meaning the heritage of the philosophers, of the French Revolution, of the science and technology descending from Greek civilization.

Our education system has taught us that the West rose from the darkness of the Middle Ages thanks to the Light of Reason. For some, humanist philosophical insights are a source of "darkness" for they obscure the knowledge and revelation of he who is the light of the world.

However, the identity of the fourth empire was not explicitly revealed in Daniel for the simple reason that this final empire did not exist at the time when Daniel received his visions. This fourth empire is described by the word *tehom*, meaning "abyss." It is the successor and heir of the three previous empires and particularly of Greece, which illuminated it with its darkness.

This last empire rises from the abyss, from nothingness, and goes to perdition, and in that is nihilistic. This civilization is centered on itself; its sole goal is its strength, its desire for power. It has no authentic spiritual dimension; its only ambition is world domination. This empire is beastly, dominating, and totalitarian.

The animal that represents it is a beast that isn't earthly, but supernatural. This beast is:

...one dreadful, terrible and very strong. It had two large rows of iron teeth. It devoured and crushed, and anything that was left it trampled with its feet. It was different from all the beasts that came before it, and it had ten horns. *(Daniel 7:7)*

In the intertestamental period, the Essenes of Qumran expressed the identity of this fourth empire in an apocalyptic-style book found among the Qumran scrolls discovered in the region of the Dead Sea. This work is called the fourth book of Ezra or the Apocalypse of Ezra. Among the different denominations of Christian churches, only the Ethiopian, Coptic, and several Eastern churches include this book in their biblical canon, while the others consider it apocryphal.

We read that *"the fourth beast your brother Daniel saw is none other than the Roman Empire."* The Roman Empire is also called "Edom," a small nation located south of Israel that disappeared roughly a century before Jesus, or is designated by the term *khytimes*, referring to the inhabitants of Cyprus in the coded language of the Bible, which made it possible to dodge imperial censorship.

The rabbis reached the conclusion that the Roman Empire would continue until the end of time, but in a divided, different, evolved, and adapted form. This metamorphosis is well described in chapter 7 of Daniel where we read that this empire splits into ten parts constituted by two types of different materials.

The number ten symbolizes a plurality; it is a numeral that should probably not be interpreted literally as ten countries, but rather evocatively, as "a certain number of kingdoms" that will come out of the division of the Roman Empire.

The Roman Empire saw the light in the year 27 BC. And in the year 285, having become too vast to be governed from Rome alone, the emperor Diocletian decided to divide it into a western and an eastern half. In the west, the empire disappeared in 476, while it lasted in the east in the form of the Byzantine Empire until 1453. Furthermore, the European descendants of ancient Rome conquered the Americas and founded the United States of America, a sort of extrapolation of this Western civilization. Historian Mary Beard thus shows how in the Roman Empire the democracy associated with the Republic progressively gave way to an imperial, totalitarian regime. An important factor contributed to this transition: the ascent of a military leader, a hero capable of guaranteeing victory on the battlefield and protection for Rome.

The later Roman Catholic Church, under the guidance of Pope Leo I (440–461 AD), structured itself concretely according to the centralized pattern of the Roman government and gave the pope the sacerdotal title of Pontifex Maximus. A century after the fall of the western part of the Roman Empire in 476, while the church and the residue of the empire were struggling to find a viable future, Pope Gelasius I depicted the imperial and papal functions as "two swords" that together detained sovereign power over the territory.

In the framework of this system, Europe passed from the authority of the Roman Empire to that of the Holy Roman Empire. The Holy Roman Empire lasted for a thousand years, from 800 to 1806, "more than twice the duration of Imperial Rome itself." When Pope Leo III crowned Charlemagne emperor on Christmas Day of 800, "it's quite likely that Charlemagne was convinced that he had been made Roman emperor." Wilson confirms that the European Empire was "a joint creation of Charlemagne and Leo III."

In the tenth century, the heart of the Holy Roman Empire was the Germanic kingdom, which gave birth to the Reich, whose territory ended up extending to the North and Baltic Seas and to the Mediterranean and Adriatic.

The Holy Roman Empire survived until the crisis of the French Revolutionary wars when Napoleon defeated Emperor Francis II at Austerlitz.

The heritage of the Roman Empire remains clearly recognizable today, and the European Union is a sort of modern resurgence of the Roman Empire. Since the EU's expansion in 2004 and the 2008 economic crisis, opinions regarding Europe have grown even more divided.

Wilson argues that comparisons between the Holy Roman Empire and the EU "can turn out to be instructive." First, "[...] decentralized political systems do not necessarily have peaceful intentions." The empire certainly didn't and, although the EU doesn't have its own armed forces (yet) and is entirely at peace, we should recall that France and the United Kingdom have participated in armed conflicts under EU cover.

Like the empire, the EU lacks, for the moment, a capital and a "clearly defined political heart." Throughout its history, the empire, too, remained abstract, without an established capital or a common language or culture.

Next, according to Wilson, the European Union "resembles the empire through the absence of homogeneous, organized citizens. Its relationship with its nationals is indirect since it passes through autonomous political levels, including the member states, who can still define their own criteria for citizenship, but who issue passports conferring rights applicable throughout the Union." He notes that up to the present time, the old empire seems to have had more success in encouraging a feeling of affection between its citizens.

In the Roman Empire, two cults were obligatory: the cult of the goddess Roma and the cult of the emperor. In return for their loyalty, the provinces were authorized to participate in the imperial cult, while both Nicaea and Ephesus were permitted to build temples to Julius, the deified emperor, and the goddess Roma. Thus the empire and its governors were venerated in distant regions. The presiding consul had now officially become *Imperator Caesar divi filius Augustus.*

The title "Augustus," writes the historian Goldsworthy, "brought with it weighty religious connotations" considering its link with the auguries, while *divi filius* means 'son of a god.'" According to modern criteria, *Caesar Augustus Imperator* is a military dictator; indeed, another famous dictator, Benito Mussolini, proclaimed himself "Il Duce," deliberately imitating the *Dux Augustus.* It's worth noting that Jesus Christ, called the Son of God and destined, according to the Bible, to become,

King of kings and Lord of lords *(Revelation 19:16)*

was born during the reign of Augustus, the emperor at the origin of a line of emperors who claimed to be the king of kings. Many of these human sovereigns would claim divine status and offer salvation to their people.

Israel would consider the Roman Empire as more than idolatrous; for them it was blasphemous. At the death of Augustus in the year 14, the Senate declared that he was not just the son of a god, but a god himself, which for the Jews was an unthinkable abomination.

One could say that the Babylonian Empire did not disappear completely but that Babylon metamorphosed and was reincarnated in the national confederation of the Roman Empire called in the Bible, "*The Nations*," or *Goyim* in Hebrew. Rome was a conglomerate of nations present in all of Europe, North Africa, and the Middle East. When the apostle John speaks of Babylon in Revelation, he is referring to Rome. The Roman Empire is, in his view, manipulated by a satanic creature, the dragon, the old serpent of Eden.

History gives us confirmation that pride and the desire for domination were essential components in the Roman Empire.

The modern European Union is a space of prosperity, but it doesn't genuinely offer a clear civilizational plan, nor can it offer well-founded hope to its citizens.

In this twenty-first century, our postmodern civilization is characterized by hedonism and the desire to enjoy the moment, but also by anguish and apprehension. The men of the present century live to gorge themselves on pleasure and leisure, perhaps to forget the fundamental questions inherent to human nature. They apply to the letter the expression,

…let us eat and drink, for tomorrow we die *(1 Corinthians 15:32)*

There is nothing spiritual, nothing of salvation or of God, nothing that comes after death, there is no hope. Our civilization is hemmed in by the negation of substantial biblical values, beliefs, and realities. Often pessimistic or penetrated by radical skepticism, it puts forward doubts regarding the causality, intentionality, and norms of existence. In our time, someone who has a spiritual nature is often considered a good-natured dreamer and a utopian.

Daniel's Vision of the Four Empires
Engraving by Gustave Doré

That which is serious in our civilization is power: of human science and technology. The prophet Isaiah speaks of the man who

makes a god, his idol; he bows down to it and worships it. *(Isaiah 44:17)*

As demonstrated by the philosopher Jacques Ellul, technology and its multiple applications are the idols of our time. For the first time in human history, man is capable of animating an image, of giving voice to a sort of idol created by his own hands. Technology is how he exercises his strength, his power, his domination over the world.

According to Éric Lemaître, a new man is in the process of being born, a dehumanized and materialistic man.

With the dominion of this fourth beast and the establishment of this fourth kingdom, malice will be amplified in history. This beast has teeth and claws of iron and is made of iron and clay, the iron representing the military power on which Rome based its power thanks to its legions. Its claws and teeth of iron allowed it to trample on peoples and crush what remained of them in nihilistic totalitarianism. The nations will trample Jerusalem for all "*the time of the nations.*"

With the fourth empire, sin will grow; there is an idea according to which the world will go further and further into evil over the course of human history.

General de Gaulle said: "Nations have no friends, only interests." Rome represented unlimited debauchery allied with brutal force. Its military and technological might, its thirst for debauchery and pleasure were its sole objectives.

History teaches us, in fact, that Europe has never ceased dreaming of the time when it was unified as it was in the time of the Roman Empire. Conquerors have all tried to recreate this unity, dreaming of the *Pax Romana* that brought peace, stability, and prosperity to the European continent's history: Charlemagne's Germanic Holy Roman Empire; Napoleon who, for that matter, declared himself emperor to recreate the Roman Empire; Hitler's Reich, which claimed it would last for one hundred years; and so forth.

The recreation of a monolithic state in Europe is not currently possible; it can only be a confederated block of administratively united nations. A geopolitical risk is that supranational authorities such as the IMF, WHO, NATO, and UN, which have the power and prerogatives to dictate nations' objectives, lead the West into a globalist project designed to dominate a vast portion of the world.

THE KINGDOM OF GOD

The "Kingdom of God," "Reign of God," or "Kingdom of Heaven" is a theological concept with an eschatological dimension that is present in Judaism, Christianity, and, to a lesser degree, Islam.

In ancient Judaism, the development of the notion of the kingdom of God goes back to the book of Psalms with the appearance of the idea of the God of Israel's permanent and eternal royalty. The expressions "Kingdom of God" and "Reign of God" express two expectations: the former spatial and the latter temporal of this divine royalty. The kingdom of God can be understood both as immanent reality and as transcendent reality in a conception that varies depending on whether it concerns a spiritual or a political transformation.

From the immanent viewpoint, the kingdom of God is sometimes presented as needing to be established or, indirectly, restored. In the latter case it is a political-religious expectation founded principally on the hope of the coming of a king, the "Son of David." For the Judaism of the first century, royalty belonged to God and earthly sovereigns were mere administrators of his sovereignty. The Roman occupation was considered a consequence of the sinful state of Israel, which needed to ready itself to perform the will of God that his kingdom might be established.

In the context of this conception of the kingdom, several religious groups challenged the various political authorities in place, whether Hasmonean, Herodian, or Roman. Radical currents such as the Zealots, in the hopes of speeding up Israel's eschatological liberation, conducted an armed struggle against the Romans and the self-proclaimed sovereignty of the Caesars in a combat they considered a divine commandment to establish the sole reign of God. The various political authorities therefore looked most unfavorably on this hope for the kingdom of God, as well as on the individuals who claimed to adhere to it and the groups that formed around this expectation.

Various "prophets" took part in the political and religious dimension by contesting the reigning power following the example of Theudas, who led a revolt against the Roman authority in 45 and was decapitated. Others, such as John the Baptist, belonged to the category of itinerant preachers who offered proposed absolution from sin.

The gospel of Matthew is frequently called the "Gospel of the Kingdom" due to its numerous references to this hope. The text was written by a Jew named Levi (called Matthew in our Bibles). This gospel seems to be addressed most of all to the Jews and rabbis of the synagogue, to show them with the aid of Scripture, the Hebrew Bible, that Jesus truly is the Son of God and the Emmanuel, the son of David, heir to all the kings of Israel and the Messiah that they were waiting for, in fulfillment of all the prophecies. The original milieu in which this gospel was produced was Jewish; it "advocates the full application of the Torah, in the wake of the master [Jesus] who has not come to "*abolish these things but to fulfill them* (Matthew 5:17)."[3]

This is the only one of the four Gospels that speaks of the "*Kingdom of Heaven,*" rather than the expression "*Kingdom of God,*" to ensure the rigorous respect of the commandment, "*Thou shall not take the Lord's name in vain.*"

The concept of the kingdom of God and the announcement of its coming form the core of the preaching of Jesus of Nazareth. Jesus—whose preaching reflected the Judaism of his time—substitutes the kingdom of God for the cult of the temple in a message with a universality tenor. He does not define this notion of kingdom, which was self-evident in ancient Judaism.

If he draws on the rabbinical idea of the kingdom, he sets himself apart by a prophetic dimension in explaining that not only is the end of time absolutely certain, but what's more, that the new era of redemption has already begun in the preaching of John the Baptist. Jesus, the Messiah-king, literally inaugurates the Kingdom of Heaven whose advent is presented as imminent according to a dialectic of "past" and "still to come."

In his preaching, the notion of the kingdom is the subject of numerous parables, and the miracles that he works purport to be evidence of the kingdom already at work in the present. It's also plausible that Jesus made his death a crucial condition for the establishment of the kingdom.

In his gospel, in fact, the apostle Matthew expresses that this announced supernatural kingdom does not come from man, but from heaven, because it is not humanly possible to build the kingdom of God. This entity does not belong to the earthly world, and its construction can only be divine, celestial, messianic, and exterior (transcendent).

This conception is perfectly illustrated in the famous "Our Father," which is a typically Jewish prayer. Jesus invokes God to invite him to establish his kingdom, in order that his *basilea*, his "kingdom," comes in plenitude.

Israel and the church are awaiting the same thing, the same reality. The supplication that Christ formulates to his Father in this prayer is that his sovereignty come to pass, "*May Thy will be done.*" In heaven, the will of the Father is absolutely realized in all circumstances, and it is always good, pleasant, perfect. But on earth, this is not the case. His will is not always perfectly realized. Indeed, there are two main obstacles to the Father's sovereignty: Satan, who has prerogatives in our world, and the desire of the free will of man, who has taken the side of Satan against God, his adversary since the fall.

There is the notion of the confrontation between two contradictory kingdoms in absolute opposition, the kingdom of darkness and that of light. Their leaders, the Messiah and Satan, are mortal enemies. After Jesus is baptized with water and the Holy Spirit in the Jordan, he is put to the test against the prince of darkness during forty days in the desert. The devil shows him:

> ... in a flash all the kingdoms of the world. And he said to him, "To you I will grant this whole realm—and the glory that goes along with it, for it has been relinquished to me, and I can give it to anyone I wish." *(Luke 4:5–8)*

Satan reminds Jesus that he is the prince of this earthly world, and Jesus, who is well aware of it, doesn't argue!

The power struggle between the two kingdoms, those of light and darkness, is particularly evident in the scene described in chapter 4 of Luke when the devil (who will be expelled by Jesus in the synagogue of Capernaum at the moment of the liberation of a man possessed by an impure spirit) declared:

> Ha! Leave us alone, Jesus the Nazarene! Have you come to destroy us? *(Luke 4:34)*

This power struggle is equally present in the sending of the devils into the pigs in the land of the Gergesenes:

> They cried out, "Son of God, leave us alone! Have you come here to torment us before the time?" *(Matthew 8:29)*

Jesus provides a practical demonstration that the kingdom of darkness and its creatures are now directly under attack by the supreme leader of the kingdom of God and, for that matter, the result of the struggle is quite clear for the devils: they know that the "*Saint of God*" has full authority over them to condemn them and that the time of their freedom of action is now coming to an end.

In the Gospels, on only two occasions are there mentions of the church, and it's anecdotal, but the kingdom of God is ever-present. The preaching of Jesus—his doctrine—was principally concerned with the Holy Spirit and the kingdom of God. Indeed, the Son of God went around doing good (Acts 10:38) so that

> ... the dead are raised, and the poor have good news proclaimed to them. *(Matthew 11:5)*

He drove out the devils, soldiers, and workers of Satan. Jesus would say:

> I saw Satan fall like lightning from heaven. *(Luke 10:18)*

Each time, in fact, that there is an exorcism, a conversion, a sinner forgiven, a miracle, or a supernatural healing, Satan is troubled and his authority vacillates. Satan, the enemy of man, holds humanity captive through suffering, illness, seduction, demonic possession, and death.

Lucifer has possessed a legal prerogative over our world since the fall of Adam and Eve, who chose to side with him, the serpent, their adversary, in a joint act of revolt against their Creator. Man was designed to have authority over the devil but by this act, he passed under the domination of his worst enemy, and we have inherited this state.

The gospels of Matthew and Luke teach us that, starting in the era of John the Baptist, a breech appeared in the kingdom of God and that all, using violence, can now penetrate into it. Since the fall of man, a wall of separation between the kingdom of heaven and the earthly kingdom has been built. At the coming of John the Baptist, a fracture was created, and a human being can now escape the domination of the prince of this fallen world.

By repenting, man can now flee toward the kingdom of God and escape eternal perdition. Each man now has the freedom but also the responsibility to choose his path and his side, and the coercion that man must exercise on himself is that of penance and faith. Penance is the means given by God for entering the kingdom of God through the narrow door of the breech. There is a violence that must be done to his fallen carnal nature, but the Good Shepherd invites the sheep to pass through the doorway of life for their salvation.

The Bible announces that the end days will be a period of unprecedented crisis because Satan will revolt and become very aggressive upon seeing his kingdom besieged on all sides. Revelation unveils to us that in the end times a terrible satanic power will be unleashed upon the world.

The completion and then destruction of Babylon are the indispensable conditions for the complete establishment of the kingdom of God, which is the fifth and last empire of history, according to its description in the book of Daniel:

> In the days of these kings the God of heaven will raise up an everlasting kingdom that will not be destroyed and a kingdom that will not be left to another people. It will break in pieces and bring about the demise of all these kingdoms. But it will stand forever. You saw that a stone was cut from a mountain, but not by human hands; it smashed the iron, bronze, clay, silver, and gold into pieces. *(Daniel 2:44–45)*

The fifth empire is a kingdom with peaceable human sentiments. A non-oppressive kingdom that seeks man's fulfillment, unlike the previous beastly kingdoms that sought to debase him.

In this final kingdom, the harmony of creation will finally be restored. But during the waiting period, human beings are prone to the adversary's seduction, and the prayer taught by Jesus implores God's aid: *"Deliver us from evil,"* meaning from man's bad inclination.

Just as he is under the influence of a "good inclination," the *yotser hatov,* literally, the "creator of good," man is influenced by a "bad inclination," the *yotser hara,* "creator of evil." These influences exist to offer man the opportunity to choose his path consciously, for life in this world is summed up in a series of choices tending toward good or evil, wisdom or folly.

According to Jewish tradition the *yotser hara* that negatively influences man is dual in its nature. The *yotser hara* is simultaneously internal, inherent to our nature, and is expressed through bodily impulses or desires; it's also spiritual and external, in which case it comes from the devil and troubles us from without by tempting us through seduction. For the kingdom of God to be established, the *yotser hara* must disappear completely.

The life of man, ultimately, is a choice to be made between the side of darkness and the side of light that we make at the cost of a difficult personal struggle. But we must position ourselves, for we cannot belong to these two worlds at once.

In the end times, the faithful church must increasingly purify itself as the intensity of the satanic confrontation of the *yotser hara* grows stronger. There will be a more and more extreme drive of humanity toward evil and to destroy it; the two sides will have to come face to face, clearly taking sides, as illustrated in the parable of the wheat and the chaff where it is necessary that the two opposing realities be clearly distinguished to be able to eliminate the bad grain that has ripened. This period of history is summed up by the expression "pangs of messianic childbirth."

The Bible announces that the governor of the kingdom will be the Messiah, the King of glory, who will reign with good sentiments, caring for the young and the poor, helping the weak.

> The nations will walk by its light and the kings of the earth will bring their grandeur into it. *(Revelation 21:24)*

In Genesis, we read that Jacob, while fleeing from the wrath of his brother Esau, slept one night of his exile in Bethel and that he anointed with oil the stone on which he spent the night. This anointed *"chosen"* stone is the image of the Messiah, who is the cornerstone and foundation of the world. It's this stone that

> struck the statue on its iron and clay feet, breaking them in pieces *(Daniel 2:34)*

and destroyed the statue of Daniel's vision, then

> became a large mountain that filled the entire earth. *(Daniel 2:35)*

It is the Lord who will realize man's dream, by instituting this messianic kingdom as well as its capital and eternal city: the new Jerusalem.

Jesus Cures a Mute
Engraving by Gustave Doré, 1874

BABYLON AND JERUSALEM

According to the rabbis, only two cities in the world are perfectly antagonistic to each other: Babylon and Jerusalem. These two cities cannot coexist. Historians say that Solomon was able to reign and prosper because in his day, Babylonia was in full decay.

Babylon was revived at the time of Daniel, and its king, Nebuchadnezzar, besieged Jerusalem in 588. After roughly ten years of siege, the city fell. The sons of the Jewish king Zedekiah were killed, while he was mutilated and deported to Babylon along with the majority of the kingdom's elite. Jerusalem was then burned and sacked. After the Jews' seventy-year exile in Babylon, the Persian king Cyrus destroyed that city and authorized Jerusalem's reconstruction.

Human history appears to illustrate a spiritual succession to this city: the new Babylon will be the city of Rome. The author of Revelation makes able use of this comparison and in chapter 17 compares Babylon to a

> woman [...] dressed in purple and scarlet clothing, and adorned with gold, precious stones, and pearls. She held in her hand a golden cup filled with detestable things and unclean things from her sexual immorality. On her forehead was written a name, a mystery: "Babylon the Great, the Mother of prostitutes and of the detestable things of the earth." *(Revelation 17:4–5)*

Slightly further along, it is written:

> *(This requires a mind that has wisdom.) The seven heads are seven mountains the woman sits on. (Revelation 17:9)*

Throughout antiquity, in fact, the city known for its seven hills was the imperial capital of Rome. There is certainly a coded assimilation made by the author between these two cities, the metropolis of the Roman Empire that is the new Babylon.

We read in the story of Genesis that the city of Babylon was built by the first universal dictator, Nimrod. He tried to create *"a single people and a single tongue"* to unify humanity in the communal project of recreating an ersatz version of the original paradise lost during the fall, the memory of which humanity conserves.

This plan achieves its symbolic peak with the construction of the Tower of Babel, whose summit aimed to touch heaven. The word *Babel* comes from the Akkadian word *Bab-Il-In,* "gateway of the gods" and also "upheaval."

Yet this cursed civilization also has its polar opposite: the people of Israel founded by Abram who is a man called by God to leave Ur in Chaldea, which is in Babylonia. Chaldea is a region located between the lower portions of the Euphrates and Tigris. The inhabitants who occupied this region formed the kingdoms of Sumer and Akkad. The Chaldeans originally were a tribe who lived in Babylonia, to the southwest of Babylon.

By obeying this call, Abram grasped his vocation for becoming the father of a new people in the very same period of God's dispersion of the population of Babel. Abram, "the Father is exalted," became Abraham, which means "father of a multitude of nations." The founder of Israel is he who was called by God to create a nation that was chosen and set apart among the nations.

These peoples look with hope toward the city with solid foundations, the future celestial Jerusalem, the city of God. Then

> the LORD came down to see the city and the tower that the people had started building. *(Genesis 11:5)*

The constructors of Babel declared:

> …let's make bricks and bake them thoroughly. *(Genesis 11:3)*

It is characterized, therefore, by its technical nature and technology. The city was built in brick, which is a very negative symbol in the Bible due to its association with slavery in Egypt; by the standardization of its production, it makes possible the endless construction of monuments to the glory of man. The heavenly city of the New Jerusalem, however, was built with

> living stones […] a spiritual house. *(1 Peter 2:5)*

The Tower of Babel remained incomplete because its realization was prevented by God himself who spread confusion and disorder to halt this prideful project.

In Genesis, when Babylon was destroyed, Abraham set off for Jerusalem. In Revelation the destruction of Babylon was a condition for the establishment of the fifth empire, the kingdom of God. So we see that the new Jerusalem appeared after the destruction of the utopia of Babel.

The architects of the building of the European Parliament in Strasburg seem to have tried to poke fun at this founding story by constructing the monument at the center of the EU's political power. The Louise Weiss Tower, centerpiece of the parliament's architecture, is inspired by a painting by the artist Pieter Brueghel the Elder, painted around 1563.

In this painting, the Tower of Babel is built "like an ascending spiral, it is a circular edifice, the diameter of whose levels diminishes as they rise."

The Tower of Babel
Painting by Pieter Brueghel the Elder depicting the
biblical story of the Tower of Babel, c. 1563

The arches were built perpendicularly to the slanted floor, which made them unstable; in fact, some of them have already collapsed. Perhaps even more troubling is the fact that the foundations and lower strata of the tower were not finished beforehand. While the architectural design is quite precise, it is for that no less absurd. The tower seems composed of a strange network of barrel-vaulted galleries that lead to nothing. It is clear that Brueghel did not try to reproduce an inhabitable space. The tower builders' intention, in fact, is not to create a functional building, but to penetrate the [reach up to] heaven. The painting is supposed to represent the dangers of human pride, but also, the limits of rationality in the face of the divine."[4]

The symbolism of the builders of the European Parliament, completed in 1999, could be interpreted as the will to complete Babel, this capital of a purely terrestrial and horizontal empire to unify their human community in a materialistic, humanistic, artificial paradise. We may ask some serious questions about the symbolic intentions of an institution of continental importance.

Testifying to this is the official poster, which bore the slogan "Europe: Many Tongues, One Voice," and the upside-down pentagrams, omnipresent, for that matter, in esoteric milieux.

In the Bible, we read that ultimately, at the end times, men succeed in achieving their goal of building the great global village: they manage to finish constructing Babylon. Yes, men are going to succeed; they will think they have defeated God and finally excluded him from his creation.

Today the era of nations and states is ending, and we are witnessing the emergence of immense geopolitical blocks. It is now the era of the great global village. The Babylon described in the Revelation is a city that loves debauchery, pleasure, and luxury. It is under the influence of the merchants and the commerce that have made it so rich.

Europe: Many Tongues, One Voice
Official poster associating
Europe with the Tower of Babel

> For all the nations have fallen from the wine of her immoral passion, and the kings of the earth have committed sexual immorality with her, and the merchants of the earth have gotten rich from the power of her sensual behavior. *(Revelation 18:3)*

The analogy with our materialistic Western civilization is striking. The Tower of Babel also had an observational function; its dominant position made it possible to watch over everything that happened in the city, even within the private circles of people's homes. The permanent surveillance of men is a mark and a tool of totalitarianism. Never in the history of humanity have the knowledge and the surveillance of individuals been as absolute as in this twenty-first century and, thanks to computer science, governments can monitor each house, each individual, down to their most mundane daily habits.

The Koran begins and ends in a garden. The Bible begins in a garden and ends in a city. The word "city" in Hebrew, *ir*, has the same root as the word "curse." A century ago, three-quarters of the world's inhabitants lived in the countryside and a quarter in cities; today, that proportion has been reversed.

Modern men construct a single culture with a single language, English, and undertake exchanges with instantaneous and universal means of communication.

Man's plan is to create his own paradise on earth, hence his curse. God respects and ratifies man's choice to live in a city, but it is he who is going to build it; it will be the New Jerusalem, the City of God. A sculpture by the Sotiriadis brothers dating to 2005 is displayed on Avenue Schumann in Strasburg. This sculpture represents the goddess Europa, daughter of the king of

Tyre, as a woman riding a beast. The Greek myth says that she was raped by Zeus, king of the gods.

Revelation 17 also evokes a female prostitute sitting on the great waters and astride a beast: the kidnapping of Europa. Positioned in front of the building of the Council of the EU, this work by Léon de Pas seems to symbolize the fragility of democracy and, strangely, possesses an erotic double meaning.

Man's pride brought forth other projects for Towers of Babel. In the U.S.S.R., Stalin decided to raise the Palace of the Soviets to a height of 418 meters surmounted by a statue of Lenin 100 meters tall with a 30-meter raised arm for another "Babylon"—Moscow.

Soviet Plan for the Palace of the Soviets in Moscow
Design by architect
Boris Iofan

God wants to construct the New Jerusalem with the materials of our personal history. Revelation teaches us that the New Jerusalem bears the name of the twelve apostles of the Lamb, and the name of the twelve tribes. Ultimately, all biblical history is contained and summed up in this eternal city.

In 1141, during the golden age of Spanish Judaism, Juda Halevi wrote a poem about Jerusalem titled "Ode to Zion."

Royal city, jewel of the earth, citadel of the Great King . . . ,
From the ends of the earth where I am exiled
My heart turns toward you,
When will I be able to blend my tears
with your dust?

At the end of the biblical story, it is Babylon that will lose to the gain of Jerusalem, as Handel put into music in his "Hallelujah" that sings of the fall of Babylon!

The advent of the new Jerusalem, the heavenly city, thus becomes possible through the destruction of Babylon, the earthly capital. The Bible summons, *"Come out of her, my people" (Revelation 18:4)* to follow in the footsteps of the "patriarchs [who] set off toward the city with strong foundations, of which God is architect and builder, the heavenly Jerusalem."

The Tower of Babel
Engraving by Gustave Doré, 1874

Ultimately every man is a citizen of one of these two cities, and he must choose his allegiance. If we love Babylon, its pleasures and luxury become lust with all the banquets of Belshazzar, and we are in danger.

In front of Loth, Abraham faced a similar choice when he chose the desert, the place of sobriety and silence, the place that allows you to hear the voice of God rather than the lush plains of the Jordan close by.

THE SIGN OF THE END OF TIME

The last things contain profound mysteries, as summed up thus in the gospel of Mark by Jesus himself:

> But as for that day or hour no one knows it—neither the angels in heaven, nor the Son—except the Father. *(Mark 13:32)*

The precise unfolding of events is veiled, but Jesus nevertheless provides a landmark for discerning the last events:

> Now while some were speaking about the temple, how it was adorned with beautiful stones and offerings, Jesus said, "As for these things that you are gazing at, the days will come when not one stone will be left on another. All will be torn down!" So they asked him, "Teacher, when will these things happen? And what will be the sign that these things are about to take place?" He said [. . .], "But when you see Jerusalem surrounded by armies, then know that its desolation has come near. Then those who are in Judea must flee to the mountains. Those who are inside the city must depart. Those who are out in the country must not enter it, because these are days of vengeance, to fulfill all that is written. Woe to those who are pregnant and to those who are nursing their babies in those days! For there will be great distress on the earth and wrath against this people. They will fall by the edge of the sword and be led away as captives among all nations. Jerusalem will be trampled down by the Gentiles until the times of the Gentiles are fulfilled. [. . .]" *(Luke 21:5–24)*

The historian Flavius Josephus, who was born in Jerusalem around 37 and died in Rome around 100, was a first-century Roman of Jewish origins. In his work *The Jewish War*, one of the main secular sources for the history of Judea in the first century, he relates how certain events corresponding quite closely to the fulfillment of Jesus's prophecy took place: the siege of Jerusalem by the Romans, followed by the destruction of the Temple of Herod in the year 70.

The origin of the Jewish uprising against Rome was partly linked to the categorical refusal of the cult of the emperor that had been decreed obligatory throughout the Roman Empire. The Jewish people alone had been exempted. But in the 50s, the emperor Caius Caligula decided to eliminate this status quo by obliging the Jews to provide him with an imperial cult; he had a statue realized to his own glory, portrayed with the features of the Roman god Jupiter

Capitolinus. Petronius, the governor of Syria, received the order to place this statue in the temple of Jerusalem.

For the Jews of that age, there was no doubt about the fact that the man of sin, the Impious One announced in Isaiah 11 (the Antichrist), would come from Rome. This is why, in the Jewish tradition, this evil figure has a symbolic Roman name: Arnelius. It was thus a particularly sensitive matter.

The governor Petronius was well aware that the decree would provoke a Jewish revolt, so he begged Caligula to change his mind, to no avail. The statue arrived in Israel at the port of St. John of Acre, and the Jewish leaders lay down on the road to prevent the wagons from transporting the idolatrous statue to Jerusalem.

In the sixth decade of the first century, the extremist Jewish sect of the Zealots, observing that the Messiah was late in coming to deliver the Jewish people from Roman oppression under the dominion of Emperor Nero (in power from 54 to 68), deliberately provoked a revolt against the all-powerful Roman Empire in the year 66 to tempt God, forcing him to intervene in human history.

This revolution was evidently suicidal given the scope of Roman military force and firepower. The Roman general Titus was assisted by the ex-procurator of Judea, Tiberius Alexander, an apostate from Judaism who had an excellent knowledge of the region. They were at the head of four legions: the 5th Macedonica, the 10th Fretensis, the 15th Apollinaris, and the 12th Fulminata, a force of around 24,000 men. The legions were reinforced by an equal number of men recruited by Titus as well as by men of the Alexandrian army and the Euphrates garrisons for a total of more than 50,000 soldiers, though the historian Graetz estimated more than 80,000.

The Jewish Zealots were convinced that at the last moment God would send the Messiah to save Jerusalem, the city of the saint and the children of light whom they claimed to be. Jesus, however, had clearly indicated for people to flee Jerusalem before the coming enemy troops, prophesying that the Temple of Herod would be razed and

> Jerusalem will be trampled down by the Gentiles until the times of the Gentiles are fulfilled. *(Luke 21:24)*

Flavius Josephus stated in his writings that the temple was set on fire by accident during the taking of the city and the general Titus, who would become emperor following Nero's forced suicide in 68, did everything possible to prevent this destruction. This statement, however, is contested by numerous historians because the building's destruction was likely the objective of the military campaign.

According to Josephus, the number of prisoners of war amounted to 97,000 and the number of deaths during the siege, to 1,100,000 people. This number can seem exaggerated, though it should be remembered that the siege began just before Passover, a pilgrimage feast during which Jews from throughout the empire were accustomed to traveling to Jerusalem, whose population in that period was three times more numerous than in normal times. Thus pilgrims were caught in the trap. During these four terrible years of siege, tens of thousands of Jews perished of starvation and disease, to the point that women ate their own children. As for captured fugitives, they were crucified by the Romans in view of the populace to serve as examples and terrify those under siege. When the city fell, two-thirds of its residents were exterminated, and the surviving captives were sent to the salt mines and the Roman arenas. Seven hundred Jewish prisoners were taken to Rome. According to Josephus, Titus had thousands of Jews crucified when the city was taken.

The interpretation of apocalyptic prophecies is a delicate matter because we always have the tendency to consider that the message was written for our own time. But *"this time of distress the likes of which there will be no more, shall never come again"* was well and truly fulfilled in the year 70. We can thus state that, during the eschatological war of Armageddon, this time of distress will therefore not come again, and Jerusalem will be saved as it is written at the end of the book of Ezekiel. The disaster already took place in the year 70 AD.

But Jesus's prophetic announcement of the destruction of the temple contains a significant detail. The narration parallel to Luke's text is found in Mark 13; it underlines and brings to light a point of great importance. The evangelist Mark cites a passage from the book of Daniel:

> But when you see the abomination of desolation standing where it should not be *(let the reader understand)* …

The expression *"the abomination of desolation"* is translated literally as "the droppings that sully and render arid." But surprisingly, this expression is written each time with a spelling error. When Matthew (chapter 24) and Mark (chapter 23) cite this text in Daniel, they include the spelling error as well, this time in Greek. In most of our bibles, we find this small note: *"let the reader understand."* The error is present to attract our attention to the importance of the passage. The victorious Roman legions did raise the emblems of their gods on the location of the temple. Now these emblems were blasphemous for the Jewish people and sullied the most sacred place in Judaism, like the presence of excrement in the holy site. After Titus's conquest of the city, no building replaced the Temple of Jerusalem.

However, in the second century, after the emperor Hadrian's decision to rebuild Jerusalem as a Roman city and have himself worshipped by its peoples, the Jewish leader Bar Kokhba led an uprising against the Romans, from 132 to his death in 135, after a savage war that left Judea devastated.

This military episode was that of the revolt of what remained of the Jewish people under the leadership of him whose name in Aramaic means "Son of the Star." This nickname is clearly the result of the interpretation of the biblical verse

A star will march forth out of Jacob *(Numbers 24:17)*

to which the Jewish tradition attributes messianic scope: the star of Jacob that designates the Messiah.

Bar Kokhba raised an army, established an independent Jewish state in the land of Judea, planned to rebuild the temple, and coined money. Facing a unified and highly motivated Jewish force, the Romans were caught completely off guard. The annihilation of an entire Roman legion forced Rome to send no less than twelve legions, which represented between one-third to one-half of the imperial Roman forces, to reconquer the tiny rebel province.

Penalized in numbers and suffering heavy losses, the Romans decided to adopt scorched-earth tactics, decimating the Jewish population to gradually undermine its morale and determination to pursue the war. Bar Kokhba retreated to the fortress of Betar, southwest of Jerusalem, but the Romans ended up storming it and massacring all its defenders in 135.

Following the defeat of Bar Kokhba, Jerusalem was razed, prohibited to the Jews, and a new Roman city, Aelia Capitolina, was built on its site. The emperor Hadrian had a temple dedicated to the Capitoline Jupiter erected on the site.

When the Roman Empire became Christian under Constantine I, it seems that the location of the temple was abandoned. However, after the conquest of Jerusalem by the Arabs in 637, new buildings were raised. The Dome of the Rock (in Arabic, *Qubbat As-Sakhrah*)—sometimes mistakenly called the Mosque of Omar—was completed around 691 during the reign of Abd al-Malik.

This building serves to worship the female deity of the radiant star of the moon, Allah, chosen among the hundreds of deities of Mecca, by Muhammad, under the inspiration of his uncle Abdallah, "servant of Allah," and which for the Jews is an abomination.

This monument, the Dome of the Rock, is today the most visible in Jerusalem with its golden dome. It houses the "Rock of Foundation," the site where, according to Muslim tradition, Muhammad arrived from Mecca during his night voyage, the Isra', and from where he rose to heaven during the Miraj, riding his mount, Buraq.

According to the biblical tradition, this is the location of Mount Moriah, the name given to the massif on which Abraham climbed with his son Isaac to offer him to God in sacrifice, then on which Solomon later built the old temple of Jerusalem. Christianity does not seem to have erected a monument on the exact site of the temple, which would later be used as a dump. Later, during the Crusades, the Dome of the Rock would be transformed into the Templum Domini and the al-Aqsa Mosque given to the Templars. The building fell victim to extensive destruction prior to its last great reconstruction dating to the thirteenth century.

Jerusalem's destruction lasted "the times of the Gentiles," or an important period of history extending from 70 to 1967, the date of the Six-Day War when in less than a week, the Hebrew state tripled its territorial hold. Egypt lost the Gaza Strip and the Sinai Peninsula, the Golan Heights were cut off from Syria, and Jordan lost the West Bank and East Jerusalem. The highly symbolic Arab defeat of this war was the taking of the old city of Jerusalem.

According to the prophetic chronology, *"the times of the Gentiles"* is followed by a last period of dominion by human empires: "the end times." This period will conclude, according to the Bible, with the return of Jesus, who will complete the establishment of the kingdom of God.

The Beginning of the Reconstruction of the Temple in Jerusalem
Engraving by Gustave Doré, 1874

One question often resurfaces in Christian circles: Are the Jews today making ready to build the Third Temple, as rumors sometimes suggest, even in evangelical milieux? Here the answer must be negative. According to rabbinical doctrine, it is the Messiah, and only the Messiah, who will rebuild the temple—this is one part of the Jews' two criteria for recognizing his messianism; the second key criteria is the resurrection of the dead.

Currently, on the other hand, a group called the "Faithful of the Temple" is preparing all the elements—garments, utensils, even the Brazen Sea—for the coming of the Messiah. For the Jews, the temple is a place of peace that can only be built in times of peace, as in the time of Solomon, for that was the only time of peace in all of Israel's history. According to them, the time of messianic peace will permit the temple to be rebuilt.

When Jesus speaks of the end times with his disciples, he doesn't contradict the fact that he will reestablish the political and administrative kingdom of Israel, but not before the gospel is proclaimed to the ends of the earth. According to Mark,

First the gospel must be preached to all nations. *(Mark 13:10)*

which suggests on Jesus's part a very long period! The fig tree is the image used by Jesus to be a sign of these times for Israel, in the same way Jerusalem is the sign of the times for humanity.

Ever since the Six-Day War in 1967, East Jerusalem has been controlled and administered by Israel. It was annexed in 1980. This part includes the old city and its holy places: the Holy Sepulcher, the Esplanade of Mosques, the al-Aqsa Mosque, the Temple Mount, and the Kotel. And since 1967, prophetically, due to the current geopolitical situation, the fulfillment of the last events can be triggered at any moment.

THE GREAT APOSTASY

Jesus left us with a crucial question:

> …when the Son of Man comes, will he find faith on earth? *(Luke 18:8)*

Paul reassured the Thessalonians in his letter because they were concerned about the second coming of the Messiah: Could it be that the Lord has already returned and the community is unaware of it? *"No,"* Paul responded, *"for apostasy must come before"* the return of Christ.

The term *apostasy* comes from the Greek word *apostasia* (ἀποστασία), meaning "defection," "departure," "revolt," or "rebellion." It has been described as a voluntary abandonment of Christianity or a rebellion against it. Apostasy is the rejection of Christ by a Christian. "Apostasy is the antonym of conversion; it is de-conversion."[5] Thomas Aquinas defined apostasy as a certain moving away from God and particularly distinguished between apostasy in the religious life and apostasy through unbelief.[6] In his view, the latter completely separates man from God, which does not occur with any other sin. Apostasy only concerns people who had the faith beforehand, an essential condition for later renouncing it.

According to B. J. Oropeza, warning passages in the New Testament describe at least three dangers that can lead a Christian to commit apostasy:

- Temptation: Christians were tempted to give in to various vices that were a part of their lives before becoming Christians (idolatry, sexual immorality, greed, and so forth).
- Deception: Christians have encountered various heresies and false teachings spread by false doctors and prophets that threaten to seduce them and divert them from their pure devotion to Christ.
- Persecution: Christians were persecuted for their allegiance to Christ. Numerous Christians were threatened with certain death if they didn't renounce Christ.[7]

Persecution was highlighted in the letter to the Hebrews and in the first letter of Peter. The questions of false teachers/teachings are found in the letters of John and Paul, in the second letter of Peter, and the letter of Jude. "The Christians were to persevere through various types of opposition, standing firm against temptation, false doctrine, hardships, and persecution."[8]

The writings of the early church fathers, in addition to those cited, have led Patristic scholar David Bercot to conclude: "Since the early Christians believed that our continued faith and obedience are necessary for salvation, it naturally follows that they believed that a "saved" person could still end up being lost [by apostasy]."[9] We also find such warnings in the seven letters to the seven churches.

Following in-depth research, New Testament specialist B. J. Oropeza has come to the same conclusion: "The church fathers would affirm the reality of the phenomenon of apostasy."[10] Traditional Calvinists Thomas R. Schreiner and Ardel B. Caneday advise readers to read Oropeza's "excellent history of interpretation on the matter of perseverance and apostasy."[11]

During the period of the end times, many believers will stumble, to the point of "*denying the Master who bought them*" (2 Peter 2:1). In this period, the temptation to abandon the faith in exchange for other attractions and pleasures will thus be such that "*if those days had not been cut short, no one would be saved*" (Matthew 24:22).

In the West, the greatest danger of apostasy comes far more from seduction than from persecution. Jesus cautioned us:

> But stay alert at all times, praying that you may have strength to all these things that must happen, and to stand before the Son of Man. *(Luke 21:36)*

The danger of resting on our laurels is quite real for a believer, a church, or a nation. Jesus explains this in the parable of the foolish rich man:

> And I will say to myself, "You have plenty of goods stored up for many years; relax, eat, drink and celebrate!" But God said to him, 'You fool!' *(Luke 12:19–20)*

Complacency is the worst state of spiritual danger that a man can experience, for false justice is a state of critical blindness. In his letter to Timothy Paul evoked the attitude of men in the end times who

> will be lovers of themselves, lovers of money, boastful, arrogant, blasphemers, disobedient to parents, ungrateful, unholy, unloving, irreconcilable, slanderers, without self-control, savage, opposed to what is good, treacherous, reckless, conceited, loving pleasure rather than loving God. They will maintain the outward appearance of religion but will have repudiated its power. So avoid people like these. *(2 Timothy 3:2–5)*

This is the description of the characteristics of apostasy. European countries were Christianized but they have never technically been genuinely Christian in the biblical sense of the word. Our culture has been nourished by Christian values, by its morality, and Europe has been influenced by the gospel, but what is the heritage of all this in our century? Postmodern civilization rejects its Christian roots. The church, called to take shelter from the world, nevertheless breathes in the spirit of the times. It is permeable to the influences of society, and the danger of apostasy is precisely that it may not be manifest, but creeping. It first affects society at large and morally contaminates the church with a certain lag.

In the European Union's constitution, which is its foundational text, references to the Judeo-Christian roots of European civilization were purposely suppressed in exchange for an affiliation with classical Greek thought and the Enlightenment. This is perhaps the first time in the history of humanity that a civilization has rejected its roots. We read in Psalm 2:3:

> Let's tear off the shackles they've put on us, let's free ourselves from their ropes.

Rabbinical exegesis teaches that in the end times, nations will desire to free themselves from the chains and bonds of the Torah, from the laws of God.

In the end times, nations will reject the sweet, gentle yoke of the Messiah and his Torah. From an ethnological standpoint, cutting off one's own roots is civilizational suicide.

What distinguishes the great apostasy is moral laxity. According to philosopher, theologian, and professor Jacques Elull, the democratization of sin is one of the great dangers to the church in the twenty-first century.

Jezebel, the false prophetess of the time of Elias, also had this ambition to lead the people of God to immorality with elements of popular debauchery.

The Christianity of the final church is characterized by a semblance of piety and, unlike Communism where the revolt against God is overt, in the church, apostasy is a silent rejection. In the letters to the churches in Revelation, there are only two categories of believers: on one side, the faithful, the "conquerors," and on the other, the apostates. The image employed is a bride, either faithful or not. Indeed, just as an adulterous woman hides her depravity, so the church can continue to profess the gospel despite reneging its love and what makes it strong, giving in to shameful compromises. It is perhaps completely unaware of its true spiritual state, as in the parable of the wise and foolish virgins. While we are sleeping, we don't realize that we are asleep; it's only when we awaken that we become aware of having slept.

The rebuke for the state of apostasy is particularly strong toward the Church of Laodicea, which the Lord advised *"buy gold from me refined by fire"* (Revelation 3:18).

"Believing itself rich" and *"having the appearance of piety,"* our civilization corresponds in a number of respects to the description that Paul gives of hedonism and its subscribers, *"loving pleasure rather than loving God"* (2 Timothy 3:4).

Professor Jacques Ellul also said that the second great danger for the church of the twenty-first century is becoming "the church of entertainment," awash in ease. It lives contrary to the church of discipleship which, on the other hand, works through devotion, Bible study, and prayer.

Christ denounced the Laodiceans' thinking: "*I am rich and have acquired great wealth, and need nothing*" (Revelation 3:17). The weak spiritual appetite of many Christians surely demonstrates a similar attitude, and in this sense, comfort is dangerous, for believing means committing our life to what we believe and not seeking our security in material wealth.

One of Jesus's expressions recurs regularly in the letters to the seven churches; he tells them, "*I know.*" The apostate is he who has forgotten that the Lord sees us and knows us. It behooves us to be vigilant, for it is when we are alone, in secret, that we are truly ourselves. What is important in the eyes of God is not what we say we are or appear to be, but what we *are*.

If we have chosen a wicked path or have fallen, there is nevertheless a solution offered by God, who encourages us: "*Be earnest and repent*" (Revelation 3:19). We can always come back to what we have left and, like David, pray:

> Examine me, and probe my thoughts! Test me, and know my concerns! See if there is an idolatrous tendency in me, and lead me in the reliable ancient path! *(Psalm 139:23–24)*

The Lord addresses his promises of restoration to men who have quite often been weak and overcome but who do not cheat; precisely because they recognize their miserable state and repent, the Lord grants them grace.

The great drama of Christianity is that Christians are not genuinely interested in either their Master, Jesus, or his message. They are only interested in what he can give them—healing, miracles, prosperity—but not in his teaching to become his disciples.

Some Christians have even ended up placing God outside of their church: proof is Jesus's call:

> Listen! I am standing at the door and knocking! *(Revelation 3:20)*

meaning he's outside the door!

When all is said and done, the doctrine of Christ is quite radical. Man has the choice between two fires: that of judgment and that of purification. Christ is constantly calling on us to change, to return from our wicked paths, and to accept self-renunciation at the risk, if we do not, of lapsing into half-heartedness, even the denial of the Master.

In Turkey, the Church of Philadelphia was one of just two of the seven churches faithful to the model. Yet today there are but ruins of the Church of Saint John dating back to the Byzantine era, whose only vestige is a flying buttress, and even this is half-collapsed. In the background a mosque is visible and in the foreground, a church is in ruins. Turkey, a bastion of early Christianity and the second holy land after Israel, is now 98 percent Muslim. North Africa, too, has almost completely become Islamicized from what was once the center of Christianity in Africa. Ancient Christianity's prevalence in these regions, indeed, is hard to believe today.

The greatest danger to the spiritual life of believers is a cooling through the loss of a personal relationship with Christ. The problem for the generation of Noah's time was the attraction of worldly things. Men ate, drank, and married off their children, but Jesus warns us:

The Triumph of Christianity over Paganism
Engraving by Gustave Doré, 1874

> But be on your guard so that your hearts are not weighed down with dissipation and drunkenness and the worries of this life. *(Luke 21:34)*

Eating, drinking, and marrying one's children are not bad things in and of themselves as long as they don't become the priority in life. "*Look! I am coming soon*" (Revelation 22: 12), Jesus cautions.

The problem is that we are too comfortable on earth; we want to enjoy life. And many Christians do not wish for the Lord to return, or at the very least, not right away! If this is the case, it's because the majority prefer earthly things to those of heaven.

In Cardinal Robert Sarah's book *The Day Is Now Far Spent*, he says:

> At the root of the collapse of the West, there is a cultural identity crisis. The West no longer knows who it is, because it no longer knows and does not want to know who made it, who established it, as it was and as it is. Many countries today ignore their own history. This self-suffocation naturally leads to a decadence that opens the path to new, barbaric civilizations.[12]

This is a description of what is happening in Europe.

THE ANTICHRIST

The mysterious number 666 has fueled innumerable controversies that no one can explain with precision, even if the exegetical approaches of Jewish gematria and ancient Greek isopsephy have given rise to plenty of speculation.

The following words, written in Greek by someone in love, were unearthed in Pompei: "I love the girl whose number is 545." The use of secret codes was common practice in antiquity.

The historical context in which Revelation was written has led some commentators to argue that 666 could refer to the Emperor Nero (qsar Néron = 100 + 60 + 200 + 50 + 200 + 6 = 666). After all, the cruelty of Nero's reign did strongly mark his era. While some didn't believe in his death, others believed he would be resurrected; hence, the text's potential allusion to

> the beast who had been wounded by the sword, but still lived. *(Revelation 13:14)*

The identity of the Antichrist and the precise length of his reign, however, are hidden mysteries and will only be revealed at the end.

The nineteenth-century Protestant evangelical awakening coincided with a heightened interest in eschatology. And the new consensus affirms the advent of a world dictator (the beast or the Antichrist, Revelation 13), supported by a universal religion (the great Babylon, Revelation 18), all of which culminate in the glorious return of Christ to govern the world.

The Death of Dirce
Henryk Siemiradzki's 1897 painting is a re-evocation of the mythological episode of the death of Dirce, presented as a Christian martyr, with Nero, historically associated with an antichrist.

The first reference to the Antichrist appears in Isaiah 11, where he is called *Rashà*, the "evil one" or "wicked one" by the Jews, or *Arnelius*, his Latin name, because according to Jewish tradition, he will be a figure spawned by the Rome of the West.

We have seen that humanity's aim was to complete Babel, dominated by King Nimrod, and that during the Apocalypse humanity will be able to achieve this intent. Nimrod, the "mighty hunter before the Lord," comes from the root word *linrod*, meaning "to revolt." He is a rebel against God, a wicked, satanic creature. Indeed, we are told in Genesis 10:9:

> That is why it is said, "Like Nimrod, a mighty hunter before the Lᴏʀᴅ."
> *(Genesis 10:9)*

The rabbis explained why it is written "like Nimrod": in the end times, a dictator "like Nimrod" will appear, and following the example of the first one who led humanity in a revolt against God, he will do the same at the end. The devil will be incarnated in a human being. The Antichrist is thus a remanence, a sort of resurrection of King Nimrod, the Babylonian dictator. God is excluded from Babel and man is deified. As he will be at the end.

At the end of the Bible, humanity's age-old dream, until then impeded by God, is finally a reality. The leadership of this fourth empire is actually two-headed. Under the guidance of the two beasts described in chapter 13, in the government of the Great Babylon is instituted a sort of universal caliphate. The evil man will lead humanity in a last revolt against God, and Paul described to the Thessalonians the coming of "the man of sin," "the son of perdition," "the enemy," *"the lawless one . . . whom the Lᴏʀᴅ will destroy by the breath of his mouth"* (1 Thessalonians 2:8). This is a near-literal citation of Isaiah 11, "with the rod of his mouth."

Paul said to the Thessalonians: *". . . you know what holds him back.""* (1 Thessalonians 2:6). He was referring to a mysterious obstacle that prevents the Antichrist's appearance. It's a doctrine with which the Thessalonians were familiar and which was clear to them, but it has not come down to us. This question has been a subject of debate throughout the history of the church. Before the coming of the Antichrist must be the great apostasy preceded by the announcement that "the gospel has reached the ends of the earth, only then will the end come."

Theologian Arnold G. Fruchtenbaum believes it is the government of men that is delaying him: "The mission of restraining evil was given to the government of men when God made the pact with Noah in Genesis 9:1–17. After all, human government restrains iniquity at present."

What's more, certain theologians think it is a matter of the Holy Spirit residing in the church. In their view, God alone has the power to restrain the devil's satanic spirit. Exegete Thomas Constable states: "The Holy Spirit is the only person with sufficient power to restrain him . . . it is quite clear that removing what restrains him must occur at the advent of the day of the Lord." The word "restrain" has the following meanings: "prevent from acting, keep under control, take away physical freedom as by binding with chains."

The figure of the Antichrist is also likened to Gog, king of Magog, whom we find in the prophecies of Ezekiel. Another of Paul's texts to the Thessalonians teaches us that "the spirit of the Antichrist is already at work."

John informed us that there will be several of them in history:

> They went out from us, but they did not really belong to us, because if they had belonged to us, they would have remained with us. But they went out from us to demonstrate that all of them do not belong to us. *(1 John 2:19)*

In reality, then, it is a matter of Christians who have strayed such as "the Nicolaitans":

> You have even put to the test those who refer to themselves as apostles *(but are not), and have discovered that they are false. (Revelation 2:2)*

The Antichrist will be the exact opposite of the Messiah; we sometimes find the use of the term *Antechrist*, or he who comes *before* Christ. Nimrod is the first creator of a universal empire designed to exclude God and take control of its destiny without God: "Let's . . . make a name for ourselves" contrasts with the God of Israel, "I am he who names you Israel." The anti-Nimrod, therefore, is Abraham. Paul, speaking to the Thessalonians, tells us: "We must have seen the wicked man, the adversary, who rises up against all that we call God, going so far as to sit on the throne."

In a time of globalization during which exchanges between countries have grown so tightly interlocked, catastrophes could have chain reactions with unprecedented effects, causing health, economic, and political crises that drive humanity to call on an authoritarian government to reestablish order in a period of chaos.

In 2005 historian and journalist Alexandre Adler wrote the preface for Éditions Robert Laffont's *The New CIA Report—What the World Will Be Like Tomorrow*, dealing particularly with "the outbreak of a global pandemic" evoked by CIA experts who forecast a viral pandemic of apocalyptic dimensions. A scenario that immediately brings to mind what is currently taking place in the world with COVID-19. This is what Adler says about such an epidemic:

The appearance of a new, extremely contagious human viral respiratory illness for which no adequate treatment exists could trigger a global pandemic. If such an illness appears between now and 2025, internal and cross-border tensions and conflicts will certainly arise. Nations will then make the effort— with insufficient capabilities—to control population movements, trying to avoid infections or preserve their access to natural resources.

The appearance of a pandemic depends on natural genetic mutation, the combining of viral strains already in circulation or even the irruption of a new pathogenic factors in the human population. Experts see in the highly pathogenic strains of avian flu such as H5N1 several probable candidates for this type of transformation, but other pathogenic agents, such as the SARS coronavirus and other flu strains, have the same properties.

If a pandemic illness arises, it will undoubtedly be in a zone with a high population density, with sizable animal-human proximity, as exists in China and Southeast Asia where people live in contact with livestock. Unregulated breeding practices will facilitate the circulation of a virus like H5N1 among the animal populations—increasing the chances of the mutation of a strain liable to provoke a pandemic. To spread rapidly, the illness must simply appear in population-dense regions.

In such a scenario, the illness will take time to be identified, if the country of origin doesn't possess the necessary means to detect it. It will take weeks for the laboratories to provide definitive results, confirming the existence of an illness at risk of turning into a pandemic. Meanwhile, outbreaks will appear in the cities of Southeast Asia. Despite restrictions limiting international travel, people not displaying any serious symptoms could carry the virus to the other continents.

The sick would become more and more numerous, with new cases appearing every month. The absence of an effective vaccine or immunity in the rest of the world would expose those populations to infection. In the worst-case scenario, ten to several hundreds of millions of Westerners will come down with the disease, and deaths will reach into the tens of millions. In the rest of the world, the decline of vital infrastructures and economic losses on a global scale will lead to the infection of a third of the global population and the death of hundreds of millions of human beings.[13]

The Spanish Flu was one of the most lethal pandemics in the history of humanity, causing between 20 to 40 million deaths (between 80 to 100 million according to more recent reassessments) between 1918 to 1920. Smallpox, another deadly disease, is said to have killed from 300 to 500 million over the span of the twentieth century. During the First World War, Paul Valery wrote:

> *We modern civilizations have learned to recognize that we are mortal like the others. We had heard tell of whole worlds vanished, of empires foundered with all their men and all their engines, sunk to the inexplorable depths of the centuries with their gods and their laws ... Elam, Nineveh, Babylon were vague and splendid names ... And now we see that the abyss of history is deep enough to bury all the world. We feel that a civilization is as fragile as a life.*[14]

Busy with the daily management of this ordeal, in March 2020 President Emmanuel Macron of France evoked the world after the global health crisis. And "the day after, when we have won, will not be a return to the day before." Upheavals such as 9/11 and COVID-19 give birth to a new world. History shall tell us which.

The Antichrist announced in the Bible will exploit crisis situations to offer humanity stability, to seduce men. He will also be a sort of new pharaoh of Egypt, a dictator, oppressor of the people of God, who will tyrannize the Jewish people until God's intervention frees his people in an exodus. In Islam, various prophetic traditions (hadiths) speak of *al-Dajjal* (the Imposter)—the equivalent of the Antichrist—whose coming is a turning point in Muslim eschatology. He appears at the end of time and must be eliminated by the prophet 'Isa (Jesus) during the latter's glorious return.

Klaus Schwab and Thierry Malleret, the authors of the book and political systemic concept *COVID-19: The Great Reset*[15] presented in 2021 at the World Economic Forum in Davos, Switzerland, observed that the great historical crises have each time been at the origin of a profound change in society, from the emergence of the modern state after the Black Death pandemic to the emergence of the welfare state after the Second World War. Therefore, the COVID-19 pandemic "represents a rare but narrow window of opportunity to reflect, reimagine, and reset our world."[16] The slogan that best summarizes their project to renovate our civilization is, "Welcome to 2030. You will own nothing, and you will be happy," which is reminiscent of the old promises of the communist system.

Dissenters of this worldview, labeled as conspiracy theorists, allege that "global financial elites" and world leaders planned the COVID-19 p(l)andemic or deliberately let the virus (which they claim was probably created in the Wuhan research laboratory) spread around the world to create the conditions for restructuring governments and the political system on a global scale. The question of the value of immunization and the imposition of a pass to go to the public place is the subject of a profound debate. Some see it as social engineering on a large scale. Proponents of this hypothesis believe that the main objective of the Great Reinitialization would be to take political and economic control of a very large part of the world—including the West—by establishing an "enlightened" totalitarian regime of Marxist tendency and, by extension, a new world order. Thus, the new obligation since the pandemic in 2020 to have to present digital documents to access social life (restaurants, hotels, work . . .) would be for them a massive preparation for an era where the control of individuals would become systematic as is the case in China. Digital currencies such as the digital dollar and euro would potentially allow traceability of trade and a total grip of power on individuals. People could be forced to consume their savings or would depend on their submissions to the authorities for social assistance. These digital currencies could become widespread by 2025.

This theory claims that such a regime would gradually abolish personal property and property rights. Indeed, poverty and the need for assistance are the best breeding ground for a communist system to develop, since the very definition of the poor is to be those who own nothing. One possible scenario would be for owners to be dispossessed of their property by governments to repay public debts in the name of solidarity. But these goods will always belong to a few! A "possessing" caste would thus be able to rent the goods and services necessary for the life of a large fraction of the population. They would be the plutocrats dominating the mass of the people. This model of society is only one type proposed among several other models, but at the time of this writing, countries such as Spain are already announcing in their 2050 plan that they no longer wish to have personal cars or single-family homes and that apartments should be shared in the name of solidarity for climate resilience and quality of life. Some, even more alarmist, believe that the decrease in resources will motivate the rise of an ideology aimed at restricting the world's population to guarantee a level of prosperity to the dominant.

Already in 1979, the great French ideologist Jacques Attali (who proposed Emmanuel Macron's candidacy for the presidency of France) publicly declared on television:

We will make sure, that each one of us has a "free desire to conform to the norm" which that the absolute form of dictatorship. That each one of us "freely desire to behave like a slave."

It is through medicine, through good and evil, through the relationship to death that this new form of totalitarian society will take place.[17]

One of the great risks that the church of Jesus Christ is at today, is to have a ready-made expectation of how the events of the end times will be accomplished and thus to wait for the stereotype of the antichrist in the form of a man to appear. A man will also come and he will somehow be the keystone of the Satanic edifice—while his system and spirit are already here and active now. One should not absolutely seek to see in the antichrist a man, but above all discern a system.

THE MYSTERY OF THE TWO BEASTS

In chapter 13, at the heart of Revelation, appears a satanic trinity composed of the Dragon, the Beast, and the False Prophet. We have seen in the book of Daniel that the Beast of the Fourth Empire is composed of two very different materials: iron and clay. These components are bound in a heterogeneous alliance that branches out into ten claws and ten horns, symbolizing that this empire will split "*into a certain number of nations.*" In Revelation we find this two-headed nature of the Beast of the Fourth Empire in the description of an alliance between two of Satan's monstrous allies. The first is a creature that rises from the sea; the second is terrestrial, appearing out of the desert.

In the Bible, the sea is the image of chaos, darkness, death, and the upheaval of human nations. Isaiah evokes the sea monster in chapter 27 of the homonymous book:

> At that time the Lord will punish with his destructive, great, and powerful sword Leviathan the fast-moving serpent, Leviathan the squirming serpent; he will kill the sea monster. *(Isaiah 27:1)*

These two satanic monsters in league together against humanity are unveiled at the end of the book of Job with the names of Leviathan and Behemoth, the terrestrial monster of the desert.

> Look at its strength in its loins, and its power in the muscles of its belly. It makes its tail stiff like a cedar, the sinews of its thighs are tightly wound. Its bones are tubes of bronze, its limbs like bars of iron. It ranks first among the works of God, the One who made it has furnished it with a sword. For the hills bring it food ... *(Job 40:16–20)*

From a zoological standpoint, these are clearly monsters that do not exist on earth. In Revelation, for the New World of the Fifth Empire (the kingdom of God) to appear, these two monsters must be destroyed.

Professor David Flusser has demonstrated that these two monsters also represent the two kings of the North and the South in the book of Daniel. The Leviathan, which rises from the sea, symbolizes the nations, thus Rome and the West. But the second, Behemoth, which rises from the desert, is embodied by the false prophet of this trinity. His identity is more mysterious. What is this monster?

The book of Daniel presents two eschatological enemies of Israel in the person of two kings: the first from the North and the second from the South.

They will attempt to join forces through human alliances, but these two allies of circumstance will fight against each other and end up destroying each other.

We find this idea in the Greek version of the book of Esther with the apocryphal text known by the name of the "Dream of Mordechai." In this text, two evil dragons faced off and reciprocally destroyed each other. The joint destruction of these enemies indicates that at the end of the eschatological war, Israel will be freed without any outside intervention.

We also find a similar episode in Ezekiel 37–39, when the armies of the Gentiles brought together at Armageddon eventually turned their swords against one another and God made it rain sulfur to further the armies' confusion. The prophet Zechariah reported the same event:

> On the day there will be great confusion from the LORD among them; they will seize each other and attack one another violently. *(Zechariah 14:13)*

The Roman Empire, identified with the Fourth Empire, was once unified over the whole of the Mediterranean region and broke up with the fall of Rome.

It's interesting to note that, according to the historian Bat Ye'or in a still-controversial thesis, the European Union and the nations of the Arab League,

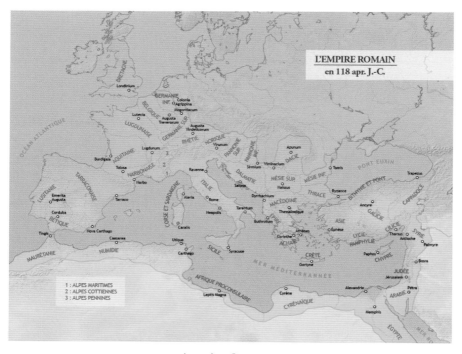

Imperium Romanum
Map of the Roman Empire at its height, one of history's largest political entities.

following the petroleum crisis of 1973, planned to unite the Mediterranean, that is, to politically join continental Europe with the countries of the Maghreb.

Nicolas Sarkozy, for example, worked to drive the progress of the "Barcelona Process" toward the project of the "Union for the Mediterranean." This intergovernmental organization founded in 2008 includes forty-three nations of Europe and the Mediterranean basin: the twenty-eight member states of the European Union and fifteen Mediterranean partner countries from North Africa, the Middle East, and southeast Europe. Its general office is in Barcelona. Its plans and initiatives are focused on six sectors of activity mandated by the UPM's member states: Business Development, Higher Learning and Research, Civil and Social Affairs, Energy and Climate Action, Urban Transport and Development, and Water and the Environment. Since 1973, the two blocs have participated in the Euro-Arab Dialogue (DEA) or Arab-Mediterranean Dialogue.

The UPM, Union for the Mediterranean, was founded in 2008 in Paris. The organization is designed to strengthen the Euromed partnership implemented in 1995 under the so-called Barcelona Process.

Historian Bat Ye'or raises the following question in her conclusion to *Eurabia*: "Why have the vast majority of Europeans never heard of the Dialogue, a policy that weighs heavily on their present and will irreversibly determine their future?"[18]

According to the author:

> *One of the Partnership's goals was to transform Muslim immigrants into a Westernized population that, after having absorbed European culture, would become the ambassador of its interest and values in Arab and Muslim countries. But this version of reality has in fact been reversed, immigration has made the host countries subservient to Arab and Muslim politics and culture, even if a significant number of these immigrants have perfectly integrated into European society and make a precious contribution.*[19]

Indeed, history professor Louis Chagnon makes the accusation that,

> *They're taking the French for complete imbeciles by extolling the angelic nature of Islamic culture and instituting a biased teaching of history, aimed at inspiring French schoolchildren with a disgust for Western culture with the current textbooks in which the West is portrayed as aggressive and violent.*[20]

According to this approach, the King of the North and iron represent Europe. The King of the South, the false prophet, and clay are supposed to represent the Arab-Muslim world.

According to certain exegetes, these two entities are currently allied in a shared political plan, which corresponds to what is written in the *Eurabia* project, aiming to fuse these two communities of the Mediterranean through culture, immigration, and even a common political system. According to the supporters of this theory, technocrats are attempting to unite once again the shores of the north and south of Europe as in the Roman Empire of the past. The Europeans' geostrategic advantage is, in their minds, clear and evident: to become an economic bloc of the first order capable of rivaling the United States and China.

According to the thesis advanced in Ye'or's *Eurabia,* the Arabs imposed the condition of aligning Europe's policy toward Israel with that of the Arab League in this political process.[21]

According to the association Portes Ouvertes, there were more than 200 million Christians persecuted in the world in 2019, the vast majority of them in Muslim countries. In the territories occupied by the Islamic State (IS), Christians were crucified solely because of their faith. In the West, these facts are generally passed over in silence. It is extremely difficult today—even impossible—to undertake a constructive critique of Islam and its texts, even with all possible respect for this civilization's beliefs. The least in-depth analysis can be accused of blasphemy, making any progressivism impossible and condemning reason to the darkest religious obscurantism.[22]

According to the Swiss doctor in theology Shafique Keshavjee, Muslims refuse to reform Islam through humanism but are determined to reform all of humanity through Islam.

Between the most liberal and the most literal forms of Islam, Muslims never cease constructing their identity. One of the most urgent tasks of our time is highlighting the "normative" Islamic dimensions resulting from foundational texts and the "practical" dimensions resulting from history.

Islam is a one-way system in which it is very easy to enter and almost impossible to exit. The great Arab historian Ibn Khaldun (1332–1406) essentially recognized that Islam's universal mission is to conquer: "In the Muslim community, holy war is a religious duty because Islam has a universal mission and all men must convert, either voluntarily or by force."[23]

The Ayatollah Khomeini said much the same: "Holy war means the conquest of non-Muslim territories. It may be declared after the establishment of an Islamic government worthy of this name, under the guidance of an Imam or at his orders. It will then be the duty of all healthy adult men to volunteer in this war of conquest whose goal is make Koranic law reign supreme to the ends of the earth."[24]

It is urgent for cultural Muslims to discover the aggressive discourses and practice of conquest in their own tradition. Surat 9 (113th): 29 is one example:

> "Fight (*qatilu*) those who believe in neither God nor the Last Day, those who do not prohibit what God and His Prophet have said to be prohibited; those who, among the peoples of Scripture, do not practice the true religion. Fight them until they pay the capitation (*jizyah*) directly in all humility!" or "The only reward for those who make war on God and His Prophet and cause disorder on the Earth is being put to death, crucified, having a hand or foot cut off by a crusader's order, or being expelled from the country."[25]

Thus the most violent interreligious wars in the history of humanity took place in India, when the monotheistic Muslim armies were confronted with the "nontheistic" Buddhists and "monopolytheistic" Hindus. Between the eleventh to sixteenth centuries, the Turkish, Afghan, and Moghul conquerors partially Islamicized India at the cost of millions of deaths.[26] There is no question that the use of terror and torture was explicitly justified by Islam's founding texts. And it is unacceptable that Muslims continue to repeat, "That has nothing to do with Islam."

According to the hadith recounted by al-Boukahri, "The Prophet ordered the nails to be heated up and, once they were red-hot, he had their eyes burned; he also had their hands and feet cut off without cauterizing the stumps. They were then cast out into the Harra (a region covered with volcanic rock near Medina), in vain they asked to drink, but they were left to die without giving them water."[27]

The seventh, sixteenth, and seventeenth centuries were historically the periods of the first and second waves of Islamic conquest. Since the beginning of Muslim history and up to the present day, these conquests have never ceased. The five Roman patriarchates have a crucial geostrategic importance in the strategy of Islamic conquest. So Jerusalem fell in 637, Antioch in 638, Alexandria in 642, and Constantinople in 1453. Based on a hadith of Mohammed recounted by al-Darimi, the declared goal is the fall of Rome: "We were with the messenger of Allah (peace and blessings be upon him), when someone asked him: Which of these two cities, Constantinople or Rome, shall be taken first? The Messenger of Allah (peace and blessings be upon him) replied: It is the city of Heraclius, Constantinople, that shall be taken first."

The Ottomans even reached the gates of Europe during their two sieges of Vienna, in 1529 and from July 14 to September 12, 1683. This was one of the most striking episodes of the wars between the Ottoman and Holy Roman Empires. It represents the farthest western advance of the Ottoman military campaigns into Europe. The Battle of Kahlenberg put an end to the siege and saved the city of Vienna, blocking the progress of the Ottomans who were bogged down in the very heart of Europe.

The Protestant Reformation, galvanized by Luther, considered Islam to be an aspect of the Antichrist. Luther said that God used this barbaric people to punish the dozing, decadent European church.

Sultan Mehmed II Entering Constantinople on May 29, 1453
Oil on canvas by Benjamin Constant, 1876

But the dream of the conquest of Rome continues to fuel the motivations of numerous Muslims who know and accept these founding texts. We are witnessing, in the beginning of the third millennium, a third period of active Islamic expansion supported by the immense wealth linked to oil and international geopolitical alliances, undertaken outside of the democratic framework, in a European context marked by the loss of faith. In the twenty-first century, we have seen the infiltration into the West of an intolerant, radical Islam whose goal is to Islamicize our countries.

Both Abu Bakr Al-Baghdadi (self-proclaimed caliph of the Islamic State) and Yusuf Al-Qaradawi (spiritual leader of the Muslim Brotherhood) cultivated the dream of the conquest of Rome. Here is how Al-Qaradawi interprets the hadith on the fall of Rome for today: "It means that Islam will return to Europe as conqueror and victor, after being expelled two times—once in the south, from Andalusia, and a second time in the east, when it knocked at the gates of Athens. [. . .] I believe that the conquest this time will not take place by the sword, but by preaching and by ideology . . . " For this reason, the jihad must remain alert in the *umma*.

Clay and iron: this motley blend of the fourth empire of Daniel—the one described in the book of Revelation—cannot remain united for long because it is a heteroclite and unnatural alliance. Even in the second century AD, Rabbi Eliezer Ben Hurcanos had already identified that the first element of this Fourth Empire would be founded by the sons of Esau (Westerners) and the sons of Ismael (Arabs). At the time, Arabs were nothing more than an insignificant tribe, and Islam would only appear five centuries later. The rabbis of the period drew the conclusion that the king of the Arabs and the king of Rome would unite in the end times against Israel and against God.

THE HEAVENLY TRIBUNAL

In the book of Exodus, Moses saw the sky open up over Mount Sinai and transcribed the vision of the celestial temple that will later be built by Solomon. But the temple, like any synagogue, also functions as a tribunal, the equivalent of a court of justice with a supreme judge who hands down final sentences: the Antichrist rebels against God, and a proud and blasphemous horn rises up to heaven.

Faced with this final provocation, a tribunal is established in the heavenly temple and the sentence is passed: the beast is condemned to death. In the book of Revelation a judgment is pronounced against the beast and the accusations are presented; the books are opened for judgment and, finally, the sentence is pronounced: the beast must be put to death.

The Son of Man is chosen to carry out this sentence against the beast and put it to death. The Messiah is the executor of judgments, the judge of the last days.

The Baptism of Christ
Engraving by Gustave Doré

[He] has assigned all judgment to the Son. *(John 5:22)*

Christ's vocation is to carry out the sentence of the divine judgment.

THE SYNAGOGUE AND THE CULT OF HEAVEN

The research conducted by Pierre Prigent, professor emeritus of the faculty of Protestant theology in Strasburg, demonstrates that the celestial cult in heaven and the cataclysms that befall the earth unfold simultaneously. There is a permanent contrast between the scourges that strike the earth and worship that takes place in heaven.

John is a Jew and during his vision on Patmos, he sees something that is familiar to him: an act in heaven in which he recognizes a synagogal cult. Contrasting Christianity and Judaism is commonplace, but Christianity is a Jewish religion, and it behooves us to rediscover in what ways it is essentially Jewish without trying to change the essence of its substance. It was only in the fourth century, in fact, with the Archbishop of Constantinople, John Chrysostom, under Emperor Theodosius (who reigned from 379 to 395), that frequenting a synagogue became prohibited.

The cult described in Revelation is wholly consistent with the synagogal cult of Jewish tradition and is integrated between the lines throughout the book. The seven shofars recall the ritual of Yom Kippur, as do the seven cups used to pour libations at the base of the altar. References to the Hebraic cult are numerous in the text. A second recurring theme is the judgment of the unjust. It speaks "of the day" that bears this expression (*yoma* = the day), which is actually "the day": Yom Kippur.

Yom Kippur is known as an austere holiday; it is a symbolic repetition of eschatological events. The ritual is animated by seven trumpets, the shofars, which blow the evening of Yom Kippur to seal the destinies of the Jewish people. People wish one another "a good signature": *May your name be inscribed in the book of life!* Then when the last shofar blows, the dice are cast, you can no longer repent; it is too late, at that point the judgment of God is definitive, irrevocable.

In chapters 4 and 5 of Revelation, there is a search in heaven for a reader worthy of opening the book of the Torah and breaking its seals, as occurs in the synagogue. Unfortunately, no one is found worthy of what seems to be the book of Daniel:

> ...close up these words and seal the book until the time of the end. Many will dash about, and knowledge will increase. *(Daniel 12:4)*

John cried with grief because no one was found worthy of opening the seals of the scroll. Then appeared the Lamb, who was the only one considered worthy of unveiling the text. Each seal that is opened triggers a catastrophe on earth.

The cult of the Jewish synagogue unfolds in several stages.

The *Yotzer,* "the potter," is the first stage of the synagogal cult. It celebrates God the creator by evoking the first chapter of Ezekiel in which the prophet sees the glory of God, the *Kavod* with some *Haïots,* the supernatural animals that pull the throne of God mounted on the *Merkava* (the Lord's chariot), with wheels covered in eyes (the *Ophnai*), among the Seraphim (the protector cherubs).

They celebrate the Lord and his creative power. It is an evocation of the creation of the world, and all is in movement, dynamic. The participants pray: "Blessed are you, our King, king of the universe who formed the light and created the darkness, such that each day you renew your creation. May your works be numerous, all things you have created with wisdom," an allusion to Psalm 104, glorifying the work of creation. For God is he who renews creation daily.

We also find this notion in the feast of Yom Kippur in which each man takes stock of his life. He comes before God, in the evening at the moment the shofar is blown, and emerges from this ceremony a new creature. The cult is the moment when God comes toward us, sends out his Spirit, his breath, and recreates us in his image during this period of communion and visitation. He makes of us new creatures according to his will.

The second stage is the *Kedusha,* or sanctification. The participants chant: "Here may you be blessed, Creator King . . . Holy, Holy, Holy is the lord, all of the world is filled with his glory." A third category of angels, the *Seraphim* (a term that means "burning, ardent") are ardent and burning with the holiness of God. The Jewish cult always reminds us that God is a holy God. Nature is seized with fear and trembling, for the Saint of Israel is coming to judge the world with justice.

The third stage of worship is the *Gueoulah,* the redemption that glorifies the God who saves. He comes to liberate his people, and this redemption is carried out by the Messiah. There is the opening of a holy, covered cupboard containing the scrolls of the Torah in the back of the synagogue, and the book is carried to the reading stand. A sequence of seven people is called to read the weekly *parasha.* The readers are called up to the Torah: they are the *Rata Torah,* the spouses of the Torah, who have been found worthy of reading it.

In the gospel, Jesus, who had returned to the town of Nazareth, was invited to read the Torah standing up and did his commentary on it seated. During his various voyages, Paul, too, was invited to comment on the Torah in the synagogues to reveal his interpretation of it and unveil its hidden meaning. The Torah scroll, after all, includes two faces: one revealed and one hidden. Jesus evokes this dual reality of the world with Nicodemus:

> If I have told you people about earthly things and you don't believe, how will you believe if I tell you about heavenly things? *(John 3:12)*

In the ancient church, even the liturgy was modeled on the synagogal cult. The proof lies in an unique document dating to the late first century called "The Didache" containing the "Lord's Teaching Through the Twelve Apostles to the Nations." It is a noncanonical document of early Christianity, described as being composed by the apostolic Fathers. It presents the foundations of the apostolic constitutions of the ancient church. In it, apostles explained how Christian worship was to unfold.

Thomas O'Loughlin argues that it is a sort of handbook for new converts, an introduction to the Christian community to be partially memorized. The text is divided into four parts:

- Moral teachings, "the two paths" of life and death;
- Liturgical prescriptions: food, baptism, fasting, prayer, and the Eucharist;
- Disciplinary prescriptions, namely on hospitality for itinerant preachers, the gathering on the "Day of the Lord," the election of bishops and deacons;
- The final eschatological parenesis.

According to Professor Prigent, the original Christian cult took place in four stages like at the synagogue with an addition, communion, taken with these words spoken to the gathering: "If someone is holy let them come, if someone is not, let them repent,"

> Let anyone who has no love for the LORD be accursed. Our LORD, come! *(1 Corinthians 16:22)*

> The Lord comes!

Communion was taken with these words: "Just as these ears previously disseminated in the mountains and these clusters already dispersed in the hills are now reunited on this table in this bread and this wine, may all your church, from the four corners of the earth, soon be gathered in your Kingdom."

The Lord is he who wants to come into our "present"; he comes to those who seek him out by his Spirit. Communion is presented as a holy moment of togetherness; it is a time of uniting with God, a solemn moment, a holy moment.

Paul said this is why there are many sick people—even dead people—in certain gatherings; it is because the Lord comes, and he comes as savior but also as judge. Thus the warning given to the church is that everyone must examine himself, to make the decision to change, if necessary, in order to appear worthily before the Lord.

The 24 Thrones of the Elders and 4 Creatures Performing Acts of Grace
Engraving by unknown artist

THE SECOND EXODUS

The themes of the Passover, the escape from Egypt, and the Exodus are omnipresent in Revelation. Just as in Jewish culture, these themes and references give shape to the Apocalypse of John.

Among the Jews, in fact, there are two fundamental certainties: the first is that God has acted in the past; the second is that he will act in the same way in the future.

According to this analogy, then, there will be a second Moses, a second Redeemer who will save the Jewish people in the last days. In the desert, Moses questioned God during the apparition of the burning bush:

> What is [your] name? *(Exodus 3:13)*

he asked. God replied:

> I AM! *(3:14)*

In the Hebrew language, no one can exist on their own, man being the shadow of God. Without him, he would disappear. So you cannot say "*I am.*" The name of God is contained in the tetragram YHWH, but it is unpronounceable. Its translation is the Lord, "*he that was, that is and is to come.*"

And it is God who came to judge the pharoah and to liberate his people. In the Ten Commandments, there are nine commandments and one promise:

> I am the LORD your God, he who brought you from the land of Egypt, from the place of slavery. *(Deuteronomy 5:6)*

Jewish thought counsels: "*You shall remember the flight from Egypt every day,*" because every day the enemy of your soul is trying to encircle you. And God comes still to liberate his people from slavery and establish his kingdom among them.

Chapter 12 of Revelation introduces a woman fleeing in the desert, pursued by the dragon:

> Then a great sign appeared in heaven: a woman clothed with the sun, and with the moon under her feet, and on her head was a crown of twelve stars. She was pregnant and was screaming in labor pains, struggling to give birth…the dragon stood before the woman who was about to give birth, so that he might devour her child as soon as it was born. *(Revelation 12:1–2, 4)*

There are two possible interpretations of this scene. The first is the Catholic approach that sees the Virgin Mary, presented with the features of the queen of heaven with twelve stars and the sun and moon. The second views the woman as representing the people of Israel according to the dream given to Joseph. According to this second interpretation, the

> son, [. . .] who is going to rule over all nations with an iron rod *(Revelation 12:5)*

is quite clearly the Messiah, liberator of the Jewish people.

It should be noted that we find this symbol of the twelve stars against the blue background of the sky on the flag of European Union, as a sort of symbolic attempt to claim for Europe the heritage of the chosen people.

The gospel must reach the ends of the earth according to the command-ment given by Jesus in Matthew 28:

> Therefore go and make disciples of all the nations, baptizing them in the name of the Father and the Son and the Holy Spirit, teaching them to obey everything I have commanded you. And remember, I am with you always, to the end of the age. *(Matthew 28:19–20)*

If the good tidings must spread throughout the world, the Jewish diaspora needed to reach all nations as well. It was necessary that Israel be strewn to the ends of the earth, in the great desert of the world, for God to be able to speak to the heart of his people as in the book of Hosea, and that dispersed Israel serves as a sign among the nations.

> But the woman was given the two wings of a giant eagle so that she could fly out into the wilderness . . . *(Revelation 12:14)*

Then in reference to the text in Exodus: "*I lifted you on eagles' wings.*" It would go into the desert of peoples. In parallel, the gospel of the kingdom needs to be preached until the ends of the earth.

Egypt will experience the fullness of God's judgment with the ten plagues. And seven of these ten we find in Revelation.

In the Apocalypse, the plagues returned gradually, striking first a third of men and then the whole earth: there was hail, the waters turned to blood, dark-ness, locusts, sores, frogs, and the waters turned bitter after the fall of a star. The water became bitter as it did in Marah in the desert in Exodus 15:

> Then they came to Marah, but they were not able to drink the waters of Marah, because they were bitter. *(That is why its name was Marah.) (Exodus 15:23)*

It is this list of scourges that gave the idea that the Apocalypse is something terrible, but it is also the liberatory story of a God who wants to save his people.

The Apocalypse is also a second Passover. Thanks to the power of the consumption of the lamb eaten on the eve of the departure from Egypt, the people of Israel received supernatural strength to undertake this long journey. There also exists a parallel between the Sea of Reeds and the sea of glass.

The Apocalypse is thus a second exodus. Through the exodus of the Jewish people, God makes a new creation; he creates a people in the desert by giving them his law, the Torah. The apostle John wrote:

> I am making all things new! *(Revelation 21:5)*

In the Apocalypse, God destroys the old world and old humanity. He creates a new world, a new city—the New Jerusalem—a paradise, a new earth and, finally, a new people in this final exodus.

The two witnesses of chapter 11, who were Moses and Elijah, played a large role in the Jewish Apocalypses. Jesus likened John the Baptist to Elijah. On the night of Pesach, the Jewish Passover, poems are read that remind how the Messiah will be welcomed by Moses and Elijah at his coming. And it is they who will attest to the people that the candidate in question truly is the veritable Messiah. During the transfiguration, *"Elijah and Moses spoke with Jesus of his departure."* The Messiah is thus a second Moses who organizes a second departure—a second exodus—on the mountain of the transfiguration.

What's more, it's on Easter that Jesus's messianic nature manifested itself fully. The night of Easter is a night of vigil during which the people are on alert: will this be the night when God carries out the final liberation of his people? For

> [You must] remember that you were slaves in Egypt and that the LORD your God redeemed you from there. *(Deuteronomy 24:18)*

In Hosea, the people of God are compared to an unfaithful spouse:

> ...I will allure her; I will lead her back into the wilderness. *(2:14)*

The flight in the desert provided the occasion for a new encounter with God. And once again, the new exodus will be the occasion for a new coming together of the chosen people with their Lord. The glory of the first exodus will be forgotten in the face of the glory of the second. This second exodus will be led by a second liberator, a mysterious figure who appears as a second Moses: the servant of the Lord.

Certain commentators, moreover, have claimed that the Bible could have begun with the book of Exodus instead of the book of Genesis, for this book, too, is the story of a creation: it relates the creation event of the people of Israel.

In the letters to the seven churches, it is written:

> The one who has an ear had better hear what the Spirit says to the churches. To the one who conquers, I will give some of the hidden manna... *(Revelation 2:17)*

This hidden manna refers to the Jewish tradition according to which, following the destruction of the temple by Nebuchadnezzar in 586 BC, angels came to collect and protect the manna by concealing it in heaven.

There is yet another allusion to Passover when the Son of Man appeared as a lamb in reference to the pascal lamb.

The book of Exodus sums it up:

> ... I said to you, 'Let my son go that he may serve me' *(Exodus 4:23)*

Therein lies God's entire plan for his redeemed people, composed of Israel and his church.

In chapter 12 of Revelation:

Pharoah's Army Engulfed
Engraving by Gustave Doré

> Now when the dragon realized that he had been thrown down to the earth, he pursued the woman who had given birth to the male child. *(Revelation 12)*

If we consider that the woman represents the Jewish people, the dragon's persecution of it heralds the great episodes of Christian and political antisemitism: the pogroms of the Middle Ages and the Holocaust.

As in the time of the Pharoah, the clash between the oppressor and the chosen people of God must be exacerbated: "*So the dragon became enraged at the woman and went away to make war on the rest of her children, those who keep God's commandments and hold to the testimony about Jesus*" (Revelation 12:17). We can conclude here that the chosen people of God are composed of the Jews (those who keeps God's commandments) and the faithful church (those who hold to the testimony of Jesus).

During the age of the nations, there is a diabolical opposition against these two entities that serves as testimony to the glory of God, as the power of God served as testimony of the time of the Pharoah's oppression in Egypt.

Revelation's author exhorts its readers to depart from Babylon as the angels exhorted Lot to leave Sodom:

> Come out of her, my people, so you will not take part in her sins and so you will not receive her plagues. *(Revelation 18:4)*

It is a call for a new exodus toward a new promised land that is the New Jerusalem, the eternal city.

The book of the Apocalypse is thus a good tiding because it announces the triumph of God and his people over the satanic tyranny that oppresses humanity.

SEPTEMBER 11, 2001

Revelation 16 speaks of demonic spirits stirring up nations to create upheaval among them.

> Then I saw three unclean spirits that looked like frogs coming out of the mouth of the dragon, out of the mouth of the beast, and out of the mouth of the false prophet. For they are the spirits of the demons performing signs who go out to the kings of the earth to bring them together for the battle that will take place on the great day of God, the All-Powerful. *(Revelation 16:13–14)*

On September 11, 2001, four suicide attacks were perpetrated in the United States in less than two hours, between 8:14 to 10:03 AM, by members of the Al-Qaida jihadist network. They targeted symbolic buildings in the northeastern U.S. (including the World Trade Center, already attacked in 1993). The "Bojinka" plot is considered a precursor to these attacks, committed two days after the suicide attack that killed Commander Ahmad Shah Massoud.

On the morning of Tuesday, September 11, 2001, nineteen terrorists hijacked four commercial airliners. Two of the planes were flown into the "twin towers" of the World Trade Center in Manhattan, New York, and a third into the Pentagon, seat of the Department of Defense, in Washington, D.C., killing all the people aboard and numerous others in these buildings. The two towers—both over 415 meters tall—collapsed less than two hours later, causing the destruction of two other buildings. The fourth plane, flying toward Washington, D.C., crashed in the countryside in Shanksville, Pennsylvania, after passengers and crew members, alerted by phone of what was happening elsewhere, tried to retake control of the plane.

The September 11, 2001, attacks are the deadliest ever perpetrated in history. The number of people injured during these attacks was 6,291, which also caused the death of 2,973 people (or 2,992 deaths if we include the terrorist hijackers), from ninety-three countries of which 343 were members of the New York City Fire Department, 37 were members of the Port Authority Police Department, and 23 were members of the New York City Police Department according to the official numbers of the report by the National Commission on the Terrorist Attacks against the United States, delivered on July 22, 2004. The site of the September 11 memorial, constructed on the location of the World Trade Center's Twin Towers, ultimately reports 2,977 victims (including nearly 2,200 employees working in the World Trade Center).

On October 17, 2001, the UN High Commissioner for Human Rights, Mary Robinson, defined the attacks as crimes against humanity; they have, on the other hand, also been the subject of multiple conspiracy theories and decried as "revisionist," even "negationist."

The National Commission on Terrorist Attacks Upon the United States was created in 2002 to explain how these attacks could have happened and to prevent such events from reoccurring. In its report published in August 2004, it established the responsibility of Al-Qaida, determining that the nineteen terrorists who carried out the suicide attacks were members of that network, and that the attacks were ordered by Osama bin Laden, who claimed them on multiple occasions. Khalid Sheikh Mohammed was indicated as the attacks' principal organizer and admitted to it, under torture, during preliminary questioning leading to his trial.

Vision of the Four Chariots of Zechariah (Ch. 6)
Engraving by Gustave Doré, 1874

The events of September 11 were experienced nearly in real time by hundreds of millions of television viewers throughout the world. They provoked considerable psychological shock as the images of the plane crashing into the second tower of the World Trade Center, as well as those of the collapse of both towers in the span of a few seconds, were broadcast live.

The U.S. federal government and those of numerous other countries reacted by reinforcing their anti-terrorist legislation and applying laws of mass computer surveillance. The American administration then launched a "war on terrorism" beginning in October 2001 in Afghanistan, where the Taliban regime favorable to Al-Qaida was suspected of harboring the latter's charismatic leader, bin Laden, and then in March 2003 in Iraq, whose Baathist regime the U.S. accused of supporting international terrorism and possessing weapons of mass destruction.

On September 12, 2001, nearly all Israeli newspapers published commentary on the biblical text of Zechariah:

> Once more I looked, and this time I saw four chariots emerging from between two mountains of bronze. Harnessed to the first chariot were red

horses, to the second black horses, to the third white horses, and to the fourth spotted horses, all of them strong. *(Zechariah 6:1–3)*

Indeed, there is an incredible rabbinical commentary on this passage from Zechariah 6 dating back to the Middle Ages: The "mountains of bronze" of the text, it seems, attracted the attention of Jewish commentators who gave them the following explanation with precise dates corresponding to September 11, 2001: "in the end time, the thirteenth day of the month of Elul of the year 5766, three great towers made by the hands of man shall fall on the same day; there shall be numerous deaths. A fourth tower shall also be struck, this one is connected to military power. The entire world shall see this drama unfold in real time, and this will set off a series of crucial events, but rather than coming together against the enemy, the nations will ally with their enemies against Israel."

The 9/11 attacks marked an irreversible turning point in modern history. This act triggered a series of reactions whose full consequences can still not be measured and that brought humanity into a new era, that of war against Islamic terrorism.

THE SON OF MAN

The expression "the son of man" is special because Jesus uses it to speak of his Passion and it is systematically linked to the theme of the last things in the Gospels, because it is related to the Last Judgment.

With the ascension of the Mount of Olives, which is the mountain of the last things, the Son of Man shall return into the clouds with the Holy Spirit, in all the fullness of the power of God, putting an end to humanity's revolt. In Matthew 16, we witness this dialogue:

> When Jesus came to the area of Caesarea Philippi, he asked his disciples, "Who do people say that the Son of Man is?" They answered, "Some say John the Baptist, other Elijah, and others Jeremiah or one of the prophets." He said to them, "But who do you say that I am?" Simon Peter answered, "You are the Christ, the Son of the living God." *(Matthew 16:13–16)*

Jesus responded to his disciple Peter with a beatitude and the announcement of the spiritual testament of his church:

> And Jesus answered him, "You are blessed, Simon son of Jonah, because flesh and blood did not reveal this to you, but my Father in heaven!" And I tell you that you are Peter, and on this rock I will build my church, and the gates of Hades will not overpower it. *(Matthew 16:17–18)*

More precisely, Jesus told Peter: "You are *Kéfa*," meaning "petros" in Greek, a quite ordinary stone, that on this *petra* (a great rock!) Jesus will build his community, against which the gates of *Sheol*, the underworld, shall not prevail.

"You are Peter." The Roman Church's conclusion is that Peter was the cornerstone of the Church. Herein lies the justification for the papacy by hierarchical descent from the apostle. But Jesus declared that he would found his church on the messianic rock and that despite the scarce value and ordinariness of his disciple Peter, he would nevertheless participate in this grandiose plan.

The Ascension
Engraving by
Gustave Doré

Jesus announced that his church will be the subject of ceaseless opposition during the centuries of its history.

Every individual, in fact, must build on the rock and be careful of the material with which they build their life.

> Therefore, this is what the sovereign master, the LORD, says: Look, I am laying a stone in Zion, an approved stone, set in place as a precious cornerstone for the foundation. The one who maintains his faith will not panic. *(Isaiah 28:16)*

The church fathers opposed the human entity of Jesus, "Son of Man" to his divine part, "Son of God." But nothing could be further from the truth. The term *Son of Man* as it concerns the last things underlines the humanity of the human sentiments that characterize the goodness of his kingdom to come and that contrast with the inhumanity of the four human empires, beastly and without sentiment.

THE FINAL WAR OF GOG AND MAGOG

The book of Genesis contains yet a further eschatological element: the story of the four kings who rise up and unite to make war in Abraham's time. These kings come from the same regions as those cited in the prophecy of Daniel:

- The king of Shinar comes from Babylonia, he is the king of Babylon;
- Dariok, king of Elassar, comes from Persia, present-day Iran;
- Kedarlaomer, king of Elam, from Asia Minor, Greece;
- King Tidal, who is king of the *Goyim,* the nations.

The parallel between first and last things is clear. As in the beginning, these four kingdoms will try to take over the land of Israel and will join forces in a battle that unfolds in the same place, in the region of Armageddon situated in modern-day Israel, in the same framework as the final eschatological war described in Revelation. Abraham pursued these kings and vanquished them, thus coming to rule over them. According to rabbinical tradition, the history of the patriarchs is a prophecy for their descendants that concerns the end times.

Now, Abraham was also the father of the Messiah; this story is, in that sense, a prophecy regarding the end of time. After his victory over his enemies, Abraham traveled to Jerusalem to bring offerings to

> Melchizedek, king of Salem, priest of the most high God *(Heb 7:1)*

who is often seen as a prefiguration of the Messiah. Abraham thus bears himself to Jerusalem to the "king of justice," just as humanity will bear itself to Jerusalem to bring "the glory of nations" to the Messiah king with the establishment of his kingdom on earth.

The eschatological war that marks the height of the final crisis is described in chapters 38 and 39 of Ezekiel:

> The LORD's message came to me: "Son of man, turn toward Gog, of the land of Magog, the chief prince of Meshech and Tubal. Prophesy against him and say: "This is what the sovereign LORD says: Look, I am against you, Gog, chief prince of Meshech and Tubal. I will turn you around, put hooks into your jaws, and bring you out with all your army, horses and horsemen, all of them fully armed, a great company with shields of different types, all of them armed with swords. Persia, Ethiopia, and Put are with them, all of them with shields and helmets. They are joined by Gomer with all its

troops, and by Beth Togarmah from the remote parts of the north with all its troops—many people are with you.

"Be ready and stay ready, you and all your companies assembled around you, and be a guard for them. After many days you will be summoned; in the latter years you will come to a land restored from the ravages of war, with many peoples gathered on the mountains of Israel that had long been in ruins. Its people were brought out from the peoples, and all of them will be living securely. You will advance; you will come like a storm. You will be like a cloud covering the earth, you, all your troops, and the many other peoples with you. This is what the sovereign Lord says: On that day thoughts will come into your mind, and you will devise an evil plan. You will say, "I will invade a land of unwalled towns; I will advance against those living quietly in security – all of them living without walls and barred gates—to loot and plunder, to attack the inhabited ruins and the people gathered from the nations, who are acquiring cattle and goods, who live at the center of the earth." Sheba and Dedan and the traders of Tarshish with all its young warriors will say to you, "Have you come to loot? Have you assembled your armies to plunder, to carry away silver and gold, to take away cattle and goods, to haul away a great amount of spoils?" Therefore, prophesy, son of man, and say to Gog: 'This is what the sovereign Lord says: On that day when my people Israel are living securely, you will take notice and come from your place, from the remote parts of the north, you and many peoples with you, all of them riding on horses, a great company and a vast army. You will advance against my people Israel like a cloud covering the earth. In the latter days I will bring you against my land so that the nations may acknowledge me, when before their eyes I magnify myself through you, O Gog. 'This is what the sovereign Lord says: Are you the one of whom I spoke in former days by my servants the prophets of Israel, who prophesied in those days that I would bring you against them? On that day, when Gog invades the land of Israel, declares the sovereign Lord, my rage will mount up in my anger. In my zeal, in the fire of my fury, I declare that on that day there will be a great earthquake in the land of Israel. The fish of the sea, the birds of the sky, the wild beasts, all the things that creep on the ground, and all people who live on the face of the earth will shake at my presence. The mountains will topple, the cliffs will fall, and every wall will fall to the ground. I will call for a sword to attack Gog on all my mountains, declares the sovereign Lord; every man's sword will be against his brother. I will judge him with plague and bloodshed. I will rain down on him, his troops, and the many peoples who are with him a torrential downpour, hailstones, fire, and brimstone. I will exalt and magnify myself; I will reveal myself before many nations. Then they will know that I am the LORD. "As for you, son of man, prophesy against Gog, and say: 'This is what the sovereign LORD says: Look, I am against you, o Gog, chief prince of Meshech and Tubal! I will turn you around and drag you along; I will lead you up from the remotest parts of the north and bring you against the mountains of Israel. I will knock your bow out of your left hand and make your arrows fall from your right hand. You will fall dead on the mountains of Israel, you and all your troops and the people who are with you. I give you as food to every kind of bird and every wild beast. You will fall dead in the open field; for I have spoken, declares the sovereign LORD. I will send fire on Magog and those who live securely in the coastlands; then they will know that I am the LORD.

"'I will make my holy name known in the midst of my people Israel; I will not let my holy name be profaned anymore. Then the nations will know that I am the LORD, the Holy One of Israel. Realize that it is coming and it will be done, declares the sovereign LORD. It is the day I have spoken about. 'Then those who live in the cities of Israel will go out and use the weapons for kindling—the shields, bows and arrows, war clubs and spears—they will burn them for seven years. They will not need to take wood from the field or cut down trees from the forests because they will make fires with the weapons. They will take the loot from those who looted them and seize the plunder of those who plundered them, declares the sovereign LORD.

"'On that day I will assign Gog a grave in Israel. It will be the valley of those who travel east of the sea; it will block the way of the travelers. There they will bury Gog and all his horde; they will call it the Valley of Hamon-Gog. For seven months Israel will bury them, in order to cleanse the land. All the people of the land will bury them, and it will be a memorial for them on the day I magnify myself, declares the sovereign LORD. They will designate men to scout continually through the land, burying those who remain on the surface of the ground, in order to cleanse it. They will search for seven full months. When the scouts survey the land and see a human bone, they will place a sign by it, until those assigned to burial duty have buried it in the Valley of Hamon-Gog. (A city by the name of Hamonah will also be there.) They will cleanse the land.' As for you, son of man, this is what the sovereign LORD says: Tell every kind of bird and every wild beast: 'Assemble and come! Gather from all around to my slaughter, which I am going to make for you, a great slaughter on the mountains of Israel! You will eat flesh and drink blood. You will eat the flesh of warriors and drink the blood of the princes of the earth—the rams, lambs, goats, and bulls, all of them fattened animals of Bashan. You will eat fat until you are full, and drink blood until you are drunk at my slaughter which I have made for you. You will fill up at my table with horses and charioteers, with warriors and all the soldiers,' declares the sovereign LORD.

"I will display my majesty among the nations. All the nations will witness the judgment I have executed, and the power I have exhibited among them. Then the house of Israel will know that I am the LORD their God, from that day forward. The nations will know that the house of Israel went into exile due to their iniquity, for they were unfaithful to me. So I hid my face from them and handed them over to their enemies; all of them died by the sword. According to their uncleanness and rebellion I have dealt with them, and I hid my face from them. Therefore this is what the sovereign LORD says: Now I will restore the fortunes of Jacob, and I will have mercy on the entire house of Israel. I will be zealous for my holy name. They will bear their shame for all their unfaithful acts against me, when they live securely on their land with no one to make them afraid. When I have brought them back from the peoples and gathered them from the countries of their enemies, I will magnify myself among them in the sight of many nations. Then they will know that I am the LORD their God because I sent them into exile among the nations and then gathered them into their own land. I will not leave any of them in exile any longer. I will no longer hide my face from them, when I pour out my Spirit on the house of Israel, declares the sovereign LORD."

Ezekiel describes the episode of a world war at the end of time. It is a war of blocs of which certain commentators say will spread out for the time it lasts.

The prophecy evokes a distant time, after the resurrection of the dry bones of chapter 37, which concerns the resurrection of the State of Israel (1948).

A missionary in China, Hudson Taylor, at the end of the nineteenth century had a vision of the map of Europe. He saw a very black cloud coming over Russia. As he prayed, he saw the cloud depart, then return definitively. The history of the twentieth century would give ample confirmation to this prophetic announcement the Russian Revolution of 1917 will lead to the USSR and its famous Iron Curtain, which has been open since 1991 but which we don't know if it will remain so. There certainly is a risk of the reappearance of the great dark cloud. The prophet Jeremiah named it "the great land of the North," for it plays a crucial role in the end times.

> You will say, "I will invade a land . . . at the center of the earth . . ." *(Ezekiel 38:12)*

Literally the center of the world, Israel truly is an incomparable geostrategic lock. To travel by land from Europe and Russia to Africa, or from Africa to Asia, you must pass through the thin strip of land of the territory of Israel; it is the only route possible. The military coalition described by Ezekiel has the same aim: controlling this crossroads that, in addition, belongs to a land that's become prosperous thanks "to the Russian revolution" of the 1990s, marking the great return of Russian Jews who resettled in Israel with a great mastery of Soviet science.

During the exodus, at their departure from Egypt, the Israelites were caught in a trap, a sliver of land in the Red Sea in the Mediterranean facing the Sinai. The temptation was irresistible for the pharoah who, envisaging an easy victory, set out to destroy the Hebrews. If the pharoah's army had not been destroyed, it would have continued to pose a threat to the survival of the people of Israel during the period of the exodus just as there will be during the war of Gog. When Israel experienced an exodus from the great country of the north, against its will the ex-USSR had to let a fraction of the country's intellectual elite leave.

Gog, the king of Magog, does not correspond to any historical figure, aside, possibly, from the king Gugu who made war in the Black Sea region. The word's etymology means "root" or "he who is raised up."

The figure of Magog, on the other hand, has been well known since the twelfth or fourteenth century BC. He is already found in the book of Genesis with the offspring of Japheth, Noah's son:

> This is the account of Noah's sons Shem, Ham, and Japheth. Sons were born to them after the flood. The sons of Japheth were Gomer, Magog, Madai, Javan, Tubal, Meshech, and Tiras. *(Genesis 10:1–2)*

Gog is the prince of Meshech (the Akkadians, modern-day Iran) or perhaps of Moshoi in the Caucasus. At the time, it was one of the limits of the world known to Israel. These frontiers are evoked in Psalm 120:

> How miserable I am! For I have lived temporarily in Meshech [the extreme north]; I have resided among the tents of Kedar [the extreme south]. *(Psalm 120:5)*

For these are warrior peoples, hostile to Israel.

The children of Seth are the people constituting Gog and Magog. They thus correspond to Persia, modern-day Iran, and we can also imagine Russians, who are a Nordic people with respect to Israel. This army will come *"from the far north."*

Political Iran is today a state ready to sacrifice itself for the destruction of Israel. Indeed, according to certain doctrines of the Shi'ite Muslim hadiths, the end of the world must be triggered by a chaos filling the earth to hasten the arrival of the *Mahdi*. The latter is a longed-for guide, an eschatological redeemer, a sort of Islamic messiah, awaited by all Muslim confessions, except for the Koranites, and identified in the last imam in Twelver Shiism.

Turkey is also showing a growing hostility toward Israel. Turkish President Recep Tayyip Erdogan declared in July 2018, "Without leaving any room for doubt, that Israel is the world's most Zionist, most fascist, and most racist state," during a speech before his parliamentary group in Ankara, and during which some deputies yelled: "May Israel be cursed." The Israeli prime minister Benyamin Netanyahu then responded to the Turkish president, affirming that Turkey, under Recep Tayyip Erdogan, was becoming a "dark dictatorship."

The text of Ezekiel also refers to Gomer, a land in the Caucasus peopled by redoubtable Scythian warriors. In addition to Turkey, north of Israel lies Iran, an ally of Russia. If we take a ruler and draw a line on a map north from Jerusalem, we go straight to Moscow.

Hudson Taylor thus had a vision according to which, after a period of thawing out, Russia would again be covered by dark clouds. And indeed, after a period of relative calm after the collapse of the Soviet bloc in 1991, a politics of force is currently underway that might inaugurate a new Cold War that would open a dangerous phase in international relations,

The text of Ezekiel 38 quite clearly evokes an international coalition against the land of Israel:

Judah Maccabee
Engraving by Gustave Doré

> . . . you will take notice and come from your place, from the remote parts of the north, you and many peoples with you, all of them riding on horses, a great company and a vast army. You will advance against my people Israel like a cloud covering the earth. *(Ezekiel 38:15)*

During the formation of this eschatological conflict, there is also another camp, that of the allies:

> Sheba and Dedan and the traders of Tarshish with all its young warriors [. . .] *(Ezekiel 38:13)*

This second coalition is the one that inhabits "the islands." They are trading people for whom the economy is essential. At the time of the prophet, Tarshish lay at the extreme west of the known world; it was the terminus of long-distance commerce by the ships of Israel. The "islands" represent all the lands on the sea (such as France, Italy, Spain, England). The expression "traders of Tarshish" can easily incorporate the present-day U.S. with its vassals and allies.

Tarshish is allied with the people of Sheba and Dedan, which are the populations of the Arabian peninsula, the oil-producing nations of the Persian Gulf. The modern world economy depends to a great extent on oil, and any military maneuver in the Middle East brings international reactions.

The attack on Israel by Gog initially leaves the camp of Tarshish indifferent. We may remember the Yom Kippur War, in which the Arab armies attacked like a great wave, to everyone's surprise. Russia was then quite close to Egypt and strongly supported the 1973 Arab attack. When the tides of battle suddenly changed direction, the Arab armies found themselves threatened by Israel. The Russians observed the situation closely, and their planes and combat parachutists were readying to set off to intervene and help the Arabs, but the American president, Nixon, threatened Russia with nuclear war, stopping the Russian intervention.

Later in the conflict described by Ezekiel, Tarshish must react, because the situation has gone too far:

> I will send fire on Magog [. . .] *(Ezekiel 39:6)*

The hypothesis of the evocation of a nuclear response is possible. The attack on Israel provokes the wrath of the Lord, who proclaims:

> . . . my rage will mount up in my anger, In my zeal, in the fire of my fury, I declare that on that day there will be a great earthquake. *(38:18–19)*

Finally, among the enemies of Israel, who come together on the plain of Armageddon for the final assault,

> ... every man's sword will be against his own brother. I will judge him with plague and bloodshed. I will rain down on him, his troops and the many peoples who are with him a torrential downpour, hailstones, fire, and brimstone. I will exalt and magnify myself; I will reveal myself before many nations. Then they will know that I am the LORD. *(Ezekiel 38:21–23)*

This coordinated elimination of Gog, by the mutual destruction of the armed in league against Christ and by divine cataclysms, will allow the advent of the Lord's glory and the establishment of the kingdom of God on earth. Following that there will reign the time of peace of the millennium in which, *"those who live in the cities of Israel will go out and use the weapons for kindling."*

It must be specified that, for some people, the events describing the war of Gog and Magog also concern the period that follows the millennium according to Revelation 20:

> Now when the thousand years are finished, Satan will be released from his prison and will go out to deceive the nations at the four corners of the earth, Gog and Magog, to bring them together for battle. They are as numerous as the grains of sand in the sea. *(Revelation 20:7–8)*

The prophecy thus seems to impact the period preceding and following the millennium, in which there will probably be similar events.

THE RESURRECTION OF THE DEAD

During his trial, Paul declared to Agrippa:

> And now I stand here on trial because of my hope in the promise made by God to our ancestors, a promise that our twelve tribes hope to attain as they earnestly serve God night and day. Concerning this hope the Jews are accusing me, Your Majesty! Why do you people think it is unbelievable that God raises the dead? *(Acts 26:6–8)*

The Greek term for resurrection is *anastasis*, composed of *ana*, meaning "erect," and *stasis*, meaning "to get up." It is important to note that, in Jesus's time, the Sadducees were opposed to this teaching and rejected outright the doctrine of the resurrection. Indeed, this teaching is purely Pharisee, the faith in which Paul was taught by the famous Gamaliel, grandson of Hillel, the dominant intellectual figure under the reign of Herod, founder of the pragmatic school of interpretation of Jewish law as well as a dynasty of patriarchs who would assure spiritual authority over Judea until the fourth century.

The Jewish religion is the only one that has never claimed something as irrational as the physical, corporeal resurrection of the dead. In our own times as well, in our churches, few people consider that this doctrine is serious—rather than simply symbolic—and truly announces a real event. It is nevertheless a fundamental doctrine in Jesus's teaching and one of those best established in the entire New Testament.

When Paul spoke of his belief in the resurrection before Agrippa, he provoked the same reaction of rejection as when he expounded it before the Greek philosophers of the Areopagus in Athens:

> Also some of the Epicurean and Stoic philosophers were conversing with him, and some were asking, "What does this foolish babbler want to say?" Others said, "He seems to be a proclaimer of foreign gods." (They said this because he was proclaiming the good news about Jesus and the resurrection.) So they took Paul and brought him to the Areopagus, saying, "May we know what this new teaching is that you are proclaiming?" [. . .] [God has] provided proof to everyone by raising him from the dead." Now when they heard about the resurrection from the dead, some began to scoff, but others said, "We will hear you again about this." *(Acts 17:18, 19, 31)*

The Jewish doctrine of the resurrection, indeed, is in total opposition to Greek thought, whose conception opposes physical matter, which is bad, with the immaterial spirit, which is good.

According to Plato, disciple of the moral philosopher Socrates, man is a good and perfect spiritual being but he is imprisoned in a clay prison, the body. In 399 BC, Socrates is put on trial with the following accusations: "not recognizing the same gods as the State, [...] introducing new divinities and [...] corrupting youth."

Plato described the death of Socrates, sentenced to drink hemlock, a "State poison" that probably contained a preparation of hemlock juice, associated with some datura and opium to increase the toxic effect while reducing suffering and neutralizing the spasms caused by its absorption. While his disciples were already mourning his death, Socrates said: "No, I'm going to be freed of this terrible prison and I will join the world of the pure spirits."

Death is perceived as a liberation in Greek philosophy. This is why, at the Areopagus, the "Epicurean and Stoic philosophers" conversing with Paul considered the idea of resurrection as pure madness.

Greek philosophy nevertheless made its way into Christianity, and in the Middle Ages, it was thought that what was physical, material, and bodily was bad. Certain monks mortified their flesh, fasted for long periods of time, and lived on half a fig and a glass of water per day, because it was necessary to mortify the carnal body to subjugate it and turn it into a place of abstinence.

This notion of the subordination of the body, of the flesh by the spirit, which is supposedly superior to it, is still quite present even today in Christian thought. The hymn "Some Day the Silver Cord Will Break" (also known as "Saved by Grace"), written by Fanny Jane Crosby, effectively expresses this Socratic conception:

> Verse 1
>> Some day the silver cord will break
>> And I no more as now shall sing;
>> But, O the joy when I shall wake
>> Within the presence of the King!
>> [...]

> Verse 2
>> Some day my earthly house will fall
>> I cannot tell how soon 'twill be,
>> But this I know, my All in all
>> Has now a place with Him for me.
>> [...][28]

This is exactly what Plato might have said. Now it is not at all what the Bible teaches, and it's precisely the error of the Corinthians that Paul corrects in chapter 15. This glorified body will indeed have properties similar to Jesus's after the resurrection.

Our understanding of the spiritual notion of death is rooted in Greek thought and not in Jewish thought, for the material is not bad; when God created the world, he declared it to be "good"! The material domain thus awaits redemption; nature is subjected to the vanity of corruption, but creation as a whole longs to take part in the glorious freedom of the children of God. For this world will take part in the "re-establishment of all things," the *Tikkun Olam*, the repairing of the original breaking of the world! This restoration will concern not only man, but all of creation, meaning the plant and animal world as well, the biological and organic balance.

The spiritual body that we will wear at the resurrection will be a physical body with flesh and bone like that of the resurrected Christ, who bears the marks of his wounds during his apparition to the disciples in the high chamber. The doors of the high chamber are then closed, for the disciples fear the Roman reprisals due to the disappearance of the body of their Master from the tomb. The glorified body of Jesus is nevertheless absolutely constituted "of flesh and bone" and capable of consuming food, as Jesus demonstrates:

Do you have anything here to eat? *(Luke 24:40)*

Jesus displayed the stupefying properties of his glorified body: He was capable of disappearing and reappearing at will, of changing his appearance to the point that Mary Magdalene takes him for a gardener, to pass through closed doors, and to rise and descend from the kingdom of God to earth, instantaneously. He lives in another physical reality, in another supernatural and heavenly, but very real, dimension, but he can appear and interact just the same with the earthly and natural world.

The glorious body with which Jesus, the second Adam, is enveloped is material and spiritual. He can live in a different, purely immaterial world—the kingdom of heaven—but natural as well. It seems that Jesus can pass from one to the other with no constraints of distance:

I have not yet ascended to my Father. *(John 20:17)*

The laws of conventional physics are jeopardized with the manifestation of "quantum" laws completely beyond our comprehension.

Paul tells the Corinthians that if the body is

… sown in dishonor, it is raised in glory; it is sown in weakness, it is raised in power. *(1 Corinthians 15:43)*

But in this we know that we are going to undergo a metamorphosis similar to that which Jesus begins, paving the way through his victory to a new humanity. According to Paul,

> ...there is going to be a resurrection of both the righteous and the unrighteous. *(Acts 24:15)*

At this stage it's necessary to highlight a very important nuance. The term employed to translate the word "resurrection" is actually erroneous:

> My aim is to know him, to experience the power of his resurrection, to share in his sufferings, and to be like him in his death, and so, somehow, to attain to the resurrection from the dead. *(Philippians 3:10–11)*

It isn't a matter of *anastasis* but of *exanastasis*. Paul goes much further with the use of the prefix *ex*, which changes the meaning of the phrase to "outside of resurrection." By doing so Paul affirms that in the *anastasis*, the resurrection of humanity composed of the "righteous and the unrighteous," a fraction of the righteous will be separated from humanity in an *exanastasis*, an outside of resurrection in a minority group. Those called the "outsiders" will be among the resurrected.

This particular status has to do with the victory that certain of the righteous will have secured over the three enemies that are the world, the flesh, and the devil. The victorious will be elevated to a status of prestige above the righteous and the rest of humanity. Paul seems quite concerned by the goal that he sets himself to participate in this *ex-anastasis*. He declares:

> ...with this goal in mind, I strive toward the prize of the upward call of God in Christ Jesus. *(Philippians 3:14)*

But he himself isn't certain of being found worthy of this election because he merely hopes "*somehow, to attain to the resurrection from the dead.*"

The process of resurrection ultimately unfolds in three stages, and the chronology of these events is related to us in this manner:

The first act constitutes the premise, the first beginning of the resurrection. It is initiated by Jesus, whose date of death isn't known with certainty. Historians today generally place it around the year 30, most often April 7, 30 or April 3, 33.

It should be noted that Christ's sacrifice on the cross is accompanied by the triggering of the resurrection of a certain number of the righteous in Jerusalem:

> Then Jesus cried out again with a loud voice and gave up his spirit. Just then the temple curtain was torn in two, from top to bottom. The earth shook and the rocks were split apart. And tombs were opened, and the

bodies of many saints who had died were raised. (They came out of the tombs after his resurrection and went into the holy city and appeared to many people.) *(Matthew 27:50–53)*

The second act will take place before the Millennium during the advent of the Lord known as the Parousia, when the righteous will be instantly taken up to meet the Lord and will join him up in the air in a fraction of a second, in an *atomos* of time:

Listen, I will tell you a mystery: We will not all sleep, but we will all be changed—in a moment, in the blinking of an eye, at the last trumpet. For the trumpet will sound, and the dead will be raised imperishable, and we will be changed. *(1 Corinthians 15:51–52)*

The blessed dead return with Christ for the deliverance of Israel. This first resurrection is the *exanastasis* of which Paul speaks. We find this notion again in Revelation:

I also saw the souls of those who had been beheaded because of the testimony about Jesus and because of the word of God. These had not worshiped the beast or his image and had refused to receive his mark of their forehead or hand. They came to life and reigned with Christ for a thousand years. (The rest of the dead did not come to life until the thousand years were finished.) This is the first resurrection. Blessed and holy is the one who takes part in the first resurrection. The second death has no power over them, but they will be priests of God and of Christ, and they will reign with him for a thousand years. *(Revelation 20:4–6)*

The Vision of the Valley of Dry Bones
Engraving by Gustave Doré

It should be noted that, during this act, the "catching up" of the church is merely a secondary event in the principal phenomenon of the *exanastasis* of the righteous from the resurrection of the dead in Christ who will precede the living:

> For we tell you this by the word of the LORD, that we who are alive, who are left until the coming of the LORD, will surely not go ahead of those who have fallen asleep. For the LORD himself will come down from heaven with a shout of command, with the voice of the archangel, and with the trumpet of God, and the dead in Christ will rise first. Then we who are alive, who are left, will be suddenly caught up together with them in the clouds to meet the LORD in the air. And so we will always be with the LORD. *(1 Thessalonians 4:15–17)*

The lapse of time separating the stages of the return of Christ from the *exanastasis* resurrection is a controversial subject. Professor David Flusser said that this chronology is one of the most difficult points in the New Testament to explain, because "it is intended by Jesus himself that we always be ready."

The third and final act will play out after the millennium and will be the final resurrection of the dead from all places and all times who will then appear before the celestial tribunal:

> And I saw the dead, the great and the small, standing before the throne. Then books were opened, and another book was opened—the book of life. So the dead were judged by what was written in the books, according to their deeds.
>
> The sea gave up the dead that were in it, and Death and Hades gave up the dead that were in them, and each one was judged according to his deeds. *(Revelation 20:12–13)*

This final act will come in the last times of the history of humanity after the last world war of Gog and Magog when Satan regains, for a limited period, his power. He will seduce humanity one final time in a last revolt:

> Now when the thousand years are finished, Satan will be released from his prison … And the devil who deceived them was thrown into the lake of fire and sulfur, where the beast and the false prophet are too … *(Revelation 20:7, 10)*

During this last resurrection, all humans of all places and times will be called to appear in judgment before the Messiah who will sort mankind, as we read in Matthew 25:

> All the nations will be assembled before him, and he will separate people one from another like a shepherd separates the sheep from the goats. He will put the sheep on his right and the goats on his left. Then the king will say to those on his right: "Come, you who are blessed by my Father, inherit

the kingdom prepared for you from the foundation of the world. *(Matthew 25:32–34)*

This sorting out will be done in view of an eternal, definitive destiny:

If anyone's name was not found written in the book of life, that person was thrown into the lake of fire. *(Revelation 20:15)*

In the Jewish tradition, the genuine Messiah must give two signs to prove his identity. These two signs are those that the enemies of Jesus demand from him in the Gospels: the first being to rebuild the temple, and the second to resurrect the dead. This is why Jesus clearly affirms his messianism when he declares:

Destroy this temple and in three days I will raise it up again [...] But Jesus was speaking about the temple of his body. *(John 2:19–21)*

Zechariah teaches us that,

Then the Lord my God will come with all his holy ones with him . . . On that day his feet will stand on the Mount of Olives . . . *(Zechariah 14:4)*

The Jews believe that it is at this moment that the dead will be raised. This is why thousands and thousands of tombs are situated on the slopes of the Mount of Olives in Jerusalem. The Jewish people are animated by the hope of resurrection, to the extent of wanting to be buried on the sides of this hill, at great expense, to be as close as possible to the event and get the most out of it when it occurs.

It should be noted that the Mount of Olives is the mountain of the last things. After all, it's in "*Bethany . . . less than two miles from Jerusalem*" that Jesus resurrects Lazarus, who had already been in the tomb for four days.

It's also in the village of Bethany, on the Mount of Olives, that Jesus declares to Martha: "*I am the resurrection and the life. The one who believes in me will live even if he dies . . .*" (John 11:25).

The doctrine of the resurrection is the cornerstone of Jewish and Christian theology. This entire system of belief rests wholly on this central foundation. "If the dead are not raised, *let us eat and drink, for tomorrow we die*" (1 Corinthians 15:32), Paul said. These two religions are the only ones that have dared to affirm that the dead are physically resurrected; it is the essential element of the preaching of Jesus and the faith of Paul, who will say to the Corinthians:

But if there is no resurrection of the dead, then not even Christ has been raised. And if Christ has not been raised, then our preaching is futile and your faith is empty. Also, we are found to be false witnesses about God, because we have testified against God that he raised Christ from the dead, when in reality he did not raise him, if indeed the dead are not raised. For if the dead are not raised, then not even Christ has been raised. And if Christ has not been raised, then your faith is useless; you are still in your sins. Furthermore, those who have fallen asleep in Christ have also perished… For just as in Adam all die, so also in Christ all will be made alive. *(1 Corinthians 15:13–22)*

THE RAPTURE OF THE CHURCH

Certain doctrines are quite popular in the evangelical world, namely that of the Parousia, also known as the concept of the rapture of the church. This doctrine figures among the privileged teachings of the Pentecostals, on par with supernatural healing and the charisms.

It is said, nevertheless, that "who are alive [thus, the church] . . . will surely not go ahead of those who have fallen asleep." The principal goal of this event concerns the dead in Christ and not the living, as was stated in the previous chapter. We can easily imagine that, for the Thessalonians, given that the announced end times were late in coming and the parishioners began to die of old age, the church began asking questions about the return of the Messiah. Are the community's believers going to miss the return of the Lord?

The Greek believers, who were the Thessalonians and the Corinthians, were asking great metaphysical questions to which Paul took the responsibility of responding, with all the precision of his erudition, through two texts. The first is found in chapter 4, verse 15 of the letter to the Thessalonians:

> . . . we who are alive, who are left until the coming of the Lord, will surely not go ahead of those who have fallen asleep . . . the dead in Christ will rise first. Then we who are alive . . . will be suddenly caught up together with them in the clouds to meet the Lord in the air. *(1 Thessalonians 4:15)*

The second is found in the first letter to the Corinthians:

> We will not all sleep, but we will all be changed—in a moment, in the blinking of an eye, at the last trumpet. For the trumpet will sound, and the dead will be raised imperishable, and we will be changed. *(1 Corinthians 15:51,52)*

Quite often, in modern churches, the believers' relationships with death are distorted because they hope in it to be freed from the challenges of this world. In certain cases, death is almost glorified and presented as a liberation, but for the Bible, it is an enemy that will be condemned and a domain contrary to God, for he is the God of life. Paul reminds us that "the last enemy to be eliminated is death." In order for the Kingdom to be fully established, the Lord must destroy death:

> Then comes the end, when he hands over the kingdom to God the Father, when he has brought to an end all rule and all authority and power. For he

must reign until he has put all his enemies under his feet. The last enemy to be eliminated is death. *(1 Corinthians 15:24–26)*

The Apocalypse also affirms that death is the last enemy that must be eliminated by Jesus at the end of human history:

... Death and Hades were thrown into the lake of fire. This is the second death—the lake of fire. *(Revelation 20:14)*

The question of the rapture of the church has raised a good deal of speculation over the latter's history. One of the doctrines to have dealt with this theme is dispensationalism. This was popularized by Scofield and Darby, but it stems from Pierre Poiret, a French mystic and philosopher (1646–1719), who published *L'Économie divine.* John Edwards (1639–1716), Calvinist pastor in the Anglican Church, and theologian Isaac Watts (1674–1748) developed this doctrine, which affirms that the church will escape the apocalyptic scourges because Christ will return at the end of time with a series of precursory events

The Rapture of the Church
Engraving by Gustave Doré

(rapture of the Church, war, appearance of a new world political and economic order, arrival of the Antichrist).

The postmillenarians place the rapture of the church after the thousand years of the messianic reign. In their view, this prosperous and blessed period corresponds to a temporary victory of the Church of Christ after the fall of the Roman Empire (Revelation 18:21). In sum, it is a Christian era prior to the aggressive return of the spirit of evil (Revelation 20:7).

Among these thinkers, Gaston Georgel presents his thesis in *Les quatre âges de l'Humanité*. He situates the millennium as falling between the Edict of Milan (313, phonetically, 1,000 years) and the destruction of the Order of the Templars (1313). This thesis, based on the works of a churchman, a certain Master Devoucoux, portrays the millennium as a golden age of Christianity that concludes with a prelude to the unleashing of Satan at the end of the cycle.

The premillenarians are closer to a literal reading and conceive of the return of Jesus Christ before the millennium. This approach is the one most widely followed by the evangelical movements. It indicates that first the church will be taken away (1 Thessalonians 4:16–18) and thus preserved from the judgments that will strike the world (Revelation 3:10) over seven years, then it will be united with the Messiah (Revelation 19:7–8) before he comes to bring into being the millennium (Revelation 20:1–6), a reign of peace of a thousand years on earth. To follow will come the last judgment (Revelation 20:11–15), the end of the world, and the entrance into a new world (Revelation 21:1).

Jehovah's Witnesses have inherited (and then reinterpreted) the conception of Nelson Barbour and Charles Taze Russell concerning the promise of the "return" made by Christ. For them, it is not a physical return, but taking it is control of earthly affairs by the kingdom of God. They justify this position by their translation of the word *Parousia*, generally understood as the "return," "coming," or "advent," which they render as "presence" (which can be invisible).

This long and invisible "presence," during which Christ remains in heaven, began according to them in 1914 and will conclude with the Battle of Armageddon, during which the humans in opposition to God will be destroyed. Then Christ will reign for a thousand years during which he will bring back paradisiacal conditions on Earth and raise up to perfection the survivors and the resurrected who will position themselves for the sovereignty of Jehovah. At the end of the millennium, the devil will be released to tempt humans, after which all the rebels will be eliminated. Those who survive will live forever.

For Mormons or Latter-Day Saints, during the millennium, which will begin at the second coming of the Savior and will be an era of peace on earth, Christ will reign in person on earth, and Satan will be bound, such that there will be no place in men's hearts for sin. All people on earth will be good and just, even if many of them will not have received the fullness of the gospel. Consequently, missionary work will continue, as will the construction of the temple.

At the end of the thousand years, Satan will be unleashed for a short period of time to assemble his armies. They will fight those of heaven, led by the archangel Michael. Satan and his disciples will then be vanquished forever. When Jesus Christ ascended to heaven at the end of his ministry in the mortal condition, two angels declared to his apostles:

> This same Jesus who has been taken up from you into heaven will come back in the same way you saw him go into heaven. *(Acts 1:11)*

According to the Scriptures, when Jesus Christ returns, he will come in power and glory to make the earth his kingdom. His second coming will be a time of fear and lament for the wicked, but it will be a day of peace and victory for the just.

Here is a brief look at the teaching concerning the Parousia, as it is understood at present by the Seventh-day Adventists and has been since this church's origins. The dead in Christ are raised during the "first resurrection," which takes place during Christ's glorious return, and the believers ascend to heaven to join Christ without going through death. They will then reign with Christ for a thousand years, judging the world and the fallen angels, deciding on the punishment to be carried out on them at the end of the thousand years.

During this time, Satan is enchained in the "abyss," meaning on earth. The latter, by the "judgments" of the "seven last plagues" described in chapter 16 of Revelation, and by means of what occurs during the second coming of Christ (Revelation 19:11–21), will have endured extensive devastation and thus have been partly returned to its original state, as well as stripped of the unrepentant, who will have been put to death.

When the thousand years have passed, Christ, accompanied by his chosen people, will descend from heaven to earth with the holy city. The reprobate dead will then be resurrected and, with Satan and his angels, will attack the city. But a fire from God will consume them and purify the earth. The universe will thus be liberated forever from sin and sinners.

Unlike a large part of the Christian world, the Adventists believe that this judgment will lead to total destruction, not just of Satan and his angels (the demons), but also of the unrepentant members of the human race. They conceive of death as a state of total nonexistence, and thus the judgment will not torment anyone for eternity, but it will reduce sinners to "ash," who will become as though they "had never been" (existed).

> New heavens and a new earth will emerge, by the power of God, from the
> ashes of the old, to be, with the New Jerusalem as metropole and capital,
> the eternal heritage of the saints in which righteousness truly resides
> *(Malachai 4:1,3; 2 Peter 3:13)*

and where God will offer the redeemed a definitive home and an ideal framework of life for an eternal existence made of love, joy, and progress in his presence, because God will live with his people, and their sufferings and death will
disappear. The great tragedy will come to an end and sin will be no more. All
that exists in the animate and inanimate world will proclaim that God is love,
and he will reign forever.

There are indeed numerous ways to interpret the events of the end, for
no definitive scenario is clearly expressed in Scripture, which encourages us to
openness and respect for the various beliefs and eschatological approaches.

FROM BIG DATA TO BIG BROTHER

The second Nimrod, the Antichrist, is he who bowed down to Satan and made an alliance with him to obtain the power and glory of the nations, in order to dominate over them on behalf of the devil. The British statesman Lord Acton declared in his day: "Absolute power corrupts absolutely." Technological tools will be used by the Antichrist to dominate the world, so that no one can

> …buy or sell things unless he bore the mark of the beast—that is, his name or his number. *(Revelation 13:17)*

This could not be more current. The world has indeed tumbled into a new era since the 9/11 attacks in the United States. Edward Joseph Snowden, ex-employee of the Central Intelligence Agency (CIA) and the National Security Agency (NSA), revealed the details of several American and British mass surveillance programs that were developed following the security laws passed in the wake of September 11.

Starting on June 5, 2013, Snowden made public through the media, namely the *Guardian* and the *Washington Post*, classified information of the NSA concerning the capture of metadata of United States phone traffic. He also revealed the existence of internet wiretapping systems in the Prism, XKeyscore, Boundless Informant, and Bullrun surveillance programs of the American government as well as the Tempora, Muscular, and Optic Nerve surveillance programs of the British government. To justify his revelations, he stated "my sole motive is to inform the public as to that which is done in their name and that which is done against them."[29]

The program's historical roots go back to the middle of the twentieth century, namely after the joint adoption by the United States and United Kingdom of the UKUSA accord, which was signed in secret on March 5, 1946. The latter led to the implementation of the first worldwide surveillance network codenamed "Echelon."

Scientia potentia is a Latin saying that can be translated as "knowledge is power." It is generally attributed to Francis Bacon. Nevertheless, the first written trace of this expression appears in the Latin edition of Thomas Hobbes's book *Leviathan.*

In the United States, the NSA collects the telephone data of more than 300 million Americans. The international surveillance tool XKeyscore allows American government analysts to carry out searches of immense databases containing the emails, online conversations (chats), and navigation histories of millions of people.

The British global surveillance program Tempora intercepts the traffic of the fiber-optic cables that constitute the backbone of the internet. With the NSA surveillance program Prism, data that have already reached their destinations are supposedly directly collected from the servers of the following American service providers: Microsoft, Yahoo!, Google, Facebook, Paltalk, AOL, Skype, YouTube, and Apple.

The NSA uses the analysis of phone calls and email monitoring logs of American citizens to create sophisticated graphics regarding their social connections, allowing identification of their interpersonal relations, their position at a given time, their traveling companions, and other personal information.

According to the top-secret NSA documents revealed by Edward Snowden, during just one day in 2012, the NSA collected the email address books of 22,881 Gmail accounts, 82,857 Facebook accounts, 105,068 Hotmail accounts, and 444,743 Yahoo! accounts.

Each day, the NSA collects the contacts from around 500,000 contact lists of online chat services, as well as those displayed in the inboxes of webmail accounts. Altogether, these data allow the NSA to design social graphs, which are sort of detailed maps of a person's social life, created based on personal, professional, religious, and political connections.

Following the secret treaties concluded by the NSA with foreign countries, the data collected by its surveillance programs are regularly shared with other signatories of the UKUSA accord. These countries also participated in a number of NSA programs, such as XKeyscore. A special branch of the NSA, called Follow the Money (FTM), monitors international payments and bank and credit card transactions; then it registers the data collected in the NSA's financial database, Tracfin.

Geolocating a cellphone indicates the act of obtaining its position and coordinates. According to the *Washington Post*, the NSA has monitored the positions of cellphones throughout the world, plugging into lines connecting mobile phone networks at the global level, lines used by both American and foreign phones.[30]

By doing so, the NSA can collect over five billion pieces of phone geolocation data every day. This allows the NSA's analysts to map the networks of relations of phone owners, correlating the models of their movements over time with the thousands or millions of other phone users who have crossed their paths.

When global smartphone sales began to increase, the NSA quickly decided to take advantage of this explosion in smartphone usage. This type of device, in fact, presents clear advantages for an intelligence agency because it contains data sets specific to its user, such as their social contacts, behavior, locations, photos, credit card numbers, and passwords.

According to documents revealed by Edward Snowden, the NSA was able to set up working groups dedicated to different producers and operating systems, including the Apple iPhone and the iOS system, as well as Google's Android system. Similarly, in the United Kingdom, GCHQ asked a team to study and "crack" the BlackBerry's protection system.

The NSA has other programs, smaller in size, known by the name of "scripts," which are capable of carrying out the surveillance of the thirty-eight different characteristics of the iOS3 and iOS4 systems, such as geolocating, voice messaging, and photos, as well as Google Earth, Facebook, and Yahoo! Messenger.

What's more, it has been revealed that the NSA and GCHQ were capable of retrieving user data from the most popular smartphone applications, such as the game *Angry Birds* or the cartographic application Google Maps. Depending on the applications targeted, the intelligence obtained can include geolocation, email address, contacts, the phone's unique identifier, model, operating system version, and so forth.

Documents provided by Edward Snowden and published by *The Intercept* in December 2014 revealed the existence of the secret program, Aurora Gold, which, since at least 2010, has allowed the NSA to exercise worldwide surveillance on cellphone networks. To do so, hundreds of operators and organizations such as the GSM Association have been spied on by the NSA for the purpose of finding exploitable security flaws in mobile communication systems and to secretly introduce new ones when deemed necessary.[31]

The goal of this program is to extend the NSA's surveillance and espionage capabilities over a maximum number of territories, including those of the United States and countries closely linked to it, such as the United Kingdom, Australia, New Zealand, Germany, and France. A top-secret map shows that in June 2012, the NSA's "network coverage" encompassed almost every country on all continents. In this same period, the NSA claimed to have penetrated 701 networks out of an estimated total of 985, or 71 percent of the cellphone networks in service worldwide.

Documents belonging to the NSA and the GCHQ, unveiled by *The Intercept* in February 2015, reveal that these intelligence services jointly hacked the computer networks of the multinational corporation Gemalto, the world leader in SIM card production, and possibly the network of the German company Giesecke+Devrient. Each year, Gemalto produces two billion SIM cards and is a provider for roughly 450 cellphone operators.

This intrusion, carried out in 2010, permitted the theft of a "colossal number" of SIM card code keys, known as "Kis" or "master" keys, used to secure communication between cellphones and telecommunication networks.

In possession of these keys, the NSA can listen in on conversations and intercept text messages and emails without leaving a trace. In addition, these keys allow the NSA to retroactively decipher communications received and recorded prior to their theft. They can also enable cloning a SIM card, and thus to direct or receive calls by usurping the identity of its legitimate user. These keys can be used to introduce malicious software into a phone via text messages. Finally, another point of interest in these keys is to make it possible to establish a register of users starting from their international identifier, for the purpose of monitoring precise people.

Between 2008 to 2012, the GCHQ intercepted on a massive scale the images from cameras used by internauts in Yahoo! chat rooms. This collection program, called the "Optic Nerve," reached into the data collected on underwater cables and stocked the images intercepted in the GCHQ's servers at a rate of once every five minutes for each video conversation. From this reservoir of data and images collected without distinction, the British agency was able to experiment with various facial recognition technologies.

It nevertheless failed to filter out the naked images (3 to 11 percent of the total) by automatic detection tools. According to the summary of the various revelations made in April 2013, the NSA established its "intelligence priorities" on a scale from 1 (of the greatest interest) to 5 (low interest). It categorized thirty or so countries as being "third parties" with which to cooperate, all the while spying on them.

The principal targets, which are China, Russia, Iran, Pakistan, and Afghanistan, are categorized at the highest level on the NSA's espionage list. These countries are monitored by France, Germany, Japan, and Brazil. The European Union's "economic stability" and "international commerce" are also considered to be targets of interest, alongside other high-priority targets such as Cuba, Israel, and North Korea.

From the point of view of American intelligence, countries such as Cambodia, Laos, and Nepal are considered unimportant, as are the governments of the smallest EU countries such as Finland, Denmark, Croatia, and the Czech Republic.

Other important targets include members of and subscribers to the group known on the internet by the name Anonymous, as well as potential whistleblowers. According to Edward Snowden, the NSA also targeted journalists who wrote articles critical of the American government after the 9/11 attacks.

In the framework of a joint operation with the CIA, the NSA deployed secret listening stations in eighty American embassies and consulates throughout the world. NATO headquarters was also used by NSA experts to spy on the EU.

"Yes We Scan"
Parody of Barack Obama's campaign slogan "Yes We Can."

According to a study published in June 2017 by the Institut Mines-Télécom with Médiamétrie, 86 percent of French internauts questioned have the feeling of being watched on the internet, and 91 percent of them would like to be able to maintain control over their data. More than half of them say they are "more vigilant" on the internet "compared to years past." So 61 percent now refuse to share their geolocation, 59 percent erase their navigation history, and just under half modify the privacy parameters of their social media accounts.

In 2016, China already counted 176 million surveillance cameras throughout its territory. It's an already massive number, but one that is going to grow until 2022 with the goal of deploying 2.76 billion video surveillance devices. An ubiquity of tracing technology will enable the government to monitor the country's 1.4 billion people.

The cameras will be equipped with facial recognition—as is already the case with the current cameras—which, from a database of digital images, will be capable to automatically identify the people caught on film.

Unlike in the United States, where facial recognition is principally used in airports, this form of technology is far more deeply rooted in Chinese daily life. In fact, facial recognition is already used in the scholastic context to monitor student attendance.

Evidently, we also find these cameras at border checkpoints, namely in airports, as well as on the streets and in public places. From ticket machines to the interior of train stations, hospitals, and even public restrooms, the Chinese are used to seeing their faces scanned and their actions vetted. It's interesting to think about what the Stasi or the Nazis' administrative services would have done with such tool.

THE MILLENNIUM

In our era, we can clearly conclude that Jesus has yet to fulfill the whole of the announced biblical prophecies. The Jewish people can thus rightly wonder whether Jesus of Nazareth truly is the Messiah! This connects to the critiques formulated by the Catholic priest and theologian Alfred Loisy (1857–1940), who triggered the Modernist crisis in 1902. Loisy was excommunicated *vitandus* by the Catholic Congregation of the Holy Office on March 7, 1908, for saying, among other things, that "Jesus announced the Kingdom, and it is the Church that has come." The following year, he was appointed to the Chair of History of Religions at the Collège de France, where he taught until 1932.

We could reply to Alfred Loisy's critique by saying that the church doesn't prevent the kingdom; to the contrary, it is designed to prepare humanity until the establishment of the kingdom by God at the time set by the Father. There are many who perceive the delay of the fulfillment of the eschatological prophecies as the clear proof of Christianity's error. An alternative vision, however, is to understand this delay as a grace that God accords man, providing him with time, as is the case with Jezebel:

> I have given her time to repent, but she is not willing to repent… *(Revelation 2:21)*

The great expectation of Jesus's contemporaries is that the Messiah will establish the kingdom of God on earth and restore Israel's political and administrative sovereignty. In the first chapter of the book of Acts, this political question is a principal concern, at the heart of the discussions between the resurrected Christ and his disciples:

> So when they had gathered together, they began to ask him, "Lᴏʀᴅ, is this the time when you are restoring the kingdom to Israel?" *(Acts 1:6)*

Jesus doesn't deny that he will reestablish a kingdom of Israel liberated from Roman domination.

> He told them, "You are not permitted to know the times or periods that the Father has set by his own authority…" *(Acts 1:7)*

Jesus affirms, on the other hand, that this reestablishment will take place later, after his disciples, invested with the power of the Holy Spirit, have first testified to the Gospels to the ends of the earth:

> But you will receive power when the Holy Spirit has come upon you, and you will be my witnesses in Jerusalem, and in all Judea and Samaria, and to the farthest parts of the earth. *(Acts 1:8)*

The order of Jesus's mission implies that the period necessary for the announcement of the Gospels will be long. For until the era of television, satellites, and the internet, journeys to the farthest corners of the globe were extremely difficult. This mission has taken almost 2,000 years, and today there is practically nowhere on earth that has not been reached. This great apostolic mission is thus nearly accomplished today, and Israel has been reestablished politically since 1948.

The time of the millennium will be that of the establishment of a messianic reign of 1,000 years over the nations. According to the Bible, after the time of crisis associated with the pains of giving birth to a new world in which

> I will make Jerusalem a heavy burden for all the nations. *(Zechariah 2)*

and concluding in the global crisis, ending with the glorious return of the Messiah, the devil, who is the father of the revolt, will be bound and reduced to impotence for a thousand years. He will thus make way for the establishment of a world of peace, justice, perfection, beauty, and goodness. By the Messiah, the world will rediscover its original harmony. God will take up once more the reins of humanity and govern a world that's finally regenerated. The consequences of the fall will be erased.

The millennium is a notion that has led to the spilling of a great deal of ink, but it is also a doctrine that is little taught in the modern church. The term *millennium* is a word that does not appear textually in the Bible. Nevertheless, it is a reality that is explicitly described in Revelation and, in that, is one of the most precisely established doctrines in the entire New Testament. The most suggestive passage is found in Revelation 20:2–6:

> He seized the dragon—the ancient serpent, who is the devil and Satan—and tied him up for a thousand years. The angel then threw him into the abyss and locked and sealed it so that he could not deceive the nations until the one thousand years were finished. (After these things he must be released for a brief period of time.) Then I saw thrones and seated on them were those who had been given authority to judge. I also saw the souls of those who had been beheaded because of the testimony about Jesus and because of the word of God. These had not worshiped the beast or his image and had refused to receive his mark on their forehead or hand. They came to life and reigned with Christ for a thousand years. (The rest of the dead did not come to life until the thousand years were finished.) This

is the first resurrection. Blessed and holy is the one who takes part in the first resurrection. The second death has no power over them, but they will be priests of God and of Christ, and they will reign with him for a thousand years.

Faith in the doctrine of the millennium was the firm belief of the first Christians. But the Roman priest Caius and then Saint Augustine would fight zealously against the Chiliasts who believed in a concrete messianic reign of 1,000 years on earth. According to the majority of history's churches, and particularly the Catholic Church, humanity is already within the era of the millennium, and the Lord is presently reigning on earth through his interposed church whose function is to administer the kingdom of God in the world.

Christianity rediscovered the doctrine of the millennium in the mid-nineteenth century with the evangelical movements, particularly under the influence of Darby, founder of the Exclusive Brethren, and with the American Congregationalist pastor Scofield. This millenarian belief has diminished today in many congregations, which have aligned themselves with the positions of the great historical churches.

The amillenarians, for their part, deny the idea of a reign of Jesus Christ on earth. They conflate the millennium with the eternal kingdom (chapters 21 and 22 of Revelation) and apply the prophecies concerning the reestablishment of Israel to the Church. This is the doctrine of the Catholic Church,

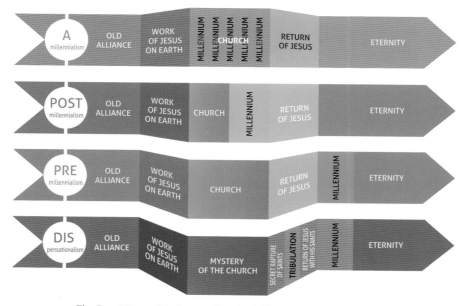

The Four Ways of Understanding the Millennium of Revelation 20
Graphic by the GBU (Groupe Biblique Universitaire)

the Orthodox Church, the Anglican Church, the Reformed Church, and the Lutheran Church.

From a historical viewpoint, the millennium's ideological influence was at the origins of the Nazi propaganda dream of the *Tausendjährige Reich*, which fated the Third Reich to last "a thousand years." Ultimately, it lasted twelve. This messianism is also present in Israel, in its secular variants; with the Communist revolution, the latter supposedly leading to messianic times by dissolving all nationalities in a great international fraternity; and in Zionism, which aims to reestablish Jewish sovereignty in the land of Israel, leading through the Jewish people to an era of peace and fulfillment.

During the millennium, there will be, in our view, three distinct entities: Israel, the chosen people, the church confessing Christ and the righteous

The Fall of Babylon
Engraving by Gustave Doré

among the nations, or a remainder of the nations who have survived the great eschatological war. The church of the Lord and Israel will reign with the Messiah over the righteous of the nations. Humanity will then develop afresh for ten centuries.

Jewish exegetes, for their part, have also concluded that the millenniium truly will last for 1,000 years. According to them, the whole of the history of humanity will last for 7,000 years, according to the analogy with the creation of the world, which emerged from the Creator's hands in seven days and the verse that associates a day with a thousand years: "A thousand years are like a single day." According to this approach, the first 6,000 years are times of suffering and servitude, while the seventh millennium will be like the day of Shabbat: a period of peace, of rest, of benediction for humanity.

In the Middle Ages, the calculation of the calendar was considered a secret reserved to an elite few.

The Jews make year one correspond to the supposed date of the creation of the World (*Anno Mundi*, often abbreviated AM). This date has been calculated using all the dates cited in the Torah concerning various persons and lineages to reach all the way back to Adam. The first day of the calendar, thus calculated, corresponds to Monday, October 7—3761 of the proleptic Julian calendar. The day of the world's creation is reputed to be Sunday, October 6—3761, the first day of the first year of the calendar began the evening of this first day and finished the evening of Monday, October 7—3761. This calculation is late arriving since it was carried out by the patriarch Hillel II in the year 358 of the Julian calendar.

The year 2020 corresponds to the year 5780, so a literal interpretation of this approach lets us believe that the era of the millennium should commence in 220 years.

The millennium, however, will still not be the definitive state of the world in its final and eternal configuration because during this time of the millennium, the two worlds, the Above and the Below, will cohabit: this will be the time of *Yemei Hamashiah*, the days of the reign of the Messiah.

FROM THE MILLENNIUM TO
THE ETERNAL STATE

In modern evangelic belief, the question sometimes comes up of a life after death situated beyond history. The hope of Peter, Paul, and the church fathers was that of an expectation of a place of repose, up to the goal of a physical return on earth, to reinstate a material body and reign, if possible, with the Messiah, during the 1,000 years of the millennium. These 1,000 years will be an intermediate hybrid state of cohabitation between the realities of heaven and earth, between the *olam hazeh* (this world) and the *olam haba* (the world to come).

In the beginning, God created two realities, heaven and earth, but they are separated by an abyss. During the millennium the worlds of Below and Above will come into contact in two mirror-image, symmetric realities just like *Jerushalayim*, a plural word describing two Jerusalems: one earthly, one heavenly. In the millennium, the two worlds, the celestial and the terrestrial, will communicate and interact quite directly. This is therefore not yet eternity, the definitive cosmic state.

The Last Judgment
Engraving by Gustave Doré

After the victory in the eschatological war of Armageddon and the advent of the Messiah that opens the millennium, the latter will summon those humans who have survived the war to judge them, dividing them into two groups.

When the Son of Man comes in his glory and all the angels with him, then he will sit on his glorious throne. All the nations will be assembled before him, and he will separate people from one another like a shepherd separates the sheep from the goats. He will put the sheep on his right and the goats on his left. *(Matthew 25:31–34)*

Those on the right will go to life; the others, on the left, will go to opprobrium and will have to suffer eternal torment. All the nations will be assembled, but the sentence handed down by the Messiah will only concern the pagan nations, and more precisely the righteous men of the pagan nations, and not the members of the church. For

> . . . the king will say to those on his right, "Come, you who are blessed by my Father, inherit the kingdom prepared for you from the foundation of the world. For I was hungry and you gave me food, I was thirsty and you gave me something to drink, I was a stranger and you invited me in, I was naked and you gave me clothing, I was sick and you took care of me, I was in prison and you visited me." Then the righteous will answer him, "LORD, when did we see you hungry and feed you, or thirsty and give you something to drink? When did we see you a stranger and invite you in, or naked and clothe you? When did we see you sick or in prison and visit you? And the king will answer them, "I tell you the truth, just as you did it for one of the least of these brothers and sisters of mine, you did it for me." *(Matthew 25.44)*

Indeed, if the author was addressing himself to Christians, they would have known the gospel and the example of their master who "*went around doing good.*" They would naturally have practiced divine justice and would not have been surprised to have been noticed by the Messiah for having performed good works.

The stakes of this confrontation of the surviving nations with the Messiah is thus the future of those found righteous among the pagan nations, who have not known Christ and have not been his disciples, but who spontaneously practiced justice in the world. The fate of "*the righteous into eternal life*" will be to "*inherit the kingdom prepared for you from the foundation of the world.*" These righteous of the nations will be the rest of humanity over which will reign the "*dead in Christ*" of the first resurrection, *exanastasis*, in which Paul is concerned about being found worthy enough to participate. This group will reign with the Messiah during 1,000 years over the "righteous of the nations," the part of humanity that has distinguished itself for its moral rectitude.

In the Jewish tradition as well, if someone does not know the Lord but naturally does what the Torah teaches despite not being familiar with it, this person is considered holy and able to take part in the world to come. We find this notion in the secular state of Israel, which attributes the title of "Righteous among the Nations," *Hasid Ummot Ha-Olam*—literally "the generous among the world's nations" according to an expression taken from the Talmud (*Baba Batra* tractate, 15 b)—to the benefactors of the children of Israel. The Yad

Vashem memorial in Jerusalem, dedicated to the victims of the Holocaust, is thus designed to honor "the righteous among the nations who put their lives in danger to save the Jews."

THE ETERNAL STATE

Humanity will not be entirely destroyed by the war of Armageddon preceding the millennium; a part of the nations will survive. These people and their descendants, the children of the millennium, will live in idyllic conditions, but this favored humanity will have to take up position against the satanic temptation. Just as the serpent was released at the origins of humanity, so it will be released in this second, regenerated humanity at the end of this period of peace. Men will thus once again be tempted by Satan at the end of the millennium so that they can choose between submission and revolt, and that God can probe the depths of their hearts. Unfortunately, the majority of humans will once again be seduced and carried off by the devil in a last revolt against God at the end of the millennium. Thus, at the end of humanity's history, the drama of Eden will begin again, bringing the cycle of human history to a close.

At the end of the millennium, the two Jerusalems, of which Moses had a vision on Mount Sinai, will unite to form a single entity. The two worlds, the Above and the Below, will then be fully connected. We shall be both in heaven and on earth. There, all the dead from all places and all times will come back to life, which corresponds to the second resurrection, *anastasis*.

> The rest of the dead did not come to life until the thousand years were finished. (*Revelation 20:5*)

The first resurrection, the *exanastasis*, concerns solely the "*dead in Christ*" preceding the millennium. Those whose names have not been found written in the Book of Life will then be thrown for eternity into the lake of fire created not for man, but for Satan:

> . . . and another book was opened—the book of life. So the dead were judged by what was written in the books . . . If anyone's name was not found written in the book of life, that person was thrown into the lake of fire. (*Revelation 20:12–15*)

This final episode is the terrible second death:

> The one who conquers will inherit these things, and I will be his God and he will be my son. But as for the cowards, unbelievers, detestable persons, murderers, the sexually immoral, and those who practice magic spells, idol worshipers, and all those who lie, their place will be in the lake that burns with fire and sulfur. That is the second death. (*Revelation 21:7–8*)

Jesus encourages the faithful of Smyrna to be steadfast because "*The one who conquers will in no way be harmed by the second death*" (Revelation 2:11). The second death is a definitive judgment, which it behooves us to fear above all else.

The destruction of the last enemy, death, will consecrate the absolute reign of God and open the last cosmic state of the universe: eternity. Today we live fully in a reality subjected to the laws of time that is a divine creation. In the beginning, when God created space, he also created time. Time is a state in which things are reversible, flexible, not definitive. God does not live within time, for he is "*the one who is, and who was, and who is still to come*" (Revelation 1:8). He is eternal, outside of time. In eternity, time will no longer exist. Eternity is the state of life without time where the bride will live with God in his blessed presence.

The New Jerusalem is the goal of the second, symbolic Exodus of the Apocalypse, which in that is comparable to the long exile of humanity that traverses the aridity of the suffering of the world of darkness, but where God has envisioned a new promised land for his people: the New Jerusalem. God will remain eternally bound to this city, and he

> will reign over the house of Jacob forever, and his kingdom will never end.
> *(Luke 1:32–33)*

The description of the city in the book of Revelation is quite full of imagery and difficult to grasp with the intellect. It is described as an immense cube including three gates per side and three foundations; there are twelve precious stones and on them are written the names of the twelve patriarchs of Israel, as well as the names of the twelve apostles of the Lamb.

Isaiah prophesizes about the earthly Jerusalem of his time by comparing it to a woman:

> O afflicted one, driven away, and unconsoled! Look, I am about to set your stones in antimony and I lay your foundation with lapis-lazuli. I will make your pinnacles out of gems, your gates out of beryl, and your outer wall out of beautiful stones. *(Isaiah 54:11–12)*

The Essenes of Qumran left this commentary: the storm is the opposition of the nations that rise and attempt to subjugate Jerusalem, and all the forces of Sheol, or Hades, shall be unleashed against it at the end of time. In the period in which Revelation was written, the high priest wore the pectoral of judgment, and each of its stones mentioned the names of the twelve tribes. In the same way, the names of the twelve tribes of Israel, but also those of the twelve apostles, are associated with the New Jerusalem:

> It has a massive, high wall with twelve gates, with twelve angels at the gates, and the names of the twelve tribes of the nation of Israel are written on the gates … The wall of the city has twelve foundations, and on them are the twelve names of the twelve apostles of the Lamb. *(Revelation 21:12, 14)*

Here we find the proof of the joint, eternal heritage of the church, but also of Israel: these two entities form the bride, the people of God, and are called to rejoice together and jointly for their eternal selection, thus disproving the idea according to which the church takes the place of the promises made to Israel.

The New Jerusalem is composed of three layers: the twelve tribes, the twelve apostles, and the cornerstone that is the Messiah.

The book of Exodus may be summarized thus: "*Release my people in order that they may serve me*" (8:1). And in Ezekiel, the new Exodus, it is written: "*My dwelling place will be with them; I will be their God, and they will be my people*" (37:27). God creates humanity to reside among his faithful and sanctified people: "*I saw no temple in the city, because the* Lord *God—the All-Powerful—and the Lamb are its temple*" (Revelation 21:22). The heavenly city will sparkle like a jewel, eternally.

Heaven and earth will then be reconciled. The consequences of the fall, the abyss, death, and the stormy sea of the nations shall be no longer. The function of this city is to be a place of sanctuary where "*they will bring the grandeur and the wealth of the nations.*"

The Vision of the Kingdom
Engraving by Gustave Doré

A NEW CREATION

The whole of Revelation may be summed up as follows:

> I am making all things new. *(Revelation 21:5)*

The expression of this future reality is particularly manifest in Isaiah 65:

> For look, I am ready to create new heavens and a new earth! The former ones will not be remembered; no one will think about them anymore. But be happy and rejoice forevermore over what I am about to create! For look, I am ready to create Jerusalem to be a source of joy, and her people to be a source of happiness. Jerusalem will bring me joy, and my people will bring me happiness. *(17–19)*

The Lord will take care of his people personally:

> He will wipe away every tear from their eyes, and death will not exist any more—or mourning, or crying, or pain, for the former things have ceased to exist. *(Revelation 21:4)*

Peter said in his second epistle:

> …the present heavens and earth have been reserved for fire, by being kept for the day of judgment… *(2 Peter 3:7)*

John affirmed:

> Then I saw a new heaven and a new earth, for the first heaven and earth had ceased to exist, and the sea existed no more. *(Revelation 21:1)*

God's plan is thus to create a new world. More precisely, one could even speak in cosmological terms of a new universe, replacing the current one and destined to be administered by man who has made a covenant with God. "*For he did not put the world to come, about which we are speaking, under the control of angels.*" Man's place in this new creation will be central:

> Of what importance is the human race, that you should notice them? Of what importance is mankind, that you should pay attention to them and make them a little less than the heavenly beings? You grant mankind with honor and majesty. *(Psalm 8:4–5)*

There is a crucial plan for man in this final reality; eternity will be a dynamic and quite active state with some great developments for this definitive civilization. The entire universe will be transfigured, metamorphosed, and will return to the harmonious state of Eden before the fall. It will be marked by perfection, harmony, and love—in a word, by *shalom*.

The biblical revelation begins in a garden in Eden, while, paradoxically and mysteriously, the history of humanity concludes in a city (unlike in the Koran, where it ends in a garden). The city, in fact, has a very negative connotation in the Bible, its Hebrew root coming from *ir*, meaning "curse."

The first builder of a city comes from the line of Cain, the accursed, who tries to recreate the original paradise according to the conceptions of man. His realization of a humanist culture culminates in Babylon, which is the city of man. But there is also the line of the brother whom Cain killed out of rivalry: Abel. He is replaced by Seth who gives rise to the line of the righteous, those who will be the blessed inhabitants of the heavenly Jerusalem.

In human history, God will not intervene in the choices of man, whom he hears and respects; like a father to his son, God will support man's choices.

In Genesis, Adam obeys the positive commandment:

> Be fruitful and multiply! Fill the earth and subdue it! Rule over the fish of the sea and the birds of the air and every creature that moves on the ground. *(Genesis 1:28)*

Adam calls out the animals in the garden and takes authority over them by giving them a name. Here, too, God will stand behind his choices.

Then when the Israelites ask for a king at the time of the judge Samuel, God accepts their choice here as well. But it is God who will give the king that suits man. He will be the son of David, Jesus, the Messiah king, "*the king of the Jews.*"

In the same way, man asks for a city, and God takes note of this desire: he will prepare a city for man, but it shall come down from heaven. This city is not the work of men; God is its architect and builder.

This city will be built with the materials that human history provides, the glorious elements that man contributes. Just as unworthy things (dogs, the immodest, the impure . . .) will not enter this city, dead works, those in life and of which men will not be proud, will go up in flames like straw. Men will thus find their works transfigured in the heavenly Jerusalem.

There is in fact a collaboration between God and man in the construction of this city, with God building it from the materials of the works of men, those men, sorted and found worthy, who have weight and value:

> His winnowing fork is in his hand, and he will clean out his threshing floor and will gather his wheat into the storehouse, but the chaff he will burn up with inextinguishable fire. *(Matthew 3:12)*

In the end time there will be a great selection, and men, too, will be winnowed. That which has weight, that which has substance, will take its place in eternity. All works will be judged—straw, stubble, gold—and tested by his fire. Every individual must be sure to build his own life with noble materials, consciously. Ecclesiastes encourages us to do so:

> Send your grain overseas … *(11:1)*

> For we must all appear before the judgment seat of Christ, so that each one may be paid back according to what he has done while in the body, whether good or evil. *(2 Corinthians 5:10)*

Jesus teaches us that if we give something as insignificant as a simple glass of water in the name of the Lord, that will be rewarded—counted as righteousness—and remunerated with value in eternity. It is therefore not the grandeur or the size of the work that determines its value, but the quality of heart and interior disposition with which it is realized. The clearest illustration of this notion is found in chapter 12 of the gospel of Mark:

> Then [Jesus] sat down opposite the offering box, and watched the crowd putting coins into it. Many rich people were throwing in large amounts. And a poor widow came and put in two small copper coins, worth less than a penny. He called his disciples and said to them, "I tell you the truth, this poor widow has put more into the offering box than all the others. For they all gave out of their wealth. But she, out of her poverty, put in what she had to live on, everything she had." *(Mark 12:41–44)*

What can we be proud of in our life? What things of value could we offer? Superficiality will catch fire and disappear of its own accord; it will not last. We can live only for ourselves, egotistically, for ourselves and our pleasure in this world: "*Let us eat and drink, for tomorrow we die.*" But the Bible calls on man to build with gold and precious stones for the Kingdom. It exhorts us to "*above all pursue his kingdom and righteousness,*" while being conscious of being strangers and travelers on earth and knowing that all this existence is merely a preparation—an investment—for eternity.

Jesus will say: "*You have been faithful with a few things.*" And indeed, the simple glass of water, offered to the meek and the small, shall not be without its reward. This glass of water will be transfigured; it might be transformed into a precious stone or, for example, a golden column. This is the attitude that will be evaluated, and not that which seems grand to the eyes of men. Just as the simplest drawings, often the scribblings of children offered to their parents, are a testament of their love, God will receive and transfigure our works of love done in his name. It is the intention, the love and sincerity, that we want to express through what we do that counts the most.

The same goes for when we receive a gift whose value ultimately depends less on the purchase price than on the love we perceive in its preparation. The Bible contains a prophetic inversion between the things Above and those Below:

> Blessed are the poor in spirit, for the kingdom of heaven belongs to them. *(Matthew 5:3)*

In addition,

> It must not be this way among you! Instead whoever wants to be great among you must be your servant ... *(Matthew 20:26)*

My grandmother, in her day, brought water every day with a handcart to a Rom community in her village. At her funeral, Anna, one of the women in the community who had benefitted from her care, came to the church with a bouquet of flowers that she had picked to express, with the means at her disposal, her gratitude. This gesture was very moving.

So it is important to do, but above all to be, with the ideal being to be and to do.

The Messiah will be the light of the New Jerusalem:

> Look! The residence of God is among human beings. He will live among them, and they will be his people, and God himself will be with them. *(Revelation 21:3)*

God will live among his people, made up of Israel and the church—the righteous—who will form a single entity in eternity. The people of God will celebrate the Lord; the Lamb will be the torch, the lamp of the city as it is announced in Psalm 132:

> I will make David strong ... his crown will shine. *(17–18)*

The brilliance of the Messiah's vestment will be seen by the entire earth. It's by his light that we will see the light.

There is an anecdote about the great composer Johann Sebastian Bach (1685–1750). He had been invited by Frederick the Great of Prussia, who had had him try out his numerous keyboard instruments, the harpsichords and new Silbermann pianos of which the king possessed roughly fifteen.

During the evening, Bach asked the sovereign to give him a theme played on the flute; he offered to improvise and develop a musical discourse starting with this theme chosen by the sovereign. Legend has it that Bach then improvised a series of variations of length. The sovereign had written three or four very simple measures, but starting with them, Bach was able to work over the score and improvise a breathtaking, three-hour concert. He would turn it into an important work: the *Musical Offering*, composed in 1747.

Today this piece is considered one of the composer's greatest works. It is certainly 99.9 percent Bach's, but it's also the work of King Frederick, which Bach expanded and "transfigured."

God is an artist of such mastery that he will turn our works, sincere though mediocre and clumsy, into marvelous masterpieces.

King Solomon writes to us, in Ecclesiastes, that God *"will evaluate every deed, including every secret thing, whether good or evil"* (12:14). Nothing that we do of value in this world will be lost; all shall be transformed, magnified.

In ancient times, in case of a dispute with someone, a meal was organized, and you ate together by way of reconciliation. The famous Psalm 23 also tells us of this moment of coming together: *"You prepare a feast before me in plain sight of my enemies"* (5).

A meal that the Lord offers us in this broken world is Holy Communion, with the symbolic message: *"you are reconciled with Me through the blood of my son; Take courage and mind your conduct until the end so that you can be found worthy of having a place at the King's table."*

Revelation concludes with the celebration of the marriage of the Lamb:

> Let us rejoice and exult and give him glory, because the wedding celebration of the Lamb has come, and his bride has made herself ready. *(19:7)*

The idea conveyed in Revelation is that if man repents, then God is already prepared to rehabilitate him, to make all things new in this life and in people's hearts as of right now. A believer's prayer should be to ask God how he sees us. Examining our hearts, in the light of his truth, is what leads the believer to eternal life, to victory, and to eternal communion with the Lord.

The sole thing that man risks regretting in eternity is not having given enough of his life to the Lord, as it's expressed in the canticle: "Must I go for eternity, and emptyhanded?" This song is inspired by the story of a young man of thirty, lying in his bed gravely ill with tuberculosis, an incurable illness at the time. A month before his death, he had accepted Jesus as his Savior. One day a friend who found him worried asked him if he was afraid of death. "No, I'm not afraid of dying, but oh! Must I go, and emptyhanded?" he responded.

These are the words that inspired Charles C. Luther (1847–1924), who composed "Must I Go, and Empty-Handed?" a month after the death of his friend. Here is one verse:

> O the years in sinning wasted;
> Could I but recall them now,

I would give them to my Savior,
To His will I'd gladly bow.[32]

The Lord can make new things in our lives starting today, just as he will do in the universe. And the purpose of the Apocalypse of John is to encourage us:

> For our momentary, light suffering is producing for us an eternal weight of glory far beyond all comparison. *(2 Corinthians 4:17)*

Waiting for the flight to Greece,
Zurich Airport

Aerial view of Lake Geneva in Swiss Romandie,
Between Puidoux and Mont Pelerin

Commentary on Patmos and the Seven Churches of Revelation

The following notes are the result of the preparatory work on the documentary series *Les 7 églises de l'Apocalypse*, produced by Millenium-Productions in co-production with Ze Watchers and directed by Étienne Magnin.

PATMOS

Geography

The island of Patmos (in modern Greek, Πάτμος) is located at the northern end of the Dodecanese, between the islands of Ikaria and Samos to the north and Lypsi to the east. It is a strip of land that is 12.5 kilometers long, welcoming in the waters of the Aegean Sea, which form numerous inlets and pretty bays. The whole of this coastline represents a perimeter of 65 kilometers.

In the narrowest part of the island, at its center, is the port of Skala, its economic heart and soul.

Reading Revelation,
above the port of Skala on Patmos

Sunset over one of Patmos's numerous bays.

The terrain of Patmos is mountainous, volcanic, and rocky, with numerous low mountains separated by verdant hills. The island enjoys a particularly mild climate; in the summer, winds from the north bring coolness. At present, the island numbers roughly 3,500 inhabitants. Its soil is particularly fertile and propitious for agriculture, even if the water supply is in a critical state.

It should be noted that Patmos is located at just a few cable lengths from the Turkish city of Ephesus. The tiny, fortified city of Chora has developed around the monastery whose somber edifice contrasts with the whitewashed houses with flat roofs. The island numbers more than 365 churches or monasteries, hermitages, and various sacred places. Thanks to the apostle John, the island of Patmos has become one of the most important places in Christianity, attracting tens of thousands of visitors each year.

Chapels of the island of Patmos. The small island
counts roughly 365 Christian holy places.

History

Classical history relates that, in the 90s, under the emperor Domitian, there erupted one of the gravest persecutions against the ancient church. Legend has it that Domitian vainly tried to put John, son of Zebedee, to death. John, invited to drink a cup of poison, swallowed the contents in one gulp without suffering the slightest ill effect.[33]

As the Lord said to Peter concerning John: *"If I want him to live until I come back, what concern is that of yours?"* (John 21:22). From then on, rumor spread among the disciples that the apostle hadn't died. Clement of Alexandria specifies that John was later exiled to the island of Patmos in 94. Unable to put John to death, the emperor exiled him to Patmos, where he had the vision of the Day of the Lord and received spiritual revelations about the end times (*acharit-hayamim*) in his lifetime, though he was already very old.

Recently certain exegetes have cast doubt on this tradition, hypothesizing that it was in the context of the first persecution, which took place under Nero beginning in 63, that John was exiled to Patmos. He supposedly fled Jerusalem in the year 66 at the outset of the great Jewish revolt against Rome, and then took refuge in Ephesus where he became the bishop responsible for the seven churches of Asia; he was then exiled to Patmos by the Roman authorities.

Saint John on Patmos
Engraving by Gustave
Doré, 1874

Whatever the case, the exile on Patmos is documented by the text of Revelation. According to an apocryphal text, the apostle John came to the island with his disciple Prochorus, one of the seven deacons of the ancient church of Jerusalem, who became bishop of the island after the apostle's return to Ephesus, after John was freed by Nerva, Domitian's successor.

After the death of Domitian in 96, emperor Nerva allowed John to return to Ephesus.[34] From there, he traveled around the region, invited by the local Christian communities, "sometimes to appoint bishops, sometimes to organize full churches, sometimes to choose as a priest one of those who had been designed by the Spirit."[35]

He supposedly died in Ephesus in the year 101 at the age of roughly 90. He is said to have been buried in Selçuk, near Ephesus, where there was a Basilica of St. John, today in ruins. Polycarp of Smyrna was said to have been his disciple.

John may only have remained for a short time on the island of Patmos, but he spread the gospel in Asia, thus continuing the work that Paul and his disciple

Timothy had begun. He organized the churches of Asia Minor and had to fight against the agnostics, as demonstrated by the letters he wrote on the subject.

Archaeology and John's Sojourn on Patmos

In pre-Christian antiquity, the island was the center of the cult of Apollo and Artemis, for these twins were supposedly born not far from there.

Patmos still maintains numerous traditions related to the stay of the great apostle. As with any non-biblical tradition, we cannot take them all "literally," but given the exiguity of the island, its isolation from the rest of the world, and its small population, neither can they be dismissed out of hand.

According to them, the exiled apostle spent a great deal of time praying in a cave; it was in this cavern that he received the revelation of the Apocalypse. Today this cave is the island's holiest site. A monastery was built above it, and the monks show pilgrims the traces of John's passage. A crevice in a rock is thus supposedly the place where the old man rested his head when he lay down.

Also indicated is a sort of natural desk cut into the rock, where his assistant and secretary, Prochorus, supposedly kept the manuscript and wrote, under dictation from the apostle, what the Lord revealed and which became the text of Revelation. The monks also show the recesses in which John placed his hands when he rose after praying; his old age, indeed, would have made this maneuver difficult.

It was around this sacred cave that the city of Chora developed the island's capital. Roughly two kilometers from the cave stands the monastery of St. John, dominating with its massive splendor the Bay of Skala, the island's main port. The monastery was founded in 1088.

Recess in the wall of the Cave of the Apocalypse on Patmos. Legend has it that the apostle John, given his old age, used this cavity to help himself up.

It's the island's principal monument, built like a great medieval fortress, to protect the monks from the Barbary pirates who ravaged the Aegean Sea in this period. It is a truly formidable fortress.

The monastery contains numerous artistic treasures, namely a library, among the most important in the world as far as the Christian manuscripts it contains, after that of the Vatican, the National Library in Paris, those of

City of Chora: the fortified monastery of Saint John the Theologian on Patmos, in Greece.

Athens, and the monastery of Saint Catherine on Mount Sinai. Indeed, the library of the monastery of Saint John on Patmos contains 1,100 manuscripts, including 300 parchments, 10,000 old prints, 13,000 archival pieces of biblical and patristic documents, and so on.

One of the oldest pieces is the *Codex Purpurex Petropolitanus,* which dates to the beginning of the sixth century. It contains thirty-three pages of the gospel of Mark, written on a parchment of purple vellum, the imperial color; it's one of the oldest known examples of this text. This manuscript undoubtedly comes from a workshop in Constantinople, dismantled in the twelfth century, perhaps by the Crusades.

Another quite ancient manuscript, dating to the seventh century, is a copy of the book of Job in a large format, annotated with several variants. This book is often consulted by exegetes.

Manuscript from the library of the monastery of Saint John the Theologian on the island of Patmos. The collection contains the *Codex Purpurex Petropolitanus,* the oldest known example of the gospel of Mark.

It is interesting to note that in the monastery's church you see a painting representing John's dictation to Prochorus, and that the text is that of the opening of John's gospel: "In the beginning was the Word, and the Word was with God, and the Word was fully God" (1:1). Some thus claim that the gospel of John was also written here on Patmos. Around the year 180, Irenaeus of Lyon, who had frequented Polycarp, the bishop of Smyrna who had seen John, nevertheless wrote: "After the other disciples, John, the disciple

Cross inside the chapel of the monastery of Saint John the Theologian in Chora, on the island of Patmos.

Interior of the chapel of the monastery of Saint John the Theologian in Chora, on the island of Patmos.

of the Lord who rests on his chest, gave he himself his version of the gospel during his stay in Ephesus."[36]

Local tradition says that the apostle preached the gospel on the island, leading numerous pagans to the faith in Christ. They show, in a place called Penera, the spot where John baptized the new converts. Later, it seems, a baptistry was built on this location, perhaps to commemorate the site where the apostle himself had baptized. The spot is visible at the port of Skala.

Father Philippos, a clergyman on the island, argues that the message of the Apocalypse came out of Patmos. It is "more relevant than ever, at the very moment that the world plunges into a chaos resembling that which was revealed to John as the precursory sign of the judgment that is to come."

According to an ancient tradition, John came up against strong opposition from a pagan priest named Synops, a sort of local sorcerer. The island did have an active cult to Zeus and Dionysus. But Patmos is famous in the world most of all as the island of the Apocalypse.

Aerial view of Kusadasi, Turkey, usual departure port for the Dodecanese archipelago and the island of Patmos.

According to the fathers of the church, John, son of Zebedee, after Paul had founded the church of Asia Minor, would become their bishop. He stayed in Ephesus where you can still see the tomb of Mary, mother of Jesus. Jesus, seeing his mother and near her the disciple whom he loved, said to her:

> "'Woman, look, here is your son!' He then said to his disciple: 'Look, here is your mother!' From that very time the disciple took her into his own home." *(John 19: 26–27)*

Interview with the doyen of the monastery of Saint John the Theologian on the island of Patmos.

John had received the mission of hosting Mary in his home, and she would naturally have accompanied him to Asia Minor when he succeeded Paul as bishop. Mary supposedly died in Ephesus while John was living in this city. Asia, meaning modern-day Turkey, was Christianity's second holy land after the land of Israel, and it had developed there to a considerable extent.

Interview with American Professor Mark Wilson on Patmos. He is one of the world's most renowned specialists in the archaeology of the seven churches of Revelation.

EPHESUS

Ephesus is the site of the first of the seven churches of Asia cited in Revelation. It was founded by the Greeks 1,000 years before Christ. Ephesus is the largest archaeological site of the Mediterranean basin and contains a host of veritable treasures, true pearls of antiquity.

The ancient city occupies an important place in the New Testament. The apostle Paul founded a Christian community there and traveled to the city during his second and third missionary journeys. Paul sent his assistant Timothy to Ephesus toward the end of his ministry to oversee its church. In Paul's day, the city was quite prosperous; thanks to its port, it was one of the largest cities in the world and possessed monumental public buildings, including a theater. Also built there was the Temple of Artemis, one of the wonders of the ancient world.

The city played host to the great apostle John, who would end his days in Ephesus; his tomb in Selçuk is still visible there today. But Ephesus was built on a lagoon that gradually filled in from silt and ended up being abandoned. What's more, this is certainly the origin of the biblical text's allusion to the stagnation of the first love. The fact that no modern buildings have been constructed over the site means that, here more than anywhere else, we can immerse ourselves in the realities of the ancient world.

Geography

Ephesus is located on the western coast of Asia Minor in modern-day Turkey, in the heart of Ionia, northeast of the island of Samos. It lies on one of the numerous bays on the coast of Asia Minor. It's located near the mouth of the Cayster, a river that flows through a deep, mountainous valley. The Cayster Valley constitutes a natural communications thoroughfare. Numerous roads connect Ephesus to its neighboring cities and it's a strategic stop between Greece and the Middle East.

Ephesus was a very important port in antiquity; a description of Ephesus given by Pliny the Elder, the greatest ancient historian, relates that "the sea tended to rise up to the Temple of Diana" (Artemis). But the entire zone gradually silted up, and the city now sits at roughly seven kilometers from the Aegean coast.

Indeed, the Cayster River originally poured into a gulf whose banks touched the three hills of Ephesus. At the beginning of the first millennium BC, the sea level was still two meters below its current height, and the mouth of the Cayster in the Gulf of Ephesus was then located at more than ten kilometers from its current position.

The problem of silting never ceased presenting itself throughout the city's history; it results in a migration of the port infrastructure toward various sites to the west, increasingly distant from the original urban core. The terrain thus progressively subtracted from the sea stood out for their marshy character; they posed health problems and required constant draining.

The region of Ephesus enjoys a mild Mediterranean climate, which, combined with the opportunities offered by its topography, presents numerous advantages. Due to its fertility and abundance, the wide valley of the Cayster is an ideal place for wheat farming and horse breeding. Likewise, the numerous plateaus that surround the city lend themselves quite well to sheep farming. Finally, the hills offer their gentle slopes for the cultivation of orchards and olive groves.

History

The settlement of the region of Ephesus dates back to the fifth millennium BC. Like that of other Ionian settlements, the colonization of Ephesus dates to the tenth century. The site was then occupied by autochthonous peoples, and the colonists clashed with the cult of the mother goddess Cybele, a cult then dominant over the majority of Anatolia. To reconcile themselves with the native populations, the Greeks opted for a politics of syncretism, fusing the cults of Artemis and Cybele.

Once the community was established, the city was governed by kings. Monarchy was a widespread form of government in the Mediterranean basin. Between the tenth and the early seventh century BC, the monarchy was replaced by an aristocratic oligarchy that, in turn, was overthrown by dictators.

The Persian sovereign Cyrus the Great conquered Ephesus in 546 BC; the Greek Peloponnesian War (431–404 BC) gave it the opportunity to rebel and ally with Sparta. After the fall of Athens, Ephesus came once more under Persian domination, until the conquest of the region by Alexander the Great in 333 BC. After Alexander's death, his general Lysimachus emerged victorious in the power struggles in Asia Minor, and Ephesus came under the control of the Seleucids.

In this period, the Hellenistic world found itself divided among the new dynasties created by Alexander's generals (the book of Daniel prophesied these events quite precisely). The Seleucids occupied a kingdom that extended from the Mediterranean to the Indus River. Asia Minor changed hands numerous times.

The Anatolian cities progressively gained their independence, and the King of Pergamon gained control over a part of Asia Minor.

The nascent Roman Empire's increasing interference in eastern Mediterranean affairs gradually led it to gain control over the kingdom of Pergamon. The door was then open to the integration of Anatolia and Ephesus into the Roman bosom. Rome defeated Antiochus III in 189 BC and placed Ephesus under the control of Pergamon, before taking direct control of it in 133 BC.

The framework of Roman administration was then progressively put into place. Anatolia became a full-fledged Roman province and was put under the government of a proconsul, one of whose residences was located in Ephesus.

In 88 BC the revolt of the Vespers of Ephesus took place, an episode in which all Romans of Asia Minor were massacred as a means of uniting the Greeks irreversibly, seeing as they would all have to fear Roman vengeance. Indeed, it was the beginning of a war against the latter that would last four long years.

The city was not spared by the troubles that affected the majority of the empire in the mid-third century; with its outer walls in ruins for want of upkeep, the city was hit hard in 262 under Emperor Gallienus by a maritime raid of Ostrogoths and Heruli pirates. They pillaged and set fire to the Temple of Artemis and probably ravaged other neighborhoods.

It wasn't until the reign of Diocletian, who durably reestablished the security of the empire and profoundly reformed its institutions, that the city entered a new period of prosperity that would last three centuries, until the Persian and Arab invasions. It owed its prosperity to its strategic position along the routes of commerce. The city, port of call between Rome and Egypt, remained a point of strategic importance on the eastern Mediterranean maritime routes. This central position was also the reason for which the city was chosen for the meeting of two ecumenical councils by the Christian Church in 431 and 449.

Archaeology

The silting up and abandonment of the city have been a genuine godsend for archaeologists. Today its vestiges offer us a privileged glimpse into an ancient city that played a major role in the mission of the apostles and the diffusion of Christianity.

The Artemision of Ephesus, the sanctuary dedicated to the goddess Artemis, was one of the seven wonders of the ancient world and represented for the city a great source of revenue. Greek and Roman merchants were in the habit of offering a portion of their profits to Artemis. It took 220 years to build this temple, which was also the "first bank in the world." It was possible to deposit your money there and even earn interest!

This temple had a surface area four times greater than the Parthenon in Athens. It was lined with 127 twenty-meter-high columns with a length of 138 meters and a breadth of seventy-one meters. Nothing in the Greek world could match it.

The temple housed the statue of Artemis, goddess of fertility for the Greeks. According to the Ephesians, this white marble sculpture had fallen from heaven (Acts 19:35). The goddess's chest was decorated with strange clusters. Chicken eggs? Bull testicles? Theories abound, but the symbolism was clearly connected to fertility.

To affirm the goddess's sovereignty over the city, the Ephesians instituted a sacred fire that was never to be extinguished. The priests were responsible for keeping it aflame, at the risk of being buried alive if the fire went out. There were hundreds of priests, eunuchs, guardians, musicians, and magicians employed in the goddess's service.

Tradition has it that during the annual Feast of Artemis, into the flames of a great bonfire were thrown animals, birds, and fruit, and that the priestesses walked barefoot over hot coals and initiated followers into secret rituals. Each month of May was entirely a holiday, consecrated to bacchanals that celebrated the Artemis of Ephesus. Tens of thousands of pilgrims came from throughout the Greek world to attend to the feasts given in the goddess's honor.

It was the most frequented temple in Asia Minor, a site for the practice of mystery religions, whose secrets were unveiled to followers during initiation rites. The city was a hotbed for magic and known as a veritable capital of occultism.

Paul in Ephesus

Paul worked there for three years with immense success; he founded one of the most solid communities in primitive Christianity. The Christian converts burned their books of magic on the public square (Acts 19:19) during a bonfire that destroyed grimoires for an overall value of 50,000 drachmas. Given that a good day's work was paid one drachma, we can imagine the financial equivalent today: over 3.5 million dollars! The city lived richly of the commerce of the pagan cult of Artemis. Paul's preaching disturbed this profitable market, to the point that the city's merchants stirred up a riot against Paul (Acts 19:23). Timothy and John continued Paul's work in this city, and the cult of Artemis diminished in consequence.

The prytaneum, a sort of city hall, faces the bouleuterion, or the council house, that was probably located in the position of the music hall (*odeon*) that survives today. The building was associated with the temple consecrated to Hestia Boulaia, where the perpetual fire burned, certainly the object of the allusion to the candelabra in the letter to the church.

Due to Ephesus's geographical situation, the port occupied a preponderant place in the city's economic activity. It was opened by a colossal statue of Poseidon. Ephesus possessed a good number of textile workshops whose production surpassed that of traditional domestic production.

It was in the 25,000-seat theater that the population rose up against Paul's preaching (Acts 19:28–41).

According to the Christian tradition, it was in Ephesus that John wrote the gospel that's attributed to him (some, however, believe that the text was written on Patmos). It's also where Mary is said to have resided on a hill seven kilometers south of Ephesus, on the site where you can still visit a small thirteenth-century Byzantine church known as the House of the Virgin Mary (*Meryemana Evi*), the so-called House of Mary or church of the Monastery of the Three Doors (*Monastiriüç Kapu*).

John is supposed to have been buried on the hill of Ayasuluk in Selçuk, but the identity of the deceased has been a source of debate since the second century; it's a question of knowing whether the author of Revelation is also the man who wrote the gospel, a position taken first by Irenaeus of Lyon, but also contested from that same period (late second century). While this identity is ultimately accepted, it is still contested in the fourth century by Eusebius of Caesarea. There were, according to him and other Christian authors of the time of Irenaeus, two homonymous figures: John of Zebedee and John the Presbyter (John the Elder), both buried in Ephesus. According to them, it could be this second John who worked on the final versions of the gospel known today as the gospel according to Saint John. The apostle's tomb, in any case, became an object of veneration quite early in Ephesus, and a basilica was built to aggrandize its site beginning, in all probability, in the fourth century.

The joint presence of John and Mary in Ephesus is mentioned by numerous Christian authors starting in the second century. Thus, in the fifth century, the acts of the council of 431 specified that it was being held in the city where they had both resided.

View of the agora of the city of Ephesus, where Paul worked.
In the background, the library of Celsus.

Facade of the Library of Celsus in Ephesus. It was the third-largest in the ancient
world after those in Alexandria and Pergamon.
Burned down by the Goths in 263, everything it contained was destroyed.

The building housed no less than 12,000 scrolls,
conserved in wooden cupboards set into the walls.
Built beginning in 117

In Ephesus there was a large number of artisans, particularly goldsmiths. The riot provoked by Paul's preaching testifies to the influence of this socio-professional group as well as its organization. Indeed, it was under the aegis of Demetrius, something of a "leader" of theirs—actually, the wealthiest and most prestigious practitioner—that they came together to counter the Jewish preacher.

We can wonder just how Saint Paul was disturbing the business of these professionals. The famous Demetrius mentioned previously was a goldsmith who produced small silver models of the Artemision; he trafficked in them, which certainly assured his financial well-being. Like Demetrius, the majority of Ephesus's artisans exploited the temple's image and renown to their profit. The calling into question by Paul of Artemis, her cult, and, consequently, her temple, damaged these artisans.

Effectively, their business decreased as the number of pilgrims diminished and the Ephesians themselves turned away from Artemis. They formed a privileged category within the city. Most of the artisans connected to the temple made money off it. Their significant number, turning them into an unstable and influential group, obliged the city and its administration, in both the classical and Hellenistic periods, to take them into consideration and ensure their good graces. This occurred via the conferral of certain privileges and advantages, such as fiscal discounts which, in certain cases, could be an exemption from contributing to public levies to which the city might make recourse.

These artisans, as their name indicates, lay on the boundary between artistic and commercial activities. They participated in both the economic and cultural enrichment of the city. Next on the chain were the vendors who had their stalls on the agora. Commercial exchange gave rise to the use of money.

The practice of medicine also developed in a quite unique fashion in the city. The development of schools of medicine, as well as the rise of private and public practice of medicine, could be attributed to the cultural conditions created in the city. An intellectual crossroads, Ephesus was one of cities most propitious to the development of curative practices.

Legend places the beginning of the story of the Seven Sleepers of Ephesus around the year 250, under Emperor Decius. A group of young people, persecuted for their Christian faith, took refuge in a grotto where they fell asleep and were walled in by their persecutors. According to this tradition, they woke up two centuries later, around 430, in the reign of Theodosius II, and attracted the authorities' attention by trying to use money from the reign of Decius to buy food. The emperor himself visited the site of the presumed miracle with the occasion of a pilgrimage to Ephesus. The miracles were interpreted as a prefiguration of the resurrection of the dead. This event appears at a crucial moment in the history of the church, just before an ecumenical council. This story of young people presenting themselves as survivors of persecution was particularly welcome at a time when the Origenist controversy concerning the resurrection of the body was raging.

The recognition of Christianity under Constantine didn't immediately put an end to the pagan cults, which continued to be tolerated for nearly all the fourth century. The Artemision, roughly restored after its destruction by the Goths in 262, probably continued to welcome Artemis's faithful up to the reign of Constans II, even until the laws of Theodosius I imposed Christianity as the official religion. The cult of Serapis was still alive in the fourth century judging by the extant epigraphs, and the same goes for the imperial cult: the temple of Hadrian, restored under the Tetrarchy, received at the end of the century a dedication to Theodosius, father of the homonymous emperor.

The importance of Ephesus's Christian community is confirmed by holding two important church councils in the city, metropole of Asia, in the reign of Theodosius II: on the one hand, the third ecumenical council, known as the Council of Ephesus, in 431; on the other, the second council, better known in the Catholic tradition by the name of "Robber Council of Ephesus" in 449, which concerned the settling of the question of the nature of the Holy Trinity.

It was the triumph of Alexandrine theology, the interpretation by Cyril of the Christological doctrine of the Council of Nicaea. In his view, the humanity and divinity of Christ were united by a hypostatic union that designates the union of the two natures, divine and human, in the person of Jesus Christ (meaning not just Jesus the man, but the Jesus who is recognized by Christians as "perfectly God and perfectly man"). Another important long-term consequence is the recognition of the Virgin Mary by the title of *éotokos*, "Mother of God." These doctrinal elements influenced the whole of Christianity in the centuries to come.

Commentary on the Biblical Text

We read in Revelation:

> "To the angel of the church in Ephesus, write the following: "This is the solemn pronouncement of the one who has a firm grasp on the seven stars in his right hand—the one who walks among the seven golden lampstands: I know your works as well as your labor and steadfast endurance, and that you cannot tolerate evil. You have even put to the test those who refer to themselves as apostles (but are not), and have discovered that they are false. I am also aware that you have persisted steadfastly, endured much

for the sake of my name, and have not grown weary. But I have this against you: You have departed from your first love! Therefore, remember from what high state you have fallen and repent! Do the deeds you did at the first; if not, I will come to you and remove your lampstand from its place— that is, if you do not repent. But you do have this going for you: You hate what the Nicolaitans practice—practices I also hate. The one who has an ear had better hear what the Spirit says to the churches. To the one who conquers, I will permit him to eat from the tree of life that is in the paradise of God. (2:1–7)

Ephesus means "desirable." This city occupies an important place in the New Testament; the apostle Paul establishes the church there and goes to Ephesus during his second and third missionary voyages. Toward the end of his ministry, he sends his assistant Timothy to take care of that church (1 Timothy 1:3).

John speaks to the church of Ephesus (Revelation 2:1–7), which is his church; he knows it perfectly because he is its leader. And what does the Lord tell him? Initially something quite positive: I'm familiar with your deeds, your work, and your perseverance. I know that you have endured, that you have suffered in my name. Christ begins by recalling all the virtues of this important church. And they are numerous; this is a community that has zeal, discernment, perseverance, that not only has engaged in numerous and praiseworthy acts but has not hesitated to testify in a very difficult context, one which has caused notable hardships. It is an admirable church both in acts and words.

But the reproach made by Jesus is its lack of authentic love. Christ rebukes it for its lack of profound love. Nevertheless, he recognizes its merit for having condemned the false prophets and the Nicolaitans, a little-known sect whose teachings were linked to immodesty and likely to the erotic cult of idols. These were Gnostics, a heretical sect that saw the material body not as being subject to sanctification and, was therefore, available for debauchery. This thinking was influenced by Greek thought, which viewed the material body as evil.

For more than forty years, since its foundation by Paul, this church had remained faithful to the teaching of its founding fathers and to the Lord. Through difficulties and persecution, its members had persevered, driven by good reason: the name and reputation of Christ. But something saddens the Lord:

But I have this against you: You have departed from your first love! (Revelation 2:4)

Being a Christian means loving the Lord Jesus Christ. Now the fervor and passion of the Ephesians for Christ had become a cold, mechanical orthodoxy.

Their moral and doctrinal purity, their zeal which had always been so great in favor of the truth, and their disciplined service could not replace the love for Christ that they had lost.

The Church of Ephesus had not fallen into the trap of the Nicolaitans's impure works; it had resisted their false beliefs and teachings. This heresy resembled the teachings of Balaam (see the commentary on the church of Pergamon). *Nicolas* means "conqueror of peoples."

According to Irenaeus, Nicolas, named a deacon in Acts 6, was a false believer who later sank into apostasy and deceived members of the church thanks to the credit he enjoyed. Like Balaam, he drove the believers to immorality and wickedness. The Nicolaitans probably gave themselves to immorality and assaulted the church by means of sexual temptations. Through their erroneous teachings, they perverted the meaning of grace and replaced freedom with licentiousness.

The problem inherent in this church is that it "was becoming paralyzed." It was threatened with death. Where the Spirit dwells is life, and where it is no longer, a spiritual cooling inevitably occurs. This entropic danger has always menaced the churches over the centuries. It is customary to compare the Church of Laodicea, the seventh, to a lukewarm, old church, where the Lord, who is no longer in the church, but outside, wants to come in.

To the contrary, the Church of Ephesus had, for its part, shifted its pole of interest. The Lord could have told it: you have Christian qualities, you remain virtuous, faithful. But Christ no longer held pride of place in their hearts. The Christian must love his Lord before all else, because from there springs his love for his brothers and sisters and for his neighbor. The greatest commandment in the Christian faith is to love, as Jesus himself attests:

> Now one of the experts in the law came and heard them debating. When he saw that Jesus answered them well, he asked him, "Which commandment is the most important of all?" Jesus answered, "The most important is, *'Listen, Israel, the Lord our God, the Lord is one. Love the Lord your God with all your heart, with all your soul, with all your mind, and with all your strength.'* The second is: *'Love your neighbor as yourself.'* There is no other commandment greater than these." *(Mark 12:28–31)*

This is why God, in his great mercy (Lamentations 3:33), continues to exhort and to admonish his church in order to rouse its awareness and repentance.

How is the expression "your first love" to be understood? We all know the verses of the famous French song "when love has become a habit." It isn't necessarily a matter of rediscovering the original fluster, the exuberance and enthusiasm of the first period in which we discovered the faith—for love ripens as well—but our love for the Lord must remain a priority in our lives. And this love is always an active, practical love: True love must give rise to actions.

It is also an exhortation to cultivate and conserve our hatred of evil. Today in a time of absolute tolerance, of the loss of values and refuge, where prohibiting is prohibited, in a time when one must avoid judging at all costs, it is very difficult to hate evil and even to discern it. Christianity is generally identified as a religion of love. But, according to this text, it is a religion of love and hatred (of evil). The apostle Paul said:

> Love must be without hypocrisy. Abhor what is evil . . . *(Romans 12:9)*

The text contains the warning:

> . . . if not, I will come to you and remove your lampstand from its place . . . *(Revelation 2:5)*

The Church of Ephesus was, in this period, the most important and glorious of the church of Asia. It was there that Paul dwelt longest for his ministry. It was in Ephesus that his teachings had the greatest impact since we learn, in the book of Acts, that all the inhabitants of the province of Asia heard the echo of his renown.

The lampstand, symbol of the light of the gospel that had originally been in Jerusalem then in Antioch (departure point for the first missionary journeys), had then been transferred to Ephesus. But it could be moved again. Indeed, history proves to us that it has been.

Today as you walk through the ruins of what remains of the city of Ephesus, you can't help but be moved, even overwhelmed: all the remains of the Christian presence in this city are the ruins of an immense basilica dedicated to Saint John. But all life of the Christian faith has vanished.

In listening to the warnings that the glorified Christ addresses to the Church of Ephesus, you can't help but think of the cities and villages of France, of Switzerland, of Europe. This continent was the focal point of Catholic and Protestant Christianity in a none-too-distant world. And what is left of it now? The traditional churches are nearly empty on Sunday, with Europe experiencing a genuine cooling of the Christian passion and fervor that characterized it over the centuries.

It's as though, after Ephesus and Turkey, Europe inherited this lampstand for several centuries. But the light of this lampstand was gradually replaced by the thought of the Enlightenment, humanism, and by the temptations of materialism. This thinking and this way of life are what, today, guides our civilization, and no longer the original light of the lampstand of the Christian faith.

Even if the warning is mentioned once, it is recalled two times that if the church repents, if it returns to putting love for its Lord first and flees resolutely from evil, the lampstand can remain, life can triumph, and a new beginning can flourish in the image of the Garden of Eden itself:

> To the one who conquers, I will permit him to eat from the tree of life that is in the paradise of God. *(Revelation 2:7)*

What a promise! What encouragement! What Christ promises to his church, whether to that of Ephesus or to our own, is nothing less than the life of God within us, our participation in his paradise, the fulfillment of all his promises of joy, of peace, and of happiness.

View of the ruins of the city of Ephesus with Basilica of St. John in Selçuk. In the distance, the castle of Aisasaluk. Built on the tomb attributed to the evangelist John on the hill of Ayasoluk.
Engraving by T. Allom and W. J. Cook

SMYRNA

Smyrna (*Izmir* in Turkish; in modern Greek, Σμύρνη, Smýrni): the city of the renowned poet Homer. Smyrna was a port city at the heart of a majestic bay at the foot of Mount Pagus. Its homes, as well as its superb monuments, rose on the side of the mountain, dominating the sea in a sort of magnificent crown. Smyrna means "myrrh," that is, "bitter" or "suffering." This substance was frequently used as a perfume to embalm the dead and as an analgesic in ancient pharmacopeia.

The city was nicknamed "the crown of Asia." Known in antiquity as being the most beautiful city in Asia Minor, it was an important scientific and medical hub. The city was reputed for its commerce and its exports. Also to be found there were schools of rhetoric, philosophy, medicine, and science. Many Jews lived there, and they were fiercely opposed to Christianity. It was a natural port in a fertile region, and it became one of Asia Minor's most prosperous cities.

Geography

Smyrna was located on the site of the current city of Izmir in Turkey, roughly seventy kilometers to the north of Ephesus. Izmir is Turkey's second-largest port (after Istanbul) and the third-largest Turkish city in terms of population (close to 3.1 million inhabitants in 2017). The name "Smyrna" was long preferred in English to the Turkish appellation, testifying to the city's openness to the West.

History

Smyrna was founded around 3000 BC by the Leleges on the site of Tepekule, near modern-day Bayraklı. Between 2000 and 1200 BC it was a part of the Hittite kingdom. It was then occupied by the Aeolians, who had emigrated from Greece to Anatolia in the eleventh century BC, then by the Ionians following the collapse of the Hittite state due to attacks by the Phrygians. The first Smyrna reached its height during the Ionian period. It was invaded in 600 BC by the Lydian king Alyattes II, then by the Persians in 546 BC.

Having been sacked, the city no longer occupied an important role during the classical period (fifth and fourth centuries BC). According to legend, it was Alexander the Great who decided to restore the destroyed city. But it was more likely his successors (Antigonus, then Lysimachus) who rebuilt it in the fourth century, after Alexander's death.

In 302 BC, it came under the rule of Lysimachus, ex-general of Alexander the Great, after his victory over Antigonus the One-Eyed. Then it came under the domination of the Seleucids and finally, for a short period, under the kingdom of Pergamon (late third to early second century BC).

In this period, the Seleucids attempted to regain control of the region of Ionia, but Smyrna fought on the side of the Attalids, Pergamon, and Rome. From 189 to 188 BC, the Seleucids were driven out of Ionia and Asia Minor. Smyrna then received territories for having fought alongside Rome. Its engagement permitted it to benefit from relative independence and Rome's political protection.

But as the Roman Empire grew more threatening, Smyrna, along with the rest of the cities in Asia Minor, supported the king of Pontus, Mithridates VI Eupator, in his war against Rome from 89 to 85 BC. The Roman general Silla then undertook the conquest of Asia Minor. He conquered Smyrna and forced every one of the city's inhabitants to parade naked in the middle of winter to humiliate them.

With the Peace of Dardanos (85 BC) that concluded the war between Rome and Mithridates VI, Smyrna, along with the majority of free cities in Asia Minor and the Aegean, was brought under the jurisdiction of the Roman province of Asia. Smyrna is one of the seven churches of Asia cited in the Apocalypse of Saint John who, according to Tertullian, named Polycarp the first bishop of Smyrna.

A passage in Revelation alludes to imprisoned Christians whom John lauds for their courage in the face of the persecution of Domitian or Nero, depending on the accepted dating of John's text.

Ever since the third century BC, Smyrna was famed for being a prosperous city. Artistically, it was known for its grotesques, terracotta figurines used in theater whose uniqueness lay in exaggerating a physical flaw, often linked to illness. It seems that these theatrical representations did not serve a purpose of mere art or entertainment. Smyrna possessed a famous school of medicine in Antiquity where Galen taught. It's likely that some of these sculptures served to illustrate illnesses such as hydroceles (abnormal accumulation of liquid or gas in a testicle). A collection of these objects can be seen in the Louvre in Paris.

All that's known today of the Roman city is the zone of the agora, currently under excavation, which was preserved because the site was used as a cemetery, as well as the location of the theater, currently covered by residential housing.

Turned into a province of Byzantium after the division of the Roman Empire, the city was invaded by the king of the Huns, Attila, in 440, then

The agora of Smyrna, known as the "Roman agora." It is the main archaeological site currently being excavated in the ancient city of Smyrna, modern-day Izmir, in Turkey.

by the Arabs in 695, before returning to the Byzantine fold. In 1081, it was conquered by the Seljuk Turks, before the Byzantines, taking advantage of the progress of the Crusades in Anatolia, reconquered in 1097 the territories occupied by the Turks on the coasts of the Aegean Sea. It was sacked by the Turks in 1222 and rebuilt by John Doukas who built the Kadifekale (the "velvet citadel"). In 1320, it was conquered by Mehmet Bey, emir of Aydin and Izmir.

The Castle of Smyrna
Engraving by T. Allom and W. J. Codre. An artistic
rendering of the citadel of Smyrna.

Commentary on the Biblical Text

> To the angel of the church in Smyrna write the following: This is the solemn pronouncement of the one who is the first and the last, the one who was dead, but came to life: 'I know the distress you are suffering and your poverty (but you are rich). I also know the slander against you by those who call themselves Jews and really are not, but are a synagogue of Satan. Do not be afraid of the things you are about to suffer. The devil is about to have some of you thrown into prison so you may be tested, and you will experience suffering for ten days. Remain faithful even to the point of death, and I will give you the crown that is life itself. The one who has an ear had better hear what the Spirit says to the churches. The one who conquers will in no way be harmed by the second death.' *(Revelation 2:8–11)*

The final exhortation of this letter is the same as the one to Ephesus: "*The one who has an ear had better hear what the Spirit says to the churches*" (Revelation 2:29). Why isn't it said that "the one who has an ear had better hear what the Spirit says to him"? Or that "the churches who have an ear had better hear what the Spirit says to them"? Why is each of these letters addressed first to an individual (he who has ears), and then to the communities? It's because hearing these words must be both personal and collective. This warning is valid for the believers in every community.

Indeed, you cannot be a Christian by yourself. The believer needs a community, a church. This is Jesus's plan for the disciples, and the communal project of the church is the mandate he gave to his successors. All churches are imperfect,

Jean-Marc Thobois with guide Cenk Eronat and Christophe at the agora of Smyrna.

but Christian life possesses a social, collective dimension, given that the plan described in the Bible was to unite the faithful in a sole bride for Christ.

The church, however, is neither an organization, nor a system, nor much less a piece of ecclesiastical machinery. It is a community of people called on individually to listen to Jesus Christ and his teachings, personally. This exhortation underlines the importance of a call to develop a personal faith and to maintain a personal relationship with Jesus Christ, as well as a fraternal communion with other brethren. Things are not resolved by organigrams or hierarchical decisions, but by a personal and a collective listening to the Bible's teachings.

The exhortations at the end of these seven letters aim to tell us something else as well: "*The one who has an ear had better hear what the Spirit says to the churches.*" Churches, plural. Christ is speaking to the universal church, in all places and all times. But the universal church is not a theoretical, ideal, abstract, and merely spiritual reality. It is composed of local churches.

Smyrna was filled with statues glorifying the emperors as well as a temple dedicated to Roma, "the goddess Rome." Roma was generally represented as a divine warrior, helmeted and often armed with a spear. This representation from the Republican age imitated the Greek goddess Athena, or sometimes the Amazons. This cult easily took its place in the tradition of the Hellenistic monarchies and the exaltation of the power of Rome and the creation of loyal local populations. It was an element of the imperial cult.

The emperor Augustus authorized the construction of temples or altars consecrated to the goddess Roma, in association with Caesar or himself. These cults of submission to the emperor and the goddess Roma demanded offerings and sacrifices, which posed a real problem for Christians: how does one address prayers to a man, even if he was the emperor, and offer sacrifices to a city, even if it was Rome? This caused a terrible dilemma for these believers. It was necessary to choose between loyalty to Rome and loyalty to gospel, a choice engendering no small amount of suffering.

Smyrna would experience it in a terrible manner with the martyrdom of Polycarp. Roughly fifty years after the writing of Revelation, Polycarp, one of the most wonderful figures in the early church, suffered the same martyrdom that many of those before him had. It is quite possible that he had read the letter addressed to the church of Smyrna.

Polycarp seems to have been named bishop of Smyrna around the turn of the century (c. 100), carrying out the functions of his ministry for around half a century. The bishop fought a number of sects that he judged to be heretical, particularly certain Gnostics and, notably, Marcion. When the persecution mandated by the emperor-philosopher Marcus Aurelius began, Polycarp was quite elderly. He stood up to the proconsul who interrogated him. At the time of his arrest, he was old man of eighty-six.

According to tradition, Polycarp was arrested on February 2 of the year 155 or 156; he was then dragged before the Roman magistrate and obliged to renege his Christian faith and "curse Christ" in front of a huge crowd assembled in the city stadium. This was his reply, which has since become famous: "Eighty-six years I have served him, and he never did me any wrong. How can I blaspheme my King who saved me?"[37]

Sentenced to be burned alive, he climbed atop the pyre and prayed thus:

> Lord God Almighty, Father of your beloved and blessed Child, Jesus Christ, through whom we have received full knowledge of you . . . I bless you for considering me worthy of this day and hour—of sharing with the martyrs in the cup of your Christ, so as to share in resurrection to everlasting life of soul and body in the Holy Spirit. May I be received among them into your presence today as a rich and acceptable sacrifice. For this and for everything I praise and glorify you through the eternal and heavenly high priest, Jesus Christ, your beloved Child. Through him and with him, may you be glorified with the Holy Spirit, both now and forever. Amen.[38]

When Polycarp pronounced this amen, the men tasked with his execution lit the fire, and Polycarp thus died a martyr's death consumed by the flames of the stake.

The ancient account reported by *The Book of Christian Martyrs*[39] gives another perspective on the event.

"Polycarp has confessed that he is a Christian!" The herald's declaration stirred up the crowd of pagans and Jews who lived in Smyrna. The cries rang out. "It is he, the master of Asia, the father of the Christians, the gravedigger of our gods, it is he who incites the crowds to abandon their sacrifices and worship!" In the midst of these cries, they demanded the asiarch Philip to feed Polycarp to a lion. But he objected that he did not have the right to do so because the animal fights were closed.

Then in one voice, they demanded that Polycarp perish by fire. Thus was realized the vision that had shown him with his ear aflame while he prayed, and that brought him to tell his friends prophetically: "I must be burned alive."

Events precipitated. In less time than it takes to say it, the crowd flooded into the workshops and bath houses to collect wood and kindling.

When the pyre was ready, the martyr undressed himself, took off his belt, and began to take off his shoes, a gesture of which the faithful hurriedly dispensed him; in their impatience to touch his body, they all rushed to help him. Long before his actual martyrdom, the sanctity of his conduct inspired this unanimous reverence.

The testimony of his death was an immense source of encouragement for the Christians of Asia Minor, throughout the time of the persecution and beyond.

One thing must be clear: the author's goal is not to encourage the pursuit of the condition of martyr, as was too often the case in the first centuries of Christianity, and as demonstrates the abundance of these documents of crucial importance for the history of early Christianity. The numerous accounts of this period attest to the formation of a literary genre in which, as Pierre Maraval explains in *Actes et passions des martyrs chrétiens des premiers siècles*, "the actual martyr becomes idealized martyr."[40]

History demonstrates, nevertheless, that a clear, strong declaration of the gospel today often leads, in many countries as in ancient Smyrna, to contestation and opposition. For this world does not like the message of the gospel; man does not like to hear that he is a sinner and that he needs to repent, that he cannot save himself and that only the cross of Jesus Christ is his path to salvation and freedom.

Yet the message of the Bible is objectively a message of victory and hope, as we read at the end of this letter to Smyrna. Indeed, it is in this letter that speaks of suffering, persecution, and even death that the most marvelous promises of life are announced:

> ...I will give you the crown that is life itself. *(Revelation 2:10)*

> The one who conquers will in no way be harmed by the second death. *(2:11)*

The second death, in Revelation, is the total, definitive separation from God and the definitive condemnation to eternal suffering. No, neither persecution, nor suffering, nor even death can separate believers from the love of God or take away their faith. The faithful are the conquerors who will have the right to the eternal rewards.

The cult of the emperor, which consisted in denying Christ to recognize the monarch as a sovereign deity, forced the faithful to take a stand. We find references to persecution in Hebrews 11:

> But others were tortured, not accepting release, to obtain resurrection to a better life. And others experienced mocking and flogging, and even chains and imprisonment. They were stoned, sawed apart, murdered with the sword; they went about in sheepskins and goatskins; they were destitute, afflicted, ill-treated (the world was not worthy of them); they wandered in deserts and mountains and caves and openings in the earth. *(35–38)*

As this letter expresses to these Christians, the first death is to be feared less than the second death that they risk incurring if they renege on their Savior:

> If we endure, we will also reign with him. If we deny him, he will also deny us. *(2 Timothy 2:12)*

> Do not be afraid of those who kill the body but cannot kill the soul. Instead, fear the one who is able to destroy both soul and body in hell. *(Matthew 10:28)*

The church of Smyrna is, along with that of Philadelphia, the only one to receive nothing but praise. This is due partly to the opposition that the Christians had to face. Becoming a Christian anywhere was to become an outlaw in the Roman Empire before Constantine.

Pliny the Younger (61–114), Roman governor of Bithynia (a region situated in northwestern Asia Minor, in modern Turkey), wrote to the emperor Trajan to ask for his view concerning the Christians in his *Letters*, written around 111–112 AD. The following is an excerpt:

> Sir, […], I have never been present at any legal examination of the Christians, and I do not know, therefore, what are the usual penalties passed upon them, or the limits of those penalties, or how searching an inquiry should be made. […]

> In the meantime, this is the plan which I have adopted in the case of those Christians who have been brought before me. I ask them whether they are Christians; if they say yes, then I repeat the question a second and a third time, warning them of the penalties it entails, and if they still persist, I order them to be taken away to prison. For I do not doubt that, whatever the character of the crime may be which they confess, their pertinacity and inflexible obstinacy certainly ought to be punished. […] Subsequently, as is usually the way, the very fact of my taking up this question led to a great increase of accusations, and a variety of cases were brought before me.

> A pamphlet was issued anonymously, containing the names of a number of people. Those who denied that they were or had been Christians and called upon the gods in the usual formula, reciting the words after me, those who offered incense and wine before your image, which I had given orders to be brought forward for this purpose, together with the statues of the deities - all such I considered should be discharged, especially as they cursed the name of Christ, which, it is said, those who are really Christians cannot be induced to do. Others, whose names were given me

by an informer, first said that they were Christians and afterwards denied it, declaring that they had been but were so no longer, some of them having recanted many years before, and more than one so long as twenty years back. They all worshipped your image and the statues of the deities, and cursed the name of Christ.

But they declared that the sum of their guilt or their error only amounted to this, that on a stated day they had been accustomed to meet before daybreak and to recite a hymn among themselves to Christ, as though he were a god, and that so far from binding themselves by oath to commit any crime, their oath was to abstain from theft, robbery, adultery, and from breach of faith [...]; When this ceremony was concluded, it had been their custom to depart and meet again to take food, but it was of no special character and quite harmless [...].

The matter seems to me worthy of your consideration, especially as there are so many people involved in the danger. Many persons of all ages, and of both sexes alike, are being brought into peril of their lives by their accusers, and the process will go on. For the contagion of this superstition has spread not only through the free cities, but into the villages and the rural districts [...].

Here is Trajan's response:

You have adopted the proper course, my dear Pliny, in examining into the cases of those who have been denounced to you as Christians, for no hard and fast rule can be laid down to meet a question of such wide extent. The Christians are not to be hunted out; if they are brought before you and the offence is proved, they are to be punished, but with this reservation—that if any one denies that he is a Christian and makes it clear that he is not, by offering prayers to our deities, then he is to be pardoned because of his recantation, however suspicious his past conduct may have been. [...]

Theologian Alfred Kuen writes: "In Smyrna, faith was a choice for the brave. In a city where the splendor of the pagan cult could easily have extinguished the life of a weak church, a city where the pride of the people looked down on these humble Christians, a city where every believer was threatened by the demands of the imperial cult on the one hand and the slander and wickedness of the Jews on the other, there were Christians who were faithful until death."

The church of Smyrna, as the name of the city indicates (bitter, suffering), experienced severe persecutions. Of the seven churches, it is one of only two not to be called to repentance. A church in good spiritual health, according to the criteria of these seven letters, always seems to be a church facing opposition, even persecution. Is this the case in today's world as well, with the persecuted churches ultimately enjoying better spiritual health than the churches in the West?

The message of the Lord aims to be encouragement. He says that he is aware of his children's tribulations and suffering.

Each of these seven letters is garnished with allusions to the historical, geographic, economic, religious, and even the local political situations. This is evident in the second of these letters, the one addressed to the church of Smyrna. The expression "the crown of Smyrna" was often used to describe the crownlike shape formed by its buildings. It's certainly with an eye to this expression that the promise made to the church of Smyrna specifies:

> Remain faithful even to the point of death, and I will give you the crown that is life itself. *(Revelation 2:10)*

For the inhabitants of Smyrna, this was a very evocative message. To the crown of Smyrna, admired by the travelers who disembarked in his port, Jesus contrasts the crown of life! This was even more striking because the church was threatened with death. It was a church that was persecuted, slandered, prey to terrible tribulations. But in the face of likely death, Christ promised the crown of life!

The expression "synagogue of Satan" fueled many debates and Christian anti-Semitism during the Middle Ages. The Jewish people viewed as abominable the cult of submission to Rome through the worship of a man, even the emperor. Following bloody revolts in the province of Israel, Rome had granted a special statute to the Jewish communities, which were the only ones in the empire to be legally exempted from the imperial cult. This detail is perhaps the key to understanding this passage of Revelation. This letter, then, unmistakably echoes the opposition of the Jewish community, firmly opposed to these "new" Christian believers, whom they considered at the time to be heretical sect they preferred to see disappear.

The church of Smyrna was thus caught in a vise. Two important dangers threatened it: on the one hand, the Hews, who didn't accept this new message of the gospel, and on the other, Rome, which didn't tolerate this spiritual rebellion against the imperial cult! The allusion to the "synagogue of Satan" is not an attack against Judaism, but a rebuke directed at the Jews, who certainly took advantage by accusing the Christians of Smyrna to the Roman authorities of not being true Jews.

Given that the Jews were authorized not to worship the emperor as a god, this separation exposed the Christians to death if they did not participate in the cult of submission. The imperial cult, which consisted in denying Christ to recognize the monarch as a sovereign deity, forced the faithful to take a stand in the face of a terrible dilemma: were they to deny the emperor or deny Christ? Their loyalty to Christ inevitably triggered a wave of persecution on the part of the Roman authorities.

Jesus had reminded the Ephesians that the first characteristic of a true, living church is love; to Smyrna, he underlined that the second characteristic of the faithful church is persecution by the world outside, in the face of which it must stand firm even if this gives rise to profound suffering. Unconditional love for the Lord and one's neighbor almost inevitably lead to suffering in this world of darkness. The apostle Paul had already said:

> Now in fact all who want to live godly lives in Christ Jesus will be persecuted. *(2 Timothy 3:12)*

The entirety of this letter revolves around the theme of suffering. And this suffering is going to increase further in the future, as announced in Revelation 2:10. It will last until death itself:

> Do not be afraid of the things you are about to suffer. The devil is about to have some of you thrown into prison so you may be tested, and you will experience suffering for ten days. Remain faithful even to the point of death ... *(Revelation 2:10)*

But Jesus knows this suffering; after all, this is how the letter begins: I know the distress you are suffering. Now—should we be surprised?—Jesus isn't promising deliverance. And the victory of which he speaks is not the escape from torment but facing it with loyalty and courage: "*Remain faithful even to the point of death.*"

The persecutions did not stop with the fall of the Roman Empire. Indeed, loyalty to the gospel over the centuries has often been accompanied by tremendous suffering. Such was the case, for example, at the end of the Middle Ages for the Waldensians of Piedmont or, in the sixteenth and seventeenth centuries, for the Huguenots in France.

Closer to us, some Christians took a stand against Nazism; the pastor and theologian Dietrich Bonhoeffer, executed in April 1945 by Hitler's special order, is a modern example. Here is what he wrote in his admirable book *The Price of Grace*: "Suffering is the distinctive mark of those who obey Christ." Luther counted suffering among the marks of the true church. Obeying means being bound to the suffering Christ; it's why there is nothing disconcerting about the suffering of Christians, even if it is intolerable and ought to arouse the compassion, reaction, and protection of nations.

The martyrdom of the countless unnamed in the countries where radical Islam rages, as well as the dead victims of persecution by the Islamic State, remind us that this issue is terribly current and ought to push democratic governments to radical commitments to protect persecuted Christians throughout the world. Their number is said to reach 200 million worldwide.

Other communities are also persecuted for their faith, such as the Muslim Uighurs, a million of whom it is estimated are enclosed in Chinese internment camps, out of an overall population of 14 million people.

PERGAMON

Pergamon (in Greek, Πέργαμον/*pérgamon*), literally "citadel" or "marriage," was an ancient political capital of Asia Minor, located in Aeolia, north of Smyrna, at the confluence of the Caicus and the Cetius Rivers, at roughly twenty-five kilometers from the Aegean Sea and eighty kilometers north of Ephesus. Currently its name is Bergama (Turkey, province of Izmir). At the time, Pergamon was an imperial city as well as an important administrative center.

Built on a mountain, the city had a royal air. It was considered the most illustrious in all of Asia. Distant from the sea, unlike its rivals Ephesus and Smyrna, it had to impose its power through structures and buildings to ensure its supremacy.

After Ephesus and Smyrna, the third letter is also addressed to an important city. Pergamon was the administrative and judicial capital of the province of Asia. This city was renowned throughout the Roman Empire for three reasons:

- Its library numbered 200,000 manuscripts and rivaled the famous library of Alexandria. Pergamon even organized a genuine manuscript hunt throughout the empire to enrich its library, to which Alexandria responded by ordering a stop to exports of the papyrus that grew in Egypt. Deprived of this basic material, Pergamon then invented parchment, which revolutionized bookmaking ("parchment" is *pergamenè* in Greek and *pergament* in German). It was thus a city of great culture.
- On the Acropolis of Pergamon rose a gigantic, magnificent complex of temples and an altar dedicated to Zeus the Savior, on which sacrifices were made to the sovereign of the pagan gods. Like the Temple of Artemis in Ephesus, this altar was one of the Seven Wonders of the Ancient World. It has survived up to the present day and can be admired at the Pergamon Museum in Berlin. Pergamon was thus a very religious, idolatrous city that worshipped a variety of ancient gods.

Meditation and reading in front of the structures that once housed the Altar of Zeus in Pergamon.

- Pergamon was certainly the darkest city of the entire Roman Empire but it was also the capital of psychiatric (or psychosomatic) medicine of the age.

Today it is still possible to visit the remains of the Asclepeion, an immense hospital complex dedicated to the god of medicine Asclepios (or Aesculapius), which included a treatment center, a pool, a library, and even a theater. The psychically ill from all corners of the empire came to be treated there by medicine and a blend of occult practices linked to the veneration of snakes.

In honor of what was the center of psychiatric medicine in antiquity, an international psychiatry conference is currently held in Pergamon every two years. With its great culture and numerous healers, a Catholic author can easily compare Pergamon both to Florence and Lourdes![41]

The Asclepeion of Pergamon, dedicated to the god Asclepios.
Psychiatric medicine was developed in this sanctuary of healing. Sacred snakes slithered in the dormitories where the sick slept.

Geography

Pergamon, built on a hill dominating the surround plain at an altitude of 335 meters, is the superposition of three cities with belvederes and terraces supporting two-story porticoes and connected to one another by staircases. In the upper city were the administrative buildings such as the agora, the palace, the arsenal, the library, the theater, and the temples of Dionysus, Athena Polias, and the Great Altar, also known as the Altar of Zeus. In the middle city lay a magnificent gymnasium, the temples of the Demeter and Hera Basileia—the Prytaneum.

Aerial view of the majestic acropolis of Pergamon.
At the top of the citadel rose the Temple of Trajan and Zeus Philios

Christophe contemplating the countryside of the Bergama
region from the acropolis of Pergamon.

Sunset from below the theater of Pergamon.
Overlooking the modern city of Bergama.

The lower city constituted the commercial center. An admirable architectural success, the city lay at the center of rich agricultural land marked by growing wheat, olive trees, vines, and livestock. There were a variety of industries, producing perfume, fine drapery, and parchment.

The library of Pergamon rivaled that of Alexandria, founded by Ptolemy I Soter, which aspired to make Alexandria the cultural capital of the Hellenistic world, taking the place of Athens. The collection in Pergamon included 200,000 volumes.

The royal palace enclosed a veritable museum of sculptures. It was famous for its school of rhetoric and its sculpture workshops.

History

The settlement of Pergamon is documented from the eighth century BC Though tradition holds that it was founded by Arcadian Greeks, it is unlikely that it was a Greek colony, given its distance from the sea. The king of Persia gave it to the Spartan king Demaratus around 480 BC. Another mention of the city dates to 339, a time in which it was governed by a Greek tyrant.

Pergamon emerges after the death of Alexander the Great, in 323 BC. The *diadochus* Lysimachus, one of his generals, stored his treasures there under the guard of the eunuch Philetaerus. The latter took control of Pergamon and founded, in 282 BC, the Pergamene state. Initially he reigned under the supervision of the Seleucids.

Taking advantage of the struggles between the latter, Philetaerus' nephew and adopted son, Eumenes I, veritable founder of the Attalid dynasty, defeated Antiochus I in 262 BC and thus ensured the independence of Pergamon, which would be consolidated by Attalus I Soter, first of the dynasty to take the title of king. He allied with the Romans during the First Macedonian War, against Philip V of Macedonia.

After the Roman victory at Battle of Magnesia ad Sipylum in 189 BC, sealed by the Peace of Apamea, Rome gave Pergamon jurisdiction over a large part of Asia Minor. Thanks to the victory of Attalus I Soter against the Galatians (a Celtic people originally from Gaul who had settled in central Anatolia), Pergamon extended its territory from the Hellespont to Caria and Ionia, Cappadocia and the western Phrygia. It was a continental kingdom composed of a single important port, Attalia, located on the Aegean Sea. The apogee of Pergamon was reached under Eumenes II, who ruled from 197 BC.

The city was prosperous both agriculturally and in terms of industries: the latter produced fabrics, ceramics and, above all, writing media made of

"Pergamon skin" (which, in English, became "parchment"). This industry developed after the ban promulgated by Ptolemy V, jealous of the library of Pergamon, on the exportation of Egyptian papyrus to Pergamon. The inhabitants of Pergamon thus developed their own bookmaking techniques from veal skin, to be autonomous and no longer depend on Egypt. The library of Pergamon rivaled the famous library of Alexandria in Egypt, competing with it for the best manuscripts and specialists, in two divergent visions.

In Alexandria the focus was on the study of lexicon—of texts—verse by verse and word by word. Conclusions were established through the comparison of texts undertaken in the most scrupulous manner. In Pergamon, on the contrary, scholars sought the deeper—even hidden—meaning of texts, considering that what was truly meant did not necessarily correspond to what was written.

A great builder, Eumenes II enlarged the city and consolidated its fortifications; he built the Great Altar, currently visible at the Pergamon Museum in Berlin, as well as the Temple of Athena, numerous gymnasiums, and a great library.

Eumenes II also acquired sculptures and protected Delphi. In this era, Pergamon was both allied with Rome and a promoter of Hellenism in Asia Minor to counteract this Roman alliance, which generated animosity on the part of the Greek cities. Becoming one of the greatest centers of Hellenistic culture with Athens and Alexandria, it thus attracted sculptures and philosophers. The last Attalid sovereign, Attalus III (139–133 BC), without an heir, chose Rom as the executor of his will in 133 BC, leaving it the choice of finding the best successor to govern it. The Roman Senate opted to maintain the administration of the rich kingdom, which it turned into a province of Asia.

Pergamon's prosperity and expansion continued under Roman government. The city even experienced a second peak in the second century with the

Pergamon's Red Basilica, also called the "temple of the Egyptian gods." It was probably dedicated to Isis and Serapis and must also have served the imperial cult, before being transformed into a basilica.

building of temples, including the temple known as the "Red Basilica" dedicated to the Egyptian gods.

Pergamon, home to the great doctor Galen and the sanctuary of Asclepius, would progressively become a medical hub of great renown. The inhabitants of Pergamon grew intoxicated with the rites of the worship of Aesculapius (Greek god of medicine), represented in the form of a living snake, housed and fed in the temple. This god was also known by the name of Zotair, meaning "savior." The snake was supposed to embody the god Asclepius, making it easy to comprehend the association made with Satan,

> ...the ancient serpent, who is the devil and Satan *(Revelation 20:2)*

as John calls him.

The sick spent the night sleeping in the temple where harmless snakes were raised, left to roam freely among the patients. Touching them was interpreted then as touching Asclepius as a means of healing. It was like being touched by the divine, and the sick could be cured, with the snake absorbing their illness. Doctor-priests supervised these practices of occult healing.

At the end of this same second century, Pergamon converted to Christianity. The temple of Serapis, in the sanctuary of the Egyptian gods, was transformed into an immense Christian basilica. The city then experienced the decline of the Roman Empire and was conquered by the Arabs in 716, then retaken by the Byzantines, before ending up under Ottoman rule in the fourteenth century.

Commentary on the Biblical Text

> To the angel of the church in Pergamum write the following: "This is the solemn pronouncement of the one who has the sharp double-edged sword: 'I know where you live—where Satan's throne is. Yet you continue to cling to my name and you have not denied your faith in me, even in the days of Antipas, my faithful witness, who was killed in your city where Satan lives. But I have a few things against you: You have some people there who follow the teaching of Balaam, who instructed Balak to put a stumbling block before the people of Israel so they would eat food sacrificed to idols and commit sexual immorality. In the same way, there are also some among you who follow the teachings of the Nicolaitans. Therefore, repent! If not, I will come against you quickly and make war against those people with the sword of my mouth. The one who has an ear had better hear what the Spirit says to the churches. To the one who conquers, I will give him some of the hidden manna, and I will give him a white stone, and on that stone

will be written a new name that no one can understand except the one who receives it.'" *(Revelation 2:12–17)*

It had to be particularly difficult for the Christians of Pergamon to remain faithful to Christ in this capital of culture, politics, idolatry, and occultism. Pergamon was the most troubling city in the entire Roman Empire. It's probably for all these reasons that the letter begins with this distressing statement: "*I know where you live—where Satan's throne is.*" This phrase also refers to the monument that symbolizes the city's condition: the great marble altar of Zeus.

Despite this extremely oppressive context, the Christians had held fast. The name of their martyr, Antipas, is even reported to us in the Bible. Pergamon is thus a church of faithful and courageous witness despite a particularly difficult spiritual situation. However, there, too, is a "but": the "*people there who follow the teaching of Balaam.*" Balaam was an Old Testament "prophet" whose story is related to us in chapters 22 and 23 of the book of Numbers.

Pedestal of the altar of Zeus in Pergamon, the presumed location of the throne of Satan (Revelation 2:13).

To protect his kingdom against the Israelites, Balak, king of the Moabites, called for the services of the prophet Balaam. He asked him to curse Israel, but Balaam refused. Balak asked once again, and this time Balaam accepted. On three occasions, he tried to curse Israel, but to no avail. So he conceived an insidious plan: if he managed to corrupt the people by encouraging them to transgress against God's laws, this would lead to their downfall and bring down God's judgment upon them. So he suggested that the Moabite women seduce the Israelites and marry them.

What was supposed to happen, happened. The beautiful women of Moab led Israel into debauchery and idolatry, turning the heart of Israel away from the Lord. Israel thus gave itself to idolatry on the plains of Moab, and the Lord's wrath flared up against his people.

In the church of Pergamon, it seems that a similar teaching, accepting paganism or the compromise with a deeply corrupt political power, must have been tolerated. In Pergamon, therefore, there was at the same time a solid, sincere faith and a pernicious compromise that was contrary to the will of God. Pergamon was thus supposedly prostituting itself with other gods, plunged into a religious confusion from which it would be quite diffi-cult to emerge.

In our day, too, omnipresent sexual temptation in the media and the eroti-cism offered from sexually liberated women of the world are strong temptations for the men of the church to turn away from the Lord. The danger of marrying an unbeliever remains identical to this day.

In this letter, Jesus presents himself with a two-edged sword in his mouth. The sword here, as often occurs in the Bible, symbolizes the Word of God. This echoes the letters to the Hebrews:

> For the word of God is living and active and sharper than any double-edged sword, piercing even to the point of dividing soul from spirit, and joint from marrow; it is able to judge the desires and thoughts of the heart. *(Hebrews 4:12)*

The treacherous, false teaching of the Balaamites cannot be fought or thwarted except by the Word of God. This is why the image of the double-edged sword with which Christ appears is reused as a warning in verse 16 of the letter:

> Therefore, repent! If not, I will come against you quickly and make war against those people with the sword of my mouth. *(Revelation 2:16)*

There is a quite similar idea in the history of the church when, in the Middle Ages, the papacy introduced the doctrine of the two swords. In it, temporal power was delegated to the spiritual power with the dual purpose of giving, first, preeminence to the church that wanted to control or limit royal power, but also to be the guarantor of the spiritual power. It was thus a theological means of justifying the sovereignty of the church in all spheres of society, including civil and political life.

In 310, a dark period began for the Christian church. Pergamon means "marriage," and beginning in the fourth century, political authority and religion united. It was the age in which the emperor Constantine (272–337) unified and federated the Roman Empire. Converted to Christianity, his reign witnessed the establishment of individual freedom of religion that put an end to the perse-cution of Christians. Constantine, however, did not force people to convert.

Things became far more complicated under emperor Theodosius the Great (347-–395) who furthered the process of fusion between religion and politics. In 380, he published the Edict of Thessalonica, decreeing that "All peoples must rally to the faith passed to the Roman by the apostle Peter . . . meaning the Holy Trinity of the Father, the Son and the Holy Spirit." The trinitarian Catholic faith, as it had been defined by Council of Nicaea, had now gained the upper hand on Arianism, which affirmed that God is divine, but his Son, Jesus, is originally human, but a human possessing partial divinity.

The aftermath of the imperial edict was catastrophic for the adherents of the old pagan cults. Roles were immediately and drastically reversed: now it was the adepts of the "pagan religion" and their works that were banned and eliminated, after having caused so many martyrs among the Christians, namely during the last great persecution by Diocletian (244–311) at the outset of this same fourth century. All rituals and events judged to be pagan were gradually prohibited. The church went from persecuted to persecutor.

Under Theodosius, the Empire was split in two; it was governed by the emperor Theodosius in the eastern part and by Gratian, who would head the Western Empire. Both Christian, they made the Catholic faith the only official, obligatory state religion. The pagan temples of the Roman Empire were shut down (particularly in the east under Theodosius's impulse), and the statue of the goddess Victory was removed from the Roman Senate at Gratian's order.

In Egypt, the patriarch Theophilus of Alexandria was tasked with applying Theodosius I's edict, which prohibited pagans from accessing their temples, as well as all pagan ceremonies. These temples were either destroyed or consecrated as churches. Statues of pagan deities were smashed, and the Serapeum of Memphis was destroyed at the order of the emperor himself. This intolerance provoked revolts and heightened tensions in the provinces.

The simple faith of the gospel progressively vanished behind the Roman lavishness that interfered in the church. Rebirth, the necessarily original condition for salvation, was no longer important. The imperial authority erected basilicas, paid for their decoration, provided special vestments for those who serviced them, and introduced pagan feasts and costumes to make the Christian faith more attractive.

During the Council of Nicaea, the clergy were definitively separated from laymen. This seed planted in the early history of the church gained ground and became a well-established doctrine that was never truly eliminated in the centuries to come. Thus Europe was never truly Christian in the evangelical sense of the word; it was Christianized, adopting Christian culture and traditions.

In Ephesus, it was a matter of rediscovering the fire of the first love. Genuine love would never manifest itself as indulgence, indifference, laxity, or permissiveness. The Bible teaches not to compromise with evil or immorality, even under the pretext of love and tolerance.

The apostle Paul reminded Titus, his spiritual son:

> …communicate the behavior that goes with sound teaching *(Titus 2:1)*

We must love people enough to tell them the truth. Love does not exist without truth and, vice versa, truth does not exist without love.

It's necessary to distinguish between teachings and people. The gospel encourages us to love and welcome people, whoever they are. Unconditionally. But at the same time, we must also refuse erroneous teachings that are contrary to those of the Bible.

Admittedly, it isn't easy to reconcile unconditional love with uncompromising truth. Indeed, we run a dual risk: through love and because we "don't want to judge," we're tempted by compromise and a live-and-let-live attitude. We lack the courage to stand up to evil. Is this not the current temptation in our countries and even in the Western church?

It's striking, for that matter, that in five of these seven letters, Christ calls the church to repent. Does anyone dare preach this in our churches today?

But on the contrary, out of concern for being faithful to the truth, we can be tempted to pass judgment, to be harsh, even radically so: we confuse the Bible with a book of laws and strike with biblical verses those who do not think like us. We judge them, sometimes even exclude them. Under certain skies and in certain eras, we even executed them! The model of the church, as it is understood here, is one where love and truth function together. They are like the two lungs of the church that allow it to breathe and stay alive.

But in addition to spiritual or theological teachings, Scripture also teaches ethical values that are not to be trifled with. This is exactly what the Balaamites did in following the famous prophet. They advocated such an extreme moral freedom that they became libertines. All is grace, they seem to proclaim: our actions are of no importance!

The apostle Paul had seen the danger coming. He asked the Romans who were pondering the question:

> Are we to remain in sin so that grace may increase? *(Romans 6:1)*

Far from it! he forcefully replied. Once again, we might as well be talking about the world of today. Is preaching love without truth, particularly ethical truth, still love? The apostle Paul had very strong words in this respect:

> Love must be without hypocrisy. Abhor what it evil, cling to what is good. *(Romans 12:9)*

What can be said except that love with the corollary of an abhorrence of evil is hypocritical love?

The "*throne of Satan*" has been interpreted in multiple ways. For some, it might be the temple of the god of medicine Asclepius, whose symbol was a staff with a snake wrapped around it, and the principal site of whose cult was

Pergamon. However, most experts believe it to be a reference to the great altar of Zeus Soter.

The altar is a religious monument built in the Hellenistic era on the acropolis of the city of Pergamon, undoubtedly at the beginning of the reign of Eumenes II (197–159 BC). Its monumental friezes, representing a gigantomachy, and the story of Telephus, the son of Hercules, constitute one of the masterpieces of ancient Greek sculpture and represent the height of the "Hellenistic Baroque." The altar was, at a certain point, part of the list of the Wonders of the World.

Discovered in 1871 by the German engineer Carl Humann, it was transported and reassembled in Berlin in 1886 according to the terms of an agreement between Germany and the Ottoman Empire. It is now conserved at the Pergamon Museum, one of the state museums in Berlin. For several decades, the Turkish state has been vainly calling for its restitution.

On each side of the platform, a wing encircles the monumental staircase leaning up to a closed courtyard, ringed by an external colonnade, where the sacrifices must have unfolded. The platform's friezes, 110 meters long, represent the mythological combat between the giants and the gods of Olympus. Some have lent the composition a cosmic significance. Perhaps this figuration is somehow related to the mysterious passage of Genesis:

> The Nephilim were on the earth in those days (and also after this) when the sons of God were having sexual relations with the daughters of humankind,

The Acropolis of Pergamon
Engraving by T. Allom and J. Redaway representing the city
of Pergamon with its acropolis up on a hill.

who gave birth to their children. They were the mighty heroes of old, the famous men. *(Genesis 6:4)*

This center of the imperial cult was thus significantly oriented toward occultism, that is, the worship of satanic spirits and demons. While all these spirits are divided into hierarchies, what they have in common is a hatred for human beings! Those who didn't accept to prostrate themselves before the deified emperor were likely put to death on these very steps. Legend spoke of the presence of a Moloch, a bronze bull inside of which the unfortunate victims were burned to death over a bonfire as offerings to the deity. Christians certainly numbered among the victims. Satan was concealed behind the deified emperor.

In its day, Berlin became a center of world power during the reign of the false messiah Hitler and the false prophet Goebbels with their parody of the cross and desire to establish a 1,000-year empire on earth. The roots of the Nazi movement were located in the occult ariosophy of the Thule Society (*Thule-Gesellschaft*) inspired by spiritualist ideologues such as Guido von List, Dietrich Eckart, Rudolf von Sebottendorf, Karl Maria Wiligut, and Heinrich Himmler. These dark figures immersed everyone in esoterism, occultism, and even satanism.

These dark and mysterious origins are a part of history that's little discussed, even largely ignored by studies of Nazism. Indeed it is far easier to give purely political explanations to a diabolical movement rather than to investigate the mythological and spiritual inspirations that influenced its ideology. It must be recognized, however, that many political systems are founded in irrational mythological beliefs and in religions.

According to historian Eva Kingsepp, a senior lecturer at the University of Karlsbad in Sweden, who has made a detailed study of the notebooks and personal documents of Nazi leaders to comprehend their motivations, the Nazis could be divided into two groups.

The first was influenced by Himmler, who took a close interest in occultism, particularly in the Nordic gods, myths, and eastern religions. He desired to turn the Castle of Wewelsburg into a center of research and spiritual instruction of the SS and viewed the latter as a sacred order: the regime's "guardians of the light."

Himmler was convinced that he was the reincarnation of Henry I of Saxony and was more interested in occultism than in the party's political aspects. Nazi ariosophy postulated that the "pure Aryan race" descended from interstellar divine entities whose purity could be rediscovered thanks to ethnic purges. The fascination with evil and a taste for revealed mystery and the paranormal were other aspects of Nazi esoterism.

On July 1, 1935, Himmler founded the Ahnenerbe Forschungs und Lehrgemeinschaft, the "Society for Research and Teaching of Ancestral Heritage." The goal of the institute's studies was "the sphere, the spirit, the great deeds and the heritage of the Nordic Indo-European race" via the tools of archaeological research, racial anthropology, and cultural history of the "Aryan race." Its goal was to prove the validity of Nazi theories of the racial superiority of the "Aryans" and replace one chosen people, the Jews of the Bible, with another, the Aryans.

Scandinavian cave art, Viking sites, the Externteine in Teutoburg Forest: the institute discovered in the Lake Garda region inscriptions and runes that were compared with those discovered in southern Sweden, leading to the conclusion that the Italian peoples were of Indo-Germanic origin. Considering as credible the climactic theory of the eternal ice, in July 1936, Himmler gathered the scientists who supported this thesis and enjoined them to demonstrate its veracity in the framework of the Ahnenerbe.

The institute also took an interest in the mythical continent of Atlantis and in the golden hammer, which was, according to Himmler, the most powerful weapon ever produced by the ancient Nordic tribes.

In the same way, strongly influenced by the theories of Otto Rahn concerning the Holy Grail, its existence and its power, Himmler ordered research expeditions in Languedoc and, more specifically, in the region of Montségur. In Himmler's eyes, indeed, the Grail would give Christianity an indisputably Nordic dimension. Expeditions to Tibet and the Antarctic were also organized.

Upon Himmler's demand in 1942, the Ahnenerbe proceeded with medical experiments in the concentration camps, namely at Dachau and at Natzweiler-Struthof, in Alsace.

The political side of the regime was the concern of Hitler, who led the second group within Nazism and had a different vision of the world from Himmler.

The party tolerated no opposition and considered Christianity a religion for the weak, the Christians being the successors of the Jews: thus this religion possessed something corrupt, different from the pure soul of the Germanic people. They tried to purify Christianity of its Jewish origins and replace the Christian religion with a cult to the Nordic god Baldur, who was blond like Jesus and the god of light, beauty, youth, and love.

In Nordic mythology Baldur is the son of Odin and Frigg. Killed out of jealousy, he is sent to the kingdom of the dead, but will take part in the renewal that is a fundamental hope of Nazism, as attests the symbol of the swastika

The Nazi tribune of the Zeppelinfeld in Nuremberg,
inspired by the Altar of Zeus from Pergamon.

which, for Jean Chevalier and Alain Gheerbrant, symbolizes action, manifestation, and perpetual regeneration because the form itself is an indicator of movement.

Hitler, it seems, was so impressed by the Altar of Zeus in the Berlin museum that he decided to commission a symbolic reproduction in 1934 on the old zeppelin landing site in Nuremberg, the Tribune Zeppelin. The Führer confessed that if Berlin was the head of Germany, Nuremberg was its heart; the city did, indeed, have great importance in Nazi ideology.

The leader of the Reich was fascinated by the ancient architecture of Rome and Athens, and the erection of massive monuments, inspired by antiquity, played a part in the Nazi propaganda program, aiming to arouse impressions of majesty, dynamism, and power in the crowds.

Thus in 1934, Hitler ordered his architect, Albert Speer, to reconstitute the altar of Pergamon in Nuremberg on a zeppelin landing strip as a place to hold the Nazi processions. A new religion was thus progressively established on an official basis, an insidious blend of politics and religion, with Nazism becoming an increasingly mystical political movement.

In 1936, the building was inaugurated in Nuremberg, and the hunting down of the Jews and other declared enemies of the regime was organized. It was from the tribute of this monument that Hitler publicly declared his war against the Jews and all those who lacked Aryan blood, and from there that he announced the plans for the coming Holocaust.

Even though a part of the German church supported the Führer, bewitched by the magnetism of this false messiah, savior of the Aryan race, numerous Germans from all Christian denominations, as well as many Catholic priests loyal to their Christian faith, paid with their lives to preserve their beliefs or to protect the persecuted Jews.

Some saw in the public announcement of the envisioned annihilation of the Jewish people, on this tribute inspired by the "throne of Satan," and for the first time expressed publicly by Hitler in this place, an ancient parallel with the martyred bishop Antipas, put to death in Pergamon: "*My faithful witness, who was killed in your city.*" Antipas is a first-century figure venerated both by the Catholic and Orthodox churches. The tradition holds that he was burned alive in a Moloch-type bronze bull, commonly used by Pergamon's pagan population in its occult rites.

From 1939 to 1945, the Second World War cost the lives of fifty-five million people, and the implementation of the "Final Solution," the Holocaust, led to the killing of six million Jews.

During World War II, the great altar of Zeus was protected in the vaults of the Reichsbank and then in an anti-aircraft bunker beneath the *Tiergarten* (zoo). In 1945, following Hitler's defeat and suicide, part of the Pergamon altar was dismantled and taken back as booty to Leningrad in the USSR, where Lenin and Stalin's atheistic terror reigned supreme.

The "father of the people" had mobilized his secret service to implement his enterprise of death against the Christians. Some accounts state that while the victims were still alive, their eyes were gouged out, their tongues were cut off, their hands were severed, their necks were pierced. Their companions of misfortune were sometimes forced to scalp them before being executed them-selves. Women were raped and killed in front of their husbands and children. Rivers ran red with the blood of the victims. While the majority of churches were demolished by the Soviets, a few were spared to suggest that freedom of religion had been preserved.

Hitler, according to his Luciferian plan, drew inspiration from the gulags to implement his concentration camps. The only major difference: to the Christian rebels, Jehovah's Witnesses, homosexuals, gypsies, and the mentally and physically handicapped were added the Jews.

In 1958, at Germany's request, Khrushchev agreed to give back this war booty and send the altar of Pergamon to Berlin. Had he not proclaimed, in 1964, that he would personally introduce the last Christian on television? But soon after he himself fell from power, forced to provide for his and his family's needs by cultivating tomatoes and potatoes on a 600 square meter plot of land.

The old Protestant confessions of faith specified that the Bible is the supreme authority in matters of faith and life. This is exactly what the letter to Pergamon says. The Bible's message is a call to enter into a personal, intimate relationship with God, for this is what changes the disciple's life and gives him that new name of which it is spoken. We must therefore remain within the Word, as Jesus himself reminds his disciples:

> If you continue to follow my teaching, you are really my disciples and you will know the truth, and the truth will set you free. *(John 8:31–32)*

Is there a more current, more encouraging word for our world so greedy for freedom?

So what must characterize the church of Christ, the living, faithful church, is truth and the absence of compromise. After love (Ephesus) to which suffering (Smyrna) is often linked, the third characteristic of the church is truth and integrity. This is the center of the message of the letter to the church of Pergamon.

How this message must have struck the Christians of this community! In this city that had invented the parchment and whose incredibly rich library was renowned throughout the world, Christ reminds the church that truth is the biblical truth and that this book comes from his own mouth and is thus his Word.

We can conclude that teaching within the church can only be teaching faithful to what the Bible teaches, without compromise with the human spirit of the present century and alliances with political powers, no matter how seductive they might be.

THYATIRA

Thyatira (in Greek, Θυάτειρα) is the ancient name of the contemporary Turkish city of Akhisar. In antiquity, the city lay on the border between Lydia and Mysia. It was renowned for its dyeing industry, as attested by the Acts of the Apostles and inscriptions related to the dyers' guild that have been unearthed.

Thyatira had neither the fame nor the beauty of Pergamon or Smyrna; it was an industrious, commercial city in the interior, roughly seventy-five kilometers southeast of Pergamon. One of its most important products, and one the city traded throughout the world, was purple dye. This was a luxury industry. The Roman writer Pliny the Elder writes that a pound of purple dye was worth more than a thousand denarii, the salary of a worker over roughly three years.

Geography and History

A city in the Roman province of Asia, in the western part of modern Turkey, located in a low valley, Thyatira was a Roman garrison city on the frontier region, as well as an important center for the production and dyeing of fabrics, pottery, and copperworking. Lydia (Act. 16:14) was likely the commercial agent of a Thyatira manufacturer. Purple dye was produced there up to twentieth century.

Interview with archaeologist Akın Ersoy among the ruins of ancient Thyatira, today's Akhisar, in Turkey.

Traces of human settlement dating back to the period from 3000–2500 BC have been discovered. Strabo writes that the city received a Macedonian colony that he locates in Mysia, near the confines of Lydia. Pliny the Elder mentions that it is crossed by a river called the "Lycus," and that it was nicknamed Pelopia and Euhippia. The emperor Vespasian began a construction campaign there. Hadrian visited in 123, and Caracalla in 215. The city was then at its height.

From the end of the third century, Thyatira was a bishopric suffragan of Sardis at least until the tenth century, but the date of its disappearance is unknown. It was close to this city that the Roman emperor Valens defeated the usurper Procopius in 366.

Archaeology

Excavations have been carried out in the center of the city at the site called Tepe Mezarlığı ("cemetery on the hill" in Turkish), from 1968 to 1971. Finds included a portico dating to between the second to fourth centuries and a building that was probably a civil basilica from the fourth or fifth century. The acropolis of the city was situated on a hill on which the state hospital presently stands. The great mosque was built on the bases of a building that was a pagan temple, converted into a Christian church, then a mosque in the fifteenth century by the Ottomans. Few archaeological remains of ancient Thyatira remain.

Commentary on the Biblical Text

To the angel of the church in Thyatira write the following: This is the solemn pronouncement of the Son of God, the one who has eyes like a fiery flame and whose feet are like polished bronze: "I know your deeds: your love, faith, service, and steadfast endurance. In fact, your more recent deeds are greater than your earlier ones. But I have this against you: You tolerate that women Jezebel, who calls herself a prophetess, and by her teaching deceives my servants to commit sexual immorality and to eat food sacrificed to idols. I have given her time to repent, but she is not willing to repent of her sexual immorality . . . unless they repent of her deeds. Furthermore, I will strike her followers with a deadly disease, and then all the churches will know that I am the one who searches minds and hearts. I will repay each one of you what your deeds deserve. But to the rest of you in Thyatira, all who do not hold to this teaching (who have not learned the so-called "deep secrets of Satan"), to you I say: I do not put any additional burden on you. However, hold on to what you have until I come. And to the one who conquers and who continues in my deeds until the end, I will give him authority over the nations—he will rule them with an iron rod and like clay jars he

The Death of Jezebel
Engraving by Gustave Doré

will break them to pieces, just as I have received the right to rule from my Father—and I will give him the morning star. The one who has an ear had better hear what the Spirit says to the churches. *(Revelation 2:18–29)*

Here is a church that isn't merely alive, but that is growing quickly: "*I know your deeds: your love, faith . . . and steadfast endurance. In fact, your more recent deeds are greater than your earlier ones*" (Revelation 2:19). It is thus a church that practices the quintessence of the Christian faith: faith, hope, and love.

In Genesis, Joseph, son of Jacob, possessed a purple-dyed tunic and we comprehend the great value and importance of this garment in the story. The book of Acts tells that the first person to be converted in Europe was a certain Lydia, a purple dye merchant in the city of Thyatira. She had emigrated to Philippi, probably for commercial reasons, and must have been an influential businesswoman of some importance.

But Thyatira gathered numerous other industries as well: inscriptions have been found mentioning the trades of weaver, tanner, potter, shoemaker, bronze founder, saddler, tailor, and many others. These trades were organized into guilds, all of which had very strict rules and customs. Their functions were not solely professional, but religious too.

The gatherings of these guilds always began with a sacrifice and a libation offered to the pagan gods. Quite often, these banquets concluded with orgies accompanied by more or less immoral practices. We can immediately understand the problem that must have posed itself to the Christians of Thyatira: if you were a tanner, dyer, or baker, how were you supposed to handle these ceremonies?

When an owner of one of these industries converted, could he continue going to the meetings of the confraternity where libations were made to the pagan gods or orgies took place with their bevy of immoral practices? And if he decided not to go any longer, he risked being excluded from the guild and seeing his business decline or even go bankrupt.

As for the laborers, they, too, must have participated in the guild ceremonies. And the problem must have been distressing for them as well. If they stopped going to these meetings, did they risk being fired? Or lowered to the rank of slaves?

It's easy to understand the Thyatira Christians' terrible dilemma. Was this the reason why Lydia went into exile? Chapter 16 of Acts tells us that she was a "God-fearing woman," meaning a person of pagan origin, attracted by the Jewish religion and who loyally attended the synagogue without going so far as to become a convert. It's understandable what a woman, attracted by the observance of the prescriptions of Jewish law, could have lost by staying in Thyatira.

This is highly relevant in today's world. What must be, what can be, the attitude of an owner who wants to respect all the moral rules during business transactions? There are no more libations today, but the practice of bribes, "commissions," and secret additional clauses in certain contracts are still quite present. So what must an owner's attitude be in this world of unbridled competition? The survival of the business and, consequently, the job security of the employees are sometimes at stake.

And what must be the attitude of the Christian shareholder? We no longer sacrifice to the gods in today's meetings, but we certainly do sacrifice sometimes to profit, to the God of money on the altar of prosperity. And as far as workers are concerned, can we accept any working conditions whatsoever? These questions are difficult, and each case must be examined, but the continued relevance of this letter to the church of the commercial city of Thyatira must be underlined.

The City of Thyatira and Modern Akhisar
Artist's rendering. Engraving by T. Allom and S. Fisher

There, too, however, is a "but." All these positive qualities take nothing away from the seriousness of the moral compromise there was within the community: "*But I have this against you: You tolerate that woman Jezebel, who calls herself a prophetess, and by her teaching deceives my servants to commit sexual immorality*" (Revelation 2:20). Thus, a woman of the church was teaching that there was nothing wrong with giving in to immorality or debauchery. There were even sacrifices to idols and immoral practices. It was necessary, indeed, to be tolerant; it was necessary, moreover, to live life to the fullest, was it not? Was what wrong with some self-indulgence?

So it was that, in the church of Thyatira, moral compromise, reaching as far as immorality, was not only tolerated, but even encouraged, under cover of prophecy. This is why Revelation gives this woman the terrible name of Jezebel, this pagan queen of Israel, wife of the infidel king Ahab, who encouraged idolatry and appeared as the implacable enemy of the prophet Elijah.

The story of Jezebel is told in the book of Kings. Wife of King Ahab, she introduced into the kingdom of Samaria the cult of the gods Baal and of Astarte. She persecuted the religion of the Jews and tried to have the prophet Elijah, who opposed her, put to death. Jezebel drove her husband, Ahab, to tyranny. She wrongly accused Naboth and had him put to death to take possession of his small vineyard. After the murder of Naboth, God ordered Elijah to strike down Ahab and Jezebel with a violent death. But Ahab felt remorse. So God renounced punishing him, but announced he will bring misfortune down on the house of his son.

After Ahab's death, Jezebel continued to reign with her sons Ahaziah and then Joram. Commanded by the prophet Elisha to carry out the divine vengeance, Jehu dethroned and killed Joram and then had Jezebel thrown out of a palace window. The queen's body was devoured by dogs, literally bringing to pass Elijah's prophecy concerning the cursed queen.

The Bible states that God wants the purification and sanctification of his people, as Paul wrote:

> Pursue peace with everyone, and holiness, for without it no one will see the LORD. *(Hebrews 12:14)*

What is required is by no means a life governed by legalism, austerity, and moral rigidity, but rather by a coherence between what you believe and how you live, a life in the obedience of God's word, which is always the word of life and of freedom; in short, it's a life in the communion with and dependence on the Lord. This is what the Christians of Thyatira, or at least a part of them, failed to understand. They hadn't understood that the grace of God must irrigate and transform all aspects of our life.

The history of the church is punctuated by leaders who fell into immorality, and in doing so threw shame, opprobrium, and discredit on the church.

A figure famous for his immorality was the Borgia pope, Alexander VI, elected on August 11, 1492, by a canonical two-thirds majority of the cardinals gathered in the conclave. It's not unlikely that he purchased certain votes, given that simony (the purchase and sale of spiritual goods, sacraments, church posts, or ecclesiastical offices) was a common practice until the Counter-Reformation.

In his *La véritable histoire des papes*, Jean Mathieu-Rosay wrote: "Cesare Borgia, the prototype of Machiavelli's Prince, conquered various regions of Italy. Stripping the great Roman families one by one of their possessions, he aimed at nothing less than to reign over all of Italy. Waging all these wars required money. In 1500, declared a holy year by the sovereign pontiff, he reinforces his coffers thanks to the revenues from pilgrimage. As for the sale of cardinal's hats, it brings in huge revenues to the pope and his bastard children. Offering the cardinal's purple to a candidate brought in huge sums of money. Killing him subsequently even more so, since all the cardinal's goods returned by law to the pope. Finally, there was the regular income from indulgences."[42]

One of the most credible witnesses of the conduct of Pope Alexander Borgia was Jean Burckhardt of Strasbourg. From 1483 to 1508, this prelate, master of ceremonies at the pontifical court, kept a very precise journal, day by day, sometimes hour by hour, of all the events that unfolded in the Vatican.

In 1470, when he was already an ordained priest, Rodrigo Borgia became acquainted with Vannozza Cattanei, a young Roman patrician who would give him four children while continuing to lead a conjugal life with her series of husbands who were all obliged to Borgia. He also had an affair with the young Giulia Farnese (sister of Cardinal Alessandro Farnese, the future Pope Paul III).

His private life was also a source of scandal. Francesco Guicciardini reported an episode during which Borgia attracted to Castel Santangelo the young, handsome Astorre Manfredi, Lord of Faenza, whom he proceeded to rape and had thrown into the Tiber.

Borgia also made himself known for the lavish celebrations organized for the marriage of his daughter Lucrezia to Alfonso d'Este, where his debauchery reached new heights on the orgiastic night of October 31, 1501, during which his guests were invited to demonstrate the extent of their virility with a group of around fifty nude dancers. The competition was overseen by Alexander VI's own children, Cesare and Lucrezia, which created one of the greatest scandals in Christendom.

It's easy to understand why many accounts referring to pacts with the devil began to circulate at Alexander VI's death. Likely poisoned to death, his body was so bloated that it could not fit into the coffin in which he was meant to be buried. He was thus temporarily rolled up in a carpet, while his private apartments were ransacked.

The letter to Thyatira also includes a message that's relevant today. There is no truth (the heart of the message to the church of Pergamon) without holiness. Grace does not take away the need for sanctification. Quite the contrary. But today, churches are so afraid of legalism that no one dares speak of obedience or denounce sin anymore. Tolerance and permissiveness are often confused. And even within the church itself, preaching often focuses on God's love, but forgets his demands. This leads to a "cheap" grace, which, after all, is no grace at all!

Dietrich Bonhoeffer, the modern martyr put to death by Hitler's order, made some definitive statements about the mortal danger of cheap grace: "*Cheap grace is the preaching of forgiveness without repentance, baptism without church discipline, Communion without confession. Cheap grace is grace without discipleship, grace without the cross, grace without Jesus Christ, living and incarnate.*"[43]

Repentance, namely, is opposing the moral compromise that reigns, for example, in Thyatira. The call to repent sounds three times in this letter to Thyatira, more than in any of the others, as though to underline its importance.

Repentance is by no means a popular term today! But then, has it ever been? And yet, repentance is at the heart of Jesus's preaching in the Gospels and is always an offer full of hope: it is the proof that you can change and even start over again in life. The Bible says that you can become a new creature. The call to repentance is, in the Bible, always a piece of good news, a magnificent opportunity to change by starting anew. This is how Jesus began his ministry. He said:

> The time is fulfilled and the kingdom of God is near. Repent and believe the gospel! *(Mark 1:15)*

Yes, the gospel includes repentance because this is how you can undertake a new life! How is this to be understood? What despair in saying: "You were born like this, with troubles of anger or avarice or other things. You can do nothing about it. You will not change." Some would like us to believe this in order to free us of guilt in the face of our flaws. But character can correct and master our innate temperament, with the aid of the Holy Spirit.

What makes us despair is the absence of any hope of change. Repentance, to the contrary, frees us by making us responsible, by telling us that we can change and that our past, whatever it is, can make way for a new life. There are many examples in the history of the church in which men, women, or whole churches have been profoundly transformed by the grace of God.

> So then, if anyone is in Christ, he is a new creation; what is old has passed away – look, what is new has come! *(2 Corinthians 5:17)*

Calling the church of Thyatira to repentance in the face of its moral compromise is a message of encouragement, hope, and life. And the promises that conclude this letter are commensurate with the warnings. "To the one who conquers . . . I will give him the morning star." The morning star is Christ himself who comes to establish his kingdom, according to Revelation 22:16. Faithful believers, then, do not just receive new, eternal life—they are a part of the kingdom of Christ, they participate with him in his reign of glory.

These letters show us that the church's struggle is a difficult struggle, both on a personal and a moral level. But what promises are reserved to the victors! It's undoubtedly with a consciousness of this that the apostle Paul wrote:

> For I consider that our present sufferings cannot even be compared to the glory that will be revealed to us. *(Romans 8:18)*

This church of Thyatira, then, was demonstrating faith, love, ministry, and endurance, but holiness was not among its qualities. And this is the central message of this letter: the pursuit of purity and holiness is not an option, but a central and essential prerogative of Christian life.

SARDIS

Sardis (in Greek, αἱ Σάρδεις) was an ancient city of Asia Minor, the capital of Lydia, located on the Pactolus River, in the Hermos Valley. The city was a fortress known for its invincibility in antiquity. Money was invented here.

What characterizes the city of Sardis is its glorious past. It's the city of the famous king Croesus whose proverbial wealth has remained famous to the present day. This wealth came essentially from the gold-bearing Pactolus River that flowed near the city (and whose name, too, is synonymous with riches). The acropolis of the city, situated on a rocky spur a few hundred meters above the valley, was reputed to be impregnable. The expression "taking the acropolis of Sardis" designated an impossible enterprise that was destined for failure.

Geography and History

The first written mention of the city is found in Aeschylus's *The Persians*. The city might also correspond to Homer's city of Hyde evoked in the *Iliad* as the capital of the Meonians.

The citadel's construction is attributed to King Meles, who positioned his palace and treasury on this strongly fortified site. The lower city, not as well protected, developed on the other side of the Pactolus, and it underwent the attacks of the Cimmerians in 652 BC, and later, the Persians. After the fall of the Lydian Empire in the sixth century BC, the citadel of Sardis continued to

Citadel of Sardis, built by King Meles. He is said to have positioned his palace and treasury there. The fortification would only be taken with a surprise attack by Cyrus the Great in 546.

hold out and was only taken by Cyrus the Great in a surprise attack in 546 BC. Sardis became the capital of the Persian satrapy.

During the Ionian Revolt, the lower city was once again destroyed. In 334 BC, the city was taken by Alexander the Great and then coveted by the Diadochi. Under Seleucid domination until 190 BC, it was then annexed by Pergamon, and its importance diminished to the detriment of its conqueror.

Taken by the Romans in 133 BC, Sardis was destroyed in 17 AD by an earthquake. Tiberius had it rebuilt, and Hadrian invested in its adornment. After the construction of a new road network, and with Constantinople now the capital of the Eastern Roman Empire, Sardis found itself far from the main roads and went into definitive decline. It nevertheless remained symbolically important, and from 295 became the metropolitan seat of the province of Sardis.

In the tenth century, Constantine VII Porphyrogenitus placed it on the third rung of the province of Thrace, after Ephesus and Smyrna. In 1402, it was completely destroyed by Tamerlane.

Two American teams have conducted archaeological excavations in the area, from 1910 to 1914 and then from 1958 to the present, particularly on the site of the gymnasium of Sardis. Except for a stone human head dating to the Neolithic period, the first settlement is documented in the region in the early Bronze Age thanks to the presence of burial tombs (3000–2500 BC).

Capital of the kingdom of Lydia, Sardis was one of the wealthiest cities of the ancient world; it drew its wealth from the gold extracted from the Pactolus

Sardis with the Palace of Croesus, the church of Panagia, the theater, the acropolis, the Pactolus River, and Mount Tmolos.

The Temple of Artemis in Sardis with, in the background, the ruins of the citadel.

Among the ruins of the Temple of Artemis in Sardis.

River. Croesus, famous for his riches, was its king in the sixth century BC. It was in this extremely wealthy city that the first coins were struck; money was invented here. Gold was also worked there, and the city was rich in orchards and textile handicrafts.

Completely destroyed by an earthquake in 17 AD, the city was rebuilt by the Romans and saw a strong growth in the Christian faith.

If the archaeological excavations are to be believed, a spiritual revival undoubtedly took place at a certain point. Numerous crosses have been discovered on the walls of the temple of the goddess Artemis, which suggests that Christians had taken control of the site, dedicating it to the worship of the Lord. In the fourth century, the Christians abandoned this great temple and built, in a corner of the city, a building in which to practice their faith; the vestiges of this church are still well preserved.

In addition, the city's acropolis, situated on a rocky outcropping 350 meters above the valley floor, was reputed to be impregnable. This, indeed, is what led to Croesus's downfall; he was so confident in the invincibility of his acropolis that he didn't take the trouble to defend it, which allowed the Persian emperor, Cyrus, to take it at night by surprise. It was certainly with this episode in mind that Christ made this allusion: "*Wake up then . . . If you do not wake up, I will come like a thief, and you will never know at what hour I will come against you*" (Revelation 3:2–3).

Commentary on the Biblical Text

> To the angel of the church in Sardis write the following: "This is the solemn pronouncement of the one who hold the seven spirits of God and the seven stars: 'I know your deeds, that you have a reputation that you are alive, but in reality you are dead. Wake up then, and strengthen what remains that was about to die, because I have not found your deeds complete in the sight of my God. Therefore, remember what you received and heard, and obey it, and repent. If you do not wake up, I will come like a thief, and you will never know at what hour I will come against you. But you have a few individuals in Sardis who have not stained their clothes, and they will walk with me dressed in white, because they are worthy. The one who conquers will be dressed like them in white clothing, and I will never erase his name from the book of life, but will declare his name before my Father and before his angels. The one who has an ear had better hear what the Spirit says to the churches.'" *(Revelation 3:1–6)*

At first glance, this church seemed very much alive: vitality coursed through it. There were no erroneous or heretical practices within it, as in Thyatira. Neither did this community undergo persecution or resistance (not from the exterior on the part of the pagans as in Smyrna or Pergamon, nor from the interior through rivalries or disputes). No mention is made of attacks by Satan, as occurred in nearly all the other letters. It thus seems to have been a good church, and we can imagine that it must have had an excellent reputation, praised far and wide. Its members must have been proud of its activism: "*I know your deeds, that you have the reputation that you are alive . . .*" (3:1).

Yet in his diagnosis Jesus distinguished vitality from life. This church did indeed have vitality; it certainly had interesting plans, prosperous works, well-attended services, and all other desirable deeds, but it lacked the essential—the life of the Spirit. And this sentence comes like an earthquake: "*But in reality you are dead.*"

Vitality or life? Reputation or reality? Formalism or authenticity? The praise of men or the approval of God? This question, this dilemma, is found throughout Scripture and the history of the church. Samuel says to King Saul:

> Certainly, obedience is better than sacrifice; paying attention is better than the fat of rams. *(1 Samuel 15:22)*

And God says to the prophet Isaiah:

> These people say they are loyal to me; they say wonderful things about me, but they are not really loyal to me. *(Isaiah 29:13)*

Even today ceremonies and rites can be correct, but if our hearts are not in them, they lose their value.

What happened in the church of Sardis? We do not know exactly, but it can be guessed from the rest of the letter. Verse 4 specifies: "*But you have a few individuals in Sardis who have not stained their clothes.*" What do these words reveal? That in Sardis there certainly were men who were loyal to the authentic faith and coherent life, but that there were also—and these were probably the majority—faithful who, under cover of piety and a variety of religious activities, did not live an orderly life.

In this, they did not differ significantly from the rest of the population because we know from the Greek historian Herodotus that the inhabitants of Sardis led a dissolute life. Wealth and the life of ease that it engenders led to a lapse in morals. "Living à la Sardis" had become a proverbial expression to describe a dissolute life.

And the church had been contaminated by this lifestyle; it had taken a deep breath of the atmosphere of the time. People had been converted, certainly, but this had not transformed their lives. They had taken up residence in a new culture, but they lived as they had before. Their faith had changed, perhaps, but not their lives!

What does the resurrected Christ say to this active, prosperous, renowned church, without conflict either within or without, but which appeared like an empty shell? And how did the glorified Christ want to wake up this church of Sardis, flourishing yet moribund?

The manner in which he presented himself to it is both a response and, here as well, an appeal: "*This is the solemn pronouncement of the one who holds the seven spirits of God.*" Once again, we find the number "seven," symbol of plenitude, of wholeness. Jesus presented himself as he who possessed the seven spirits of God, referring to the text that enumerates them:

> The Lᴏʀᴅ's Spirit will rest on him—a Spirit that gives extraordinary wisdom, a Spirit that provides the ability to execute plans, a Spirit that produces absolute loyalty to the Lᴏʀᴅ. *(Isaiah 11:2)*

The Messiah evoked the number "seven" to underline that he does indeed possess the plenitude, the entirety of the Holy Spirit, and that it is he, too, who gives and fills his church with the Spirit of life.

What this church of Sardis needed was a visitation, an effusion, a renewal of the Holy Spirit. Because there can be flourishing ecclesiastical activity without the life of the Holy Spirit. And the Holy Spirit, as the words of salutation remind us, is the Spirit of Christ. It is the life of Jesus in believers' hearts; it is the love, joy, and peace of Jesus within them.

The work of the Holy Spirit is precisely that of communicating the life of Jesus. It is to ensure that what Jesus carried out becomes a reality in the personal, daily life of the disciples. It is through the action of the Holy Spirit that the Christians of Sardis had come to the faith, for it is the Holy Spirit that determines sin, justice, and judgment, as Jesus told his disciples in the Upper Room.

But the Christians of Sardis tended to forget it, with ecclesiastical activity continuing to spread, even very well, but the life of Christ, the life of the Spirit, was no longer present. That's why Jesus also said: *"Remember what you have received and heard, and obey it, and repent."*

Is this message not still quite relevant as well? The church, according to the biblical model, is not an activist church that puts together work upon work and project upon project, because these works and these projects can sometimes be perfectly earthly and human, but the project of God is church-filled with the love and compassion of Christ that the Holy Spirit pours into our hearts. It is not an inactive church; in fact, it is full of works and actions, but it is the Holy Spirit that animates it. It is Christ's love that fills it, it's the Messiah's compassion that makes it turn toward others and love its neighbor. That is what the Lord expects from his bride.

The Christians of Sardis had fallen asleep despite their good reputation, and they needed to hear this exhortation. The letter thus called two times for an awakening: *"Wake up then, and strengthen what remains that was about to die . . . If you do not wake up, I will come like a thief, and you will never know at what hour I will come against you"* (3:2–3).

Just before his Passion, on the evening of his arrest in the Garden of Gethsemane, Jesus exhorted his disciples several times, knowing just how fast and easy it was to fall asleep:

> Stay awake and pray that you will not fall into temptation. The spirit is willing, but the flesh is weak. *(Matthew 26:41)*

He repeated this exhortation here, solemnly, to the church of Sardis, and through it, to the church universal. In Sardis, only a small number remained faithful. Appearances are often deceiving, and the risk is ending up with an empty container, a label without content. The example of Sardis was followed by many other churches over the centuries, displaying a Christianity of labels, of registers, a sociological or traditional Christianity, but without a profound reality. Is this not what awaits the church in Europe?

All church denominations can experience the danger of spiritual death and find themselves in a state of living death, even churches that seem the most dynamic or popular. Praise, no matter how thrilling it is, is not necessarily a sign of life. We can sing incredibly beautiful words without living what they proclaim. Similarly, prayer gatherings can be meetings in which people really do pray, but without this leading to a regeneration of the heart!

And what's true for churches is equally so for each member of the faithful individually. For each person, faith can become a routine, a tradition stripped of this living and profound communion with God.

Sardis was the first church in the history of Christianity whose members could be characterized as "nominal and administrative Christians": its parishioners were Christians in name, but no longer in their hearts! Luther said, "God does not make small children." He wanted to express with that that it behooves each generation to experience a personal encounter with God.

The history of Christianity is thus one of starts and stops, of reappraisals, of reforms and of awakenings. One of the most famous jolts in history was the Protestant Reformation, or "the Reformation," begun in the sixteenth century. It was the fruit of the desire to return to the sources of Christianity and, by extension, the need to view religion and social life in a different way.

It reflected the anguish of souls due to the question of salvation, central to the reflections of the reformers, who denounced the corruption of all of society caused by the selling of indulgences, immorality, and abuses. The reformers took advantage of the rise of the printing press to circulate the Bible in the vernacular tongues (namely German, after the first translation by Martin Luther). They showed that there was no mention of saints, of the cult of the Virgin, or even of Purgatory. Referring to the Bible as the standard, however, was one of the reformers' principal motivations.

Begun on October 31, 1517, by Martin Luther, then a Catholic monk in the Holy Roman Empire, and Ulrich Zwingli in Zurich, then Martin Bucer in Strasburg, and, later, John Calvin in Geneva, the Reformation affected the majority of northwestern Europe.

With the attempts at conciliation failed, it led to a split between the Roman Catholic Church and the Protestant churches. The Catholic

Counter-Reformation, undertaken following the Council of Trent, led only to a partial reconquest of the populations gone over to Protestantism.

Another important awakening is known as "Pentecostalism"; this is an evangelical Christian movement that came out of an awakening initiated by the American pastors Charles Fox Parham and William Joseph Seymour in the United States in 1906. The movement is characterized by the importance given to the Bible, new birth, the baptism of the Holy Spirit, the gifts of the Holy Spirit, and adult baptism as a means of voluntary witness, by the missionary spirit and a lifetime moral commitment, as well as by the churches' local autonomy and the separation of church and state.

Pentecostalism is similar to a charismatic movement, but it developed earlier (in any event, in the United States) and split off from the church's principal branch. Charismatic Christians, at least in the early period of their movements, tended to remain within their respective denominations.

The great Pentecostal revival began with the American pastor Charles Fox Parham, in Topeka, Kansas, in 1901. After a first experience of "speaking in tongues," he theorized that glossolalia is a sign of the baptism of the Holy Spirit, an essential doctrine of Pentecostalism. It was also at the root of the movement of the Apostolic Faith, which created the Assemblies of God churches after merging with other Pentecostal groups. It continued with the Welsh Revival of 1904–1905 and, above all, with that of the Azusa Street Revival in downtown Los Angeles (1906–1908) under the guidance of Pastor William Joseph Seymour.

This movement was characterized by the rediscovery of the charismatic dimension, meaning the baptism of the Holy Spirit and the gifts of the Spirit (1 Cor. 12:9–11), as on the day of the Pentecost, according to the account of the New Testament (Acts 2).

Among the various revivals mentioned, the Welsh Revival and those of Topeka and Azusa Street contributed to the genuine development of the Pentecostal movement. These last two revivals are generally attributed to a prayer camp organized under the leadership of Charles Parham (a Methodist pastor) at Bethel Bible College in Topeka on January 1, 1901. It then rapidly spread to Missouri, Texas, California, and elsewhere.

In 1906, a revival camp led by William Seymour took place at the Azusa Street Mission in Los Angeles, attracting believers from around the world. Aspects of the Pentecostal Revival were not well received by the established churches, and participants in the movement were soon forced to leave their original churches. These believers tried to establish their own places of worship and founded hundreds of specifically Pentecostal churches.

In 1914, numerous ministers and laymen began to realize just how profound the effects of the Pentecostal Revival had been. The leaders felt the need to protect and preserve the revival's results, uniting their movement into a single community. According to the statistics of Pew Research Center, the movement counted roughly 279 million members in 2011.

The severity of the glorified Christ in telling the seemingly flourishing church of Sardis that *"you are dead,"* inevitably makes us think of these other words that Jesus spoke during his earthly ministry to men; they, too, were quite religious and of an apparently intense piety:

> Woe to you, experts in the law and you Pharisees, hypocrites! You clean the outside of the cup and the dish, but inside they are full of greed and self-indulgence. *(Matthew 23:25)*

Just as Jesus expressed greater severity with religious, hypocritical Pharisees, so it is with the church of Sardis that he was the most severe. Originally, a hypocrite was an actor who wore a mask. Ancient actors used masks that served as megaphones and allowed the character they were playing to be recognized immediately. But Jesus removes these masks. He unmasks people and wants reality, not appearance. As Samuel said to David's father,

> People look on the outward appearance, but the LORD looks at the heart. *(1 Samuel 16:7)*

For Ephesus, the letter spoke of the importance of remaining within love; for Smyrna, of the reality of suffering; for Pergamon, of the need for biblical fidelity; and for Thyatira, of the importance of sanctification. Here Jesus exhorted to perseverance and to remaining in the life of the Spirit.

Interestingly, Jesus did not require the faithful residue of the Sardis community to found a new, truly living church, distinct from the one that was dead and from which nothing more could be expected! No, he retained hope, now and always. And his verdict, despite its severity, was also an appeal, as though, with God, all is never lost.

This church that received the severest verdict also was handed the most glorious of promises: *"The one who conquers will be dressed like them in white clothing, and I will never erase his name from the book of life, but will declare his name before my Father and before his angels"* (Revelation 3:5).

One of the church's oldest prayers is this invocation of the Holy Spirit: *"Veni Creator Spiritus,"* "Come, Spirit of Creation." Come into us, place within us the life of Jesus, renew us, vivify us, awaken us. Jesus does not bury dead churches; he revives them by the power of the Holy Spirit. And his faithful members, even within a difficult environment, belong to him forever. How encouraging, what a sense of security!

PHILADELPHIA

Philadelphia was an ancient Lydian city in Asia Minor. It was located along the road connecting Sardis to Colossae, corresponding to the modern Turkish city of Alaşehir. It was built on the threshold of a fertile region, perhaps an allusion to the famous open door of Revelation 3:8.

Situated in the interior, some forty-five kilometers southwest of the city of Sardis, Philadelphia was a border city between different provinces. It was the gateway to Anatolia's central plateau. It was a newer city than the others that played host to the churches of the Apocalypse, and had been founded to spread Greek culture, language, and civilization in these reputedly less advanced lands of Anatolia. It was thus a city that you could say had the purpose of communicating a culture and way of thinking, from its very beginnings.

Philadelphia is the church of reference among the seven cities of the book of Revelation, its name meaning, "he who loves his brother." After the letter to Sardis, written with a severe tone, here is a particularly encouraging letter. Indeed, it doesn't contain a single reproach. It is the only letter, along with the one addressed to Smyrna, that does not require repentance.

Philadelphia, modern-day Alaşehir. Called by the Turks "Allah Sher," or the City of God. Engraving by T. Allom and W. Floyd

Irène and Jean-Marc Thobois in ancient Philadelphia in front of the ruins of the Basilica of Saint John and, in the background, one of the numerous mosques of the city of Alaşehir.

History

The city was founded in 189 BC by King Eumenes II of Pergamon (197–160 BC). Eumenes II named the city in honor of his brother and future successor, Attalus II (159–138 BC), whose loyalty earned him the nickname *Philadelphos,* literally, "he who loves his brother."

Lacking an heir, Attalus III, last king of the Attalid dynasty, bequeathed his kingdom, including Philadelphia, to his allies of the Roman Empire at his death in 133 BC Rome founded the Province of Asia in 129 BC, including Ionia and the Kingdom of Pergamon.

The city was regularly hit by powerful earthquakes and according to historians, was completely destroyed on several occasions. Rebuilt by Tiberius, it was named *Neocæsarea*, literally "New Caesarea." Finally, under Vespasian, it bore the name of Flavia. Through its Christianization, Philadelphia gradually became a part of Byzantine civilization. In the Byzantine age, the city returned to its original name of Philadelphia.

In the twelfth century, the city was surrounded on all sides by the Turkish beylics, precursors of the Ottoman Empire, but it remained Byzantine while all the other cities of Asia Minor surrendered to the enemy. It conducted independent, neutral politics, allying itself with the mercenaries of the Catalan company.

In 1390, the Ottoman sultan Bayazet I, aided by a Christian auxiliary force commanded by the Byzantine emperor Manuel II Palaiologos, conquered it despite a prolonged resistance and gave it its current name of Alaşehir, or "excellent city."

Philadelphia was the last Byzantine stronghold in Anatolia, but it was finally conquered by Tamerlane, who built a wall with the corpses of his prisoners. A fragment of this representative structure is conserved in the library of Lincoln Cathedral in England.

In 1923, under the terms of the Treaty of Lausanne, its Greek inhabitants were expelled to Greece where some of them founded "New Philadelphia," in Athens's northern suburbs.

Philadelphia was also the name given to the American city in Pennsylvania, with a deliberate reference to the Bible. Its founder, William Penn (1644–1718), was the leader of the religious movement of the Society of Friends, the English "Quakers," a dissident religious group in Anglican England. They were interested in going further toward a return to primitive Christianity than other movements of the time, going as far as to reject professional clergy; they accepted the sole authority of the Bible.

The movement had to face persecution from various Quakers being imprisoned and mistreated, both in Great Britain and in the British colonies. In England, William Penn was imprisoned several times, and access to Parliament was prohibited to the Quakers between 1698 to 1833. In Massachusetts Bay Colony, the Quakers were banned upon pain of death. One famous victim was Mary Dyer, who was hung in Boston in 1660; she is considered the only woman executed for reasons of religion in the United States.

Pennsylvania was founded in 1682 by William Penn with a constitution that served as a foundation for that of the United States. This state was designed to be a refuge for all persecuted monotheists. Penn was particularly touched by the pitiable situation of the Anabaptists who, according to Voltaire, were the "fathers" of the Quakers. The latter achieved visibility in this period for their rejection of slavery, which led them individually and collectively to be the precursors to, and later important supporters of, Abolitionism.

Pennsylvania was nicknamed the "Quaker State," though they have long since ceased to be more numerous there than elsewhere.

Pennsylvania quickly became a refuge for all those who were oppressed for their faith. William Penn thus departed for America in 1682 and founded the city of Philadelphia. He hoped the city would serve as a port and a political center. His desire was to make the city of Philadelphia more humane, which he did by rejecting the death penalty for theft and guaranteeing freedom of worship. The city's name reflected this moral ambition.

Commentary on the Biblical Text

To the angel of the church in Philadelphia write the following: This is the solemn pronouncement of the Holy One, the True One, who holds the key of David, who opens doors no one can shut, and shuts doors no one can open: 'I know your deeds. (Look! I have put in front of you an open door that no one can shut.) I know that you have little strength, but you have obeyed my word and have not denied my name. Listen! I am going to make those people from the synagogue of Satan—who say they are Jews yet are not, but are lying—Look, I will make them come and bow down at your feet and acknowledge that I have loved you. Because you have kept my admonition to endure steadfastly, I will also keep you from the hour of testing that is about to come on the whole world to test those who live on the earth. I am coming soon. Hold on to what you have so that no one can take away your crown. The one who conquers I will make a pillar in the temple of my God, and he will never depart from it. I will write on him the name of my God and the name of the city of my God (the new Jerusalem that comes down out of heaven from my God), and my new name as well. The one who has an ear had better hear what the Spirit says to the churches.' *(Revelation 3:7–13)*

Just as the city of Philadelphia had been founded to spread Hellenism in the neighboring regions, so the church is called on to spread the gospel into the farthest regions of the world, and the Lord gives it the key and opens the door for this crucial ministry of the diffusion of the gospel. A difficult mission. How is one to be a witness in a world so often indifferent to the gospel?

The glorified Christ reminds us that the mission, bearing witness, and evangelization are primarily the business of God and not of men. It is important to retain and understand these words: it is primarily God, through his Spirit, who opens doors and hearts. All techniques, all programs, all hierarchies, all piety, all music—however necessary—will never be able to do it. It's God who opens or closes people's hearts. He is the one who holds the keys.

This notion is a piece of good news, stimulating and relaxing at once. It's stimulating because it reminds us that it's God who is the sender. The mission, evangelization, and bearing witness do not depend on our own sentiments, our diplomas, or even our gifts, but on God's call. And it's also a relaxing word because it is he who has placed an open door in front of us: We can thus go through it with confidence that he will act. This door is first the door of salvation that he has opened for us. Jesus said:

I am the door. If anyone enters through me, he will be saved, and will come in and go out, and find pasture. *(John 10:9)*

Nothing is excluded from this grace. If anyone, whoever they are, is in Christ, he is a new creature.

> For this is the way God loved the world: He gave his one and only Son, so that everyone who believes in him will not perish but have eternal life. *(John 3:16)*

What an extraordinary message, so important that it must have also fortified the Christians of Philadelphia, who lived in this city on the border of the heathen world!

The door of salvation is open to all: to the Jews, to the Greeks, and even to the heathen tribes of the Anatolian plateaus, to the oft-disparaged peoples of the nearby region of Phrygia. To all, without exception, salvation is offered to the ends of the earth.

This message is still so relevant! It is given to all those who search for meaning in their lives, to all those who are in pain and suffer, to all those whom life has wounded, to all those whose past is burdensome and are sullied with sin, to all those who feel lost and have given up hope, to all those tormented by remorse or guilt, to all those whom life or society rejects—the door of grace is open. To all without exception.

The promise of the gospel is that there is always hope, that you can always start anew, because the door of grace is open.

But this door is also the door of service. In his first letter to the Corinthians, written from Ephesus, the apostle Paul wrote:

> But I will stay in Ephesus until Pentecost, because a door of great opportunity stands wide open for me, but there are many opponents. *(1 Corinthians 16:9)*

We know that Paul stayed in Ephesus for three years and that his teachings, whose echo certainly reached as far as Philadelphia, had a powerful resonance throughout the province. As the book of Acts tells us:

> ...all who lived in the province of Asia, both Jews and Greeks, heard the word of the LORD. *(Acts 19:10)*

The appeal is all the more important, stimulating, and solemn since this letter also affirms that one day, this door will be closed:

> This is the solemn pronouncement of the Holy One, the True One...who opens doors no one can shut, and shuts doors that no one can open. *(Revelation 3:7)*

If it's God who opens the door, it's also he who shuts it! This truth runs throughout the Bible, as was the case with Noah. After the patriarch had entered the ark, the text says:

Then the Lord shut him in. *(Genesis 7:16)*

And Jesus, picking up on this theme, added:

> For in those days before the flood, people were eating and drinking, marrying and giving in marriage, until the day Noah entered the ark. And they knew nothing until the flood came and took them all away. It will be the same at the coming of the Son of Man. *(Matthew 24:38–39)*

And to truly get his point across, Jesus imagined the parable of the ten virgins in which he specified that when the five wise men had entered, the door was to be closed. And the supplications of the five foolish virgins would be unable to open it!

> But while they had gone to buy it, the bridegroom arrived, and those who were ready went inside with him to the wedding banquet. Then the door was shut. *(Matthew 25:10)*

This, too, is a restful message. It's Christ who opens and closes the doors. Not us. It's he who holds the keys in his hands. The church is called on to witness, to serve, to announce the salvation in Jesus Christ, but the result, the impact, depends neither on our techniques nor our plans, but on the action of God.

As the apostle Paul said, men are called on to sow. But it is God who makes the seed grow. This is why we can be simultaneously daring and in repose, assured and humble. It's also why bearing witness to the gospel must be

Ruins of the Basilica of Saint John in Philadelphia, now called Alaşehir. The final Byzantine enclave in Asia Minor, the city was controlled by the Order of St. John of Jerusalem until 1930.

accompanied by prayers so that the work of God takes place in people's hearts, and first in our own such that our life is a testimony that truly glorifies the Lord.

There was also an interesting custom in Philadelphia: "When a man had served the state well, when he had developed the reputation of being a good magistrate, a public benefactor or a good priest, the city offered him, in one of its temples, a memorial consisting of a pillar on which his name was engraved. Thus Philadelphia honored its children but putting their names on the pillars of its temples so that all those who entered to worship could see them and remember them."[44]

Verse 12 of the letter certainly alludes to this custom. He *"who conquers I will make a pillar in the temple of my God."* We can imagine what such a phrase might have aroused among the Christians of Philadelphia who, prior to their conversion, frequented these temples, reading the inscriptions and being proud of seeing the name of such and such a relative or ancestor engraved on one of the pillars! In the same way, Jesus promised the believers of Philadelphia that they would be columns engraved with the name of God and would never leave it, the text adds. What a promise, what security for these Christian converts of Philadelphia! There, too, this text alludes to the local life of the city.

The region of Philadelphia was frequently struck by powerful earthquakes. Those of the years 17 and 23 were particularly violent. The Roman writer Strabo recounts that between these earthquakes there were frequent aftershocks of varying magnitude and that the inhabitants of Philadelphia, traumatized by these two great quakes, lived in perpetual fear and had the habit of fleeing the city as soon as they felt a tremor. They lived in makeshift huts and, when the shaking ceased, they returned to the city, ready to leave again at the first threat.

But in the kingdom of God, there's no need for fear as no earthquake can unsettle it. God's promises are stable and sure. Verse 12 contains the words *my God* four different times: the temple of my God, the name of my God, the city of my God, the heaven of my God, underlining the solidity, the reliability of God's promises that he has proven, as opposed to the fragility and uncertainty of life in a city besieged by earthquakes.

The letter to the church of Philadelphia is a tribute to loyalty, which is one of the rarest and highest-praised values in all the Bible. Solomon will say:

> Many people profess their loyalty, but a faithful person—who can find?
> (Proverbs 20:6)

Fidelity is very rare quality that is more valuable than material riches. Here is a characteristic that Christ requires of his faithful bride: being a missionary church, a church that testifies its faith and that lives it, a church that truly is the salt of the earth and light of the world around it, and even far from it.

Even if we don't live in a region subjected to seismic risk and we can sleep peacefully in our homes, our land, like others, is subject to tremors: financial, economic, moral, climactic, or other types that profoundly shake and affect our world.

In the West, are we not witnessing a fragility of our way of life, of our security? All people are living in uncertainty, insecurity, precariousness, or anguish, in search of certainties, stability, hope, and meaning in their lives. Is it not to this world of the twenty-first century, characterized by anguish, depression, and anxiety that the reassuring message of the Apocalypse is addressed in a particularly pertinent manner? God's invitation is as follows:

> ...keep seeking the things above, where Christ is, seated at the right hand of God. Keep thinking about things above, not things on the earth ... *(Colossians 3:1–2)*

in order to invest in the eternal kingdom.

> ...accumulate for yourselves treasures in heaven, where moth and rust do not destroy, and thieves do not break in and steal... *(Matthew 6:20)*

in

> ... the city with firm foundations, whose architect and builder is God. *(Hebrews 11:10)*

the heavenly Jerusalem.

LADOICEA

The ancient city of Laodicea (in Latin, *Laodicea ad Lycum*) was the capital of Phrygia in Asia Minor. Its ruins are still visible near the famous thermal baths site of Pamukkale between the villages of Goncali and the Eskihisar (literally, "old citadel"), at six kilometers from the center of Denizli in Turkey.

The city prospered with, in the surrounding area, fertile agriculture and an important sheep-farming industry. Its geographical position between the ports of the Aegean Sea and the continent made Laodicea into a wealthy financial center, controlled by an important Jewish community.

Aerial view of Laodicea over the city basins. This wealthy
city was the capital of Phrygia in Asia Minor.

History

The city was founded in 250 BC by Seleucid Antiochus II, who gave it this name in honor of his wife, Laodice. The city was peopled by Syrians and Jews who had previously been deported to Babylon. The city quickly grew famous for weaving gleaming black wool, used to make carpets and clothing.

Around 546 BC the Persian king Cyrus II conquered Lydia after Croesus's attack against Cappadocia; the region became a Persian satrapy. Around 360 BC, Mausolus, the satrap of Caria, after allying with the revolt of the satrapies of Asia Minor against Persian central power, managed to extend his possessions to Lydia. In 334 BC Anatolia passed under the control of Alexander the Great.

In 188 BC, Laodicea became part of the kingdom of Pergamon, then it fell under Roman authority in 133 BC. Despite lacking water and being struck by several sizable earthquakes, the city was, in Antiquity, extremely prosperous. Tacitus recounts that in 61 AD the city was destroyed by an earthquake.

Due to its strongly Jewish community, it quickly became a Christian diocese. An important council took place there around 364. Laodicea prospered to the detriment of its neighbor Colossae.

In 494, the city was again destroyed by an earthquake, marking the beginning of its decline.

Following the first Turkish breakthrough in 1071, a group of Turkmens settled in its outskirts, which provoked conflicts with the Byzantines and prevented the city's development. In 1077, Laodicea became a Turkish city. In 1097, the region was reconquered by the Byzantines. In 1102, the city was conquered by the sultan, who lost it to the Byzantines once more in 1119.

The Crusaders came to Laodicea for the first time in 1148, and Frederick Barbarossa even passed beneath its wall in 1190.

Around 1335, the traveler Ibn Battuta wrote that the city was also called *Dongouzlou*, or "city of the pigs." He explained that this city produced "unparalleled cotton fabrics" and was inhabited by numerous Greeks. He condemned the lax customs of the populace; even the cadi of the city made his Greek slaves available for prostitution.

The first excavations of the city were conducted by the Canadian archaeologist Jean Des Gagniers (Laval University, Québec) from 1961 to 1963. A fourth-century church was discovered in 2011, whose Christian community is mentioned in the Epistle to the Colossians. Recent discoveries demonstrate that the archaeological site is far vaster that previously imagined, with specialists now estimating that the city contained up to 100,000 inhabitants at its height.

Cenk Eronat and Christophe among the columns of Laodicea.

Commentary on the Biblical Text

> To the angel in the church in Laodicea write the following: This is the solemn pronouncement of the Amen, the faithful and true witness, the originator of God's creation: "I know your deeds, that you are neither cold nor hot. I wish you were either cold or hot! So because you are lukewarm, and neither hot nor cold, I am going to vomit you out of my mouth! Because you say, 'I am rich and have acquired great wealth, and need nothing,' but do not realize that you are wretched, pitiful, poor, blind, and naked, take my advice and buy gold from me refined by fire so you can become rich! Buy from me white clothing so you can be clothed and your shameful nakedness will not be exposed, and buy eye salve to put on your eyes so you can see! All those I love, I rebuke and discipline. So be earnest and repent! Listen! I am standing at the door and knocking! If anyone hears my voice and opens the door I will come into his home and share a meal with him, and he with me. I will grant the one who conquers permission to sit with me on my throne, just as I too conquered and sat down with my Father on his throne. The one who has an ear had better hear what the Spirit says to the churches." *(Revelation 3:14–22)*

With the church of Laodicea, we come to the best-known and most commented upon of the seven letters, as well as the one that most naturally reaches us in our reality. Without endorsing the so-called "historical" interpretation of the Apocalypse—which associates each of the seven churches with a precise historical period in the history of the church—it is nevertheless clear that Laodicea is the church whose characteristics best correspond to the church of our era.

The letter to Laodicea is the last of the seven letters addressed to the churches of Asia. In many ways, its message is stunningly similar to that of the first letter to Ephesus; the similarities found there close the circle, in a way, of this group of letters.

These parallels are even more striking since these two churches are the only ones of the seven to be mentioned elsewhere in the New Testament. They are therefore probably among the oldest, or should we say, the most "historic," and thus those with which the apostles were quite familiar in their own time.

In addition, the diagnosis of one of them bears a strange resemblance to the diagnosis of the other: Ephesus had abandoned its first love, though it is not without value, and Laodicea had grown tepid. Both, therefore, had cooled. Can we deduce that this was the temptation of the old churches? Is this the almost inevitable pattern of the so-called "historical" churches?

When John wrote the Apocalypse, the church of Laodicea had only existed for roughly forty years; it was only a second-generation church. It was most likely founded by Epaphras, companion of the apostle Paul, native of the nearby city of Colossae located roughly ten kilometers east of Laodicea and where Philemon, to whom the apostle writes another letter, is also from.

It is also probable that the evangelist Luke, who was a doctor, sojourned in Laodicea, a city famous for its ancient faculty of medicine. In the greetings that Paul addresses to the nearby church of Colossae, the apostle greets the Christians of Laodicea. It's immediately after these greetings that he added:

> Our dear friend Luke the physician and Demas greet you. *(Colossians 4:14)*

Luke was thus known to the Christians of the church of Laodicea. So it was already a historical church at the time the apostle John wrote Revelation.

This letter is strikingly relevant for our churches of Europe. Even the churches that experienced a revival forty or fifty years ago, indeed, can resemble Laodicea today.

The first lesson this letter gives us is that each generation needs a renewal, an experience and a personal encounter with God. Just because churches were created by apostles as in Laodicea, by reformers such as the Protestant churches, or amid a revival like a significant number of evangelical churches doesn't mean that they are immune to the tepidity of the second and subsequent generations. As a commentator put it: "God makes children, not grandchildren." That is to say that each generation of believers must undergo a personal experience of communion with Christ.

Four main characteristics made Laodicea famous. First, its banks and its wealth. When the great Roman writer Cicero traveled in the east, it was in Laodicea where he cashed in his letters of credit. Also, during the great earthquakes that affected the region in the years 17 and 60, Laodicea, unlike other cities, didn't need any external aid to get back on its feet. The Roman historian Tacitus wrote: "Laodicea rose up from its ruins thanks to its own resources and without our aid." And it was very proud of this as well! This attitude of pride and self-importance was certainly reflected in the church as seen in the reproaches that Jesus directed toward it. When the Lord said: "*you say, I am rich and have acquired great wealth, and need nothing*" (Revelation 3:17), the recipients of the letter certainly understood this economic allusion right away.

Its second characteristic was its school of medicine, whose specialty was ophthalmology. The famous doctor Galen spoke of two pharmaceutical specialties that originated in Laodicea: a balm for the ears and a collyrium for the eyes. Another ancient author (whose works were falsely attributed to Aristotle) spoke of "Phrygian powder" (Laodicea was on the border of Phrygia) for treating the eyes, and which was exported, according to him, throughout the Roman Empire. The limestone from the emetic water (which provokes vomiting) that fed Laodicea was reduced to powder and used as a treatment for the eyes. Still today, you can find significant limestone deposits in the city's ancient water pipes.

Its third characteristic was its textile industry. Laodicea was famous for the black wool produced by a particular type of sheep that were raised there. The Laodiceans invented a method of weaving that prevented them from having to spin the wool first. Clothing made with this wool was highly sought-after because it was particularly soft and comfortable.

The last characteristic of Laodicea concerned its entertainment. Not one, but two theaters have been discovered there, one facing east that would benefit from the morning light and the other facing west to catch the natural light of the evening when the workers came in from the fields. The inhabitants could thus easily attend shows throughout the day; such a scenario was unique in the Roman Empire.

To such a prosperous city that's so proud of itself, what did the glorified

The Ruins of Laodicea and One of Its Two Theaters
Engraving by T. Allom and W. Miller, 1826

Christ say? What was his diagnosis? "*You are poor*" despite your banquets and riches. "*You are blind*" despite your ophthalmology faculty and your eye medications. "*You are nude*" despite your textile industry and luxurious clothing.

What a difference between the perspective of men and the perspective of God! We can ask ourselves if, today, developed countries and the countries of the global "South" are the same in the eyes of men and the eyes of God. Spiritually speaking, where are Africa, Asia, and South America? What is God's diagnosis of our countries that also have famous banks, a renowned pharmaceutical industry, and design refined textiles? Is the letter to Laodicea not stunningly current? Is spiritual tepidity not one of the characteristics of our churches on the European continent?

What does Christ propose to this lukewarm church, living in the delusion of itself and others? The Lord's message is the following: *"Take my advice and buy gold from me refined by fire so you can become rich!"* How not to be struck by the tact and delicateness of these ideas? After the severity of the verdict, we might have expected harsh words, severe exhortations, or even aggressive orders. But the Lord, to whom all power has been given in heaven and on earth, who commands the wind and the water (Luke 8:25), does not constrain; he suggests and he encourages. God never forces us, he respects our freedom, our free will.

We find this same respect of our freedom in this famous phrase at the end of the letter: *"Listen! I am standing at the door and knocking! If anyone hears my voice and opens the door I will come into his home and share a meal with him, and he with me"* (Revelation 3:20). Jesus doesn't knock down doors, he doesn't enter by force; he invites us to open them, and he waits for us to welcome him, freely.

And he advised them to buy. To this city grown wealthy by exporting its luxury products to the four corners of the empire and accustomed to selling, he suggested buying. A reversal of roles. To make sure the Laodiceans really understood, he cited three elements that characterized the city: *". . . take my advice and buy gold from me refined by fire so you can become rich! Buy from me white clothing so you can be clothed and your shameful nakedness will not be exposed, and buy eye salve to put on your eyes so you can see!"* (Revelation 3:18). By speaking of buying, Jesus used the language to which the Laodicean merchants were accustomed. But he specified quite well: I suggest you buy from me the things that have true value.

Jesus is, most of all, he who freely offers the water of life and who invites man to claim his gifts:

> . . . all who are thirsty, come to the water! You who have no money, come! Buy and eat! Come! Buy wine and milk without money and without cost . . . *(Isaiah 55:1–3)*

The theme of the water of life runs through the entire Bible. Isaiah announces:

> Joyfully you will draw water from the springs of deliverance. *(Isaiah 12:3)*

The majority of the gospel of John unfolds in Jerusalem in the framework of "the feast." This is the feast of Sukkot, the "feast of the harvest," one of the most important on the Jewish calendar. Taking place in the fall, it marks the end of the annual agricultural cycle during which thanks is given to divine providence. The culmination of this feast is the ceremony of the libation of water, the *sim'hat beit hashoëva* or "celebration of the well," which is a custom linked to the ceremony of *nissoukh hamayim*, of the "libation of water."

During the seven days of the feast of Sukkot, the people joyfully celebrated the transportation of water from the Spring of Gihon to the Temple. Through this they invoked the divine benediction for rain "in good time," meaning neither too early nor too late so that the obedience of the people allowed the blessing of the annual rains. The high priest would draw water from the Pool of Siloam, in the city of David, whose water was fed by the Spring of Gihon. The joy accompanying this ceremony was well known, as evoked in this verse:

> Joyfully you will draw water from the springs of deliverance. *(Isaiah 12:3)*

Then each night, dozens of thousands of spectators gathered in the outer courtyard of the temple to see the *sim'hat bet hashoëva* (the "rejoicing at the sight of the libation of water"); the more pious among the onlookers danced and sang praises of God. The dancers brought lit torches and were accompanied by the sounds of the harps, lyres, cymbals, and trumpets of the Levites. According to the tract *Soukka*, chapter 5, Mishna 1: "He who has not seen the rejoicing at the sight of the libation of water has never seen rejoicing in his life."

The symbol is used forcefully by Jesus who proclaimed, on the last day of the feast of Sukkot:

> If anyone is thirsty, let him come to me, and let the one who believes in me drink. *(John 7:37)*

The call to receive the water of life from the springs of salvation is one of the final phrases in Revelation. Which only serves to underline its importance:

> And let the one who is thirsty come; let the one who wants it take the water of life free of charge. *(Revelation 22:17)*

The living church is the church that has a personal relationship with Jesus Christ, it's a church that lives off grace, that is in real, profound, and permanent communion with Christ. Jesus reminds this lukewarm church that glories in its human achievements that what matters more than anything else is placing him at the center of its life.

What does the white clothing he suggests buying represent? (It's even more striking, given that the garments produced in Laodicea were of black wool.) Revelation employs this image several times: It is the new clothing received by him whose life has been purified and forgiven by Christ's sacrifice on the cross.

And what does the gold refined by fire represent, if not faith in the work of salvation achieved by Jesus, as the apostle Peter specifies in his first epistle? No, it isn't human works, no matter how generous or prosperous they might be, that edify the church, but only the work issued from the will of God welcomed in faith. John's letter to Laodicea rebukes the community for its material opulence that has caused it to lose sight of the things of the Spirit and the true priorities.

The allusions to the context of the city are even more eloquent in the letter to Laodicea than in the other letters to the churches. This is particularly true for this famous and oft-cited verse: "*So because you are lukewarm, and neither hot nor cold, I am going to vomit you out of my mouth!*" (Revelation 3:16).

The city of Laodicea did not have its own spring, it had to bring its water from the city of Hierapolis (modern Pamukkale), located about six kilometers to the north, via a terracotta aqueduct whose remains are still visible today. This was a thermal water that came out of the ground at a high temperature and reached Laodicea by way of terracotta pipes. A second aqueduct transported cold water from the nearby city of Colossae. The various types of water were mixed in Laodicea, and archaeologists have recently discovered two huge pools, surrounded by columns, in the heart of the city. This water also had emetic qualities, which provoke vomiting. According to the writer Celsus, this lukewarm water was sometimes used medically as an emetic. So when the letter evokes the tepidity of the community and threatens with being vomited out, the Laodiceans surely understood immediately the allusion in these words.

The church had "the outward appearance of religion but will have repudiated its power" and zeal (2 Timothy 3:5). It could also be, by analogy, a general criticism perfectly applicable to our own time. What is the characteristic of our century?

This letter is fundamentally quite poignant. Here is a church that had everything. From its perspective, it wanted for nothing: it had money, plans, activities, probably a sufficient number of leaders. Everything seemed to function, but Christ was outside of the church, excluded, and he knocked at the door in order to reenter and reestablish the relationship: "*Listen! I am standing at the door and knocking! If anyone hears my voice and opens the door I will come into his home and share a meal with him, and he with me*" (Revelation 3:20).

As commentator John Stott puts it, "Perhaps none of the seven letters is more appropriate to the church at the beginning of the twenty-first century than this. It describes vividly the respectable, nominal, rather sentimental, skin-deep religiosity which is so widespread among us today. Our Christianity is flabby and anemic. We appear to have taken a lukewarm bath of religion."[45] Is this not the reason why our Western Christianity is in crisis?

Then how do bring ourselves back to a boil? It isn't a matter of becoming an excited yammerer or trying to move heaven and earth in our activism, but quite simply of responding and opening up for the first time or, perhaps, all over again to Jesus Christ who is knocking on the door of our heart, of letting him in and finding true communion with him, of letting him lead our lives and that of the church, of leaving him the room to establish his will.

The Messiah invites us to let him in not as a passing guest, but as the Lord. He is not simply the Savior of our soul, but the Master of our entire life, in every domain. His love for us has been supreme; he expects us to love him as well with our whole heart, to place him in the center.

Well, what a promise! "*I will grant the one who conquers permission to sit with me on my throne, just as I too conquered and sat down with my Father on his throne*" (Revelation 3:21). Jesus promises to make us a part of his glory. This is the last promise, the most glorious of all those expressed in these letters.

This letter, like all of the Bible, offers us a choice: either to be lukewarm, self-satisfied and moderately committed, to only have

> . . . the outward appearance of religion but [repudiating] its power *(2 Timothy 3:5)*

and leave Christ outside, or to accept Christ as Savior and Master and let him guide our lives entirely and take part in his eternal glory.

The Church of Jesus Christ, in the twenty-first century as in the first century, is called to rediscover its first love as was said to Ephesus, to take on, if necessary, suffering as in Smyrna, to live in faithfulness to the word of God as in Pergamon, to cultivate holiness and vigilance as in Thyatira and Sardis, to promote evangelization and bearing witness as in Philadelphia, and to be entirely of the Lord as is reminded to Laodicea. "*The one who has an ear had better hear*," both collectively and individually.

View of the city of Istanbul
From the Bosphorus Strait

Sultanahmet Mosque, or the "Blue Mosque," in Istanbul
Built Between 1609 and 1616 during the Reign of Sultan Ahmet I

Interior of the Sultanahmet Mosque, known as the "Blue Mosque," in Istanbul.

Interior of the ancient Christian basilica Ayasofya, known as Hagia Sophia, in Istanbul. Built in the 4th century, it became a mosque in the 15th century under Mehmet II and has been a museum since 1934.

The natural site and tourist attraction of Pamukkale, "cotton palace," near Laodicea, composed of springs that form a tuff waterfall.
It has been a UNESCO World Heritage Site since 988, along with nearby Hierapolis.

Archaeological site of Hierapolis and view of the pools of Pamukkale.
In the distance, the ancient city of Laodicea.

CONCLUSION

A nineteenth-century Swiss edition of the book of Revelation.

Revelation, also known as the Apocalypse of John, is the final book of the New Testament. Besides concluding the biblical canon, it also presents a sort of synthesis of the Bible's eschatological prophecies. It is undoubtedly one of Western civilization's most important texts and has enormously influenced the West's vision of the world.

Using symbolic language with a prophetic essence, the book is written in a style similar to that of Ezekiel. It presents a "revelation of Jesus Christ," who unveils to John the divine meaning of his era and how the people of God will soon be freed, during a final, temporary period, leading up to an eternal state in which the original harmony of the Garden of Eden will be restored and the consequences of the fall will be erased.

Over the centuries, the term *Apocalypse* has been distorted, taking on a series of connotations and distortions that have distanced it from its original meaning and which have often evoked massive and violent catastrophes. The term has thus become popular, but for the wrong reasons. For believers, on the other hand, it is good news and an encouragement to await the final divine liberation. As Jesus told his disciples:

> …when these things begin to happen, stand up and raise your heads, because your redemption is drawing near. *(Luke 21:28)*

The skewed perception of the Apocalypse is probably linked to a difficulty in understanding a heavily symbolic, perplexing literary genre that has no equivalent in contemporary literature.

The book announces that humanity will be placed into two categories by Christ during the Last Judgment: the vanquished and the victors. There are both apostates and conquerors in each of the seven churches of

The Heavenly Jerusalem
Engraving by Gustave Doré

the beginning chapters, even in Laodicea's, which has fallen furthest. The text encourages loyalty, perseverance, and repentance to achieve this victory, and the righteous are those who will persevere until the end to be saved. The Apocalypse is a call to remain firm in the face of anything and everything because the righteous will reap the benefits of this liberation.

Professor Pierre Prigent has affirmed: "In recent years, newly discovered ancient Jewish writings have projected a new light on the Apocalypse: the woes of the faithful are seen as the visible, superficial part of a story that is in fact glorious; God's final intervention has begun and present history reveals the signs of it to those able to see. The Apocalypse is the Christian transposition of this message: Since the coming of Christ, the world has entered its final age, Satan is defeated, and the victory of God and his people is certain.

"It's a message that is cosmic in scope, but the imaginary is placed at the service of a gospel that needs to be experienced presently on earth. The Christians of Asia Minor of the first century risked persecution and death if they refused to worship the emperor. So the Apocalypse tells them that the totalitarianism of power is victorious in appearance only. Christ is the true conqueror and Christians can take part in this victory starting immediately and for all eternity. Far from a collection of menacing prophecies about the end of the world, Revelation is a message of life that calls for constant vigilance to better serve the Lord of the universe."

The genre of apocalyptic literature reached its height in the Old Testament with the book of Daniel. Revelation amounts to an updating of previous biblical prophecies, particularly those of Daniel, a gradual unveiling of the revelations begun in this "Jewish Apocalypse."

The book of Isaiah is also particularly present in between the lines of the text of John's Apocalypse.

Reading Revelation through the filter of the Hebrew cultural context offers new keys to understanding a number of symbols. What's more, a consideration of the historical and political contexts of the era in which it was written—with a young, dissident Jewish sect subjected to persecution by the all-powerful Roman Empire—suggests the author used masked language to speak to readers of his time, but with an eschatological scope relevant to readers of the end times.

Revelation can thus be considered as the direct heritage of Jewish beliefs, reaching as far back as the first chapter of Genesis, in which the rabbis already glimpsed prophecies concerning the end times.

Typically Jewish themes structure the text: a new, final exodus; the opposition of Babylon and Jerusalem; the unholy one (the Antichrist); the war of Gog and Magog; the coming of the Messiah; and *Tikkun Olam*, the repairing of the broken world.

And of course, there's no escaping the conclusion that the book's principal character, Jesus Christ, was Jewish. Over the centuries, the Western pagan-Christian church repeatedly posed this question to the Jews: "Why do you not believe that Jesus is the Messiah?"

According to Emmanuelle Main, professor at the Hebrew University of Jerusalem, this question may result from the fact that Christians need to be reassured of Jesus's messianism. In her view, superficial Christianity feels an underlying discomfort with the Jewish people, which is probably at the origins of anti-Semitism. Westerners may be expecting a confirmation of their own beliefs.

The divorce between Judaism and Christianity would be difficult on both sides, and the states, too, had their responsibilities (the Spanish Inquisition, the wars of religion, the Crusades, forced conversions). According to the Dominican theologian Dominique Cerbelaud, "There is a dispute over heritage." The Christians who came later laid a forceful claim to the biblical spiritual heritage. The tragedy of this history was the in the process of officializing Christianity (under Theodosius in the fourth century), during which other beliefs were suppressed.

A shift occurs, from anti-Judaism to anti-Semitism and, more recently, to modern anti-Zionism. The affirmation of Jewish identity concluded with a marginalization of Christianity's Jewish roots; there was an integration of the influence of Greek thought but a genuine forgetting in the West of this Jewish heritage.

Cerbelaud says,

"There's a paradox: the founder was Jewish, and the followers, over the centuries, will be, above all else, non-Jews. I belong to a religion whose founder did not belong to it. There will be a recurring attempt to de-Judaize Jesus and the texts and figures of the New Testament, whose Jewish aspects are erased in view of maintaining only those traits deemed useful by the Christian tradition."

The great rediscovery of our time is the quite shocking realization of Jesus's Judaism. Shocking for the Jews as well, who have found in him a Pharisee master, a rabbi. Jesus had been largely concealed as far as the Jews were concerned, and this rediscovery is not without consequences for them. We are in a new context in the bimillenarian history of Christianity: a revolution, not in the banal sense, but in the almost astronomical sense of a return to the point of departure.

In the second part of this book, our study takes a closer look at the letters written to the seven diocesan communities whose episcopal seats were located in Asia Minor, corresponding with modern Turkey.

Dictated by the resurrected Christ to the apostle John, their aim is to convey a message of encouragement, to exhort these communities to repent.

Christ spoke of multiple forms of attacks organized by the enemy, Satan, in the attempt to destroy them. These aggressions are dissimulated in a three-pronged strategy described in Revelation as:

- False doctrines symbolized by the doctrine of Balaam, a danger of seduction from without.
- Moral corruption symbolized by the seduction of Jezebel, a danger of seduction from within.
- Persecution manifested by the brutality of the Roman Empire, a danger of opposition from without.

The dangers working to destroy the church thus consist of two types: seduction and persecution.

The approach adopted in our study is that the message of the seven letters is addressed to the universal church of all times and all places. Today, in fact, the satanic strategy of destruction remains fundamentally unchanged and effective, though the means and forms employed have adapted to the different time periods and evolved over time with varying appearances, tools, and techniques. This is the strength of a system that maintains its power through its ability to blend in and conceal itself, cunningly blending the chaff with the wheat to corrupt the field of the world, because the "father of lies" "comes only to steal and kill and destroy."

Detecting this multifaceted strategy is the key to fighting it with the spiritual weapons described in Ephesians 6 and to engaging in combat per the example of the Master, who declared:

> I saw Satan fall like lightning from heaven. Look, I have given you authority to tread on snakes and scorpions and on the full force of the enemy, and nothing will hurt you. Nevertheless, do not rejoice that the spirit submits to you, but rejoice that your names stand written in heaven. *(Luke 10:18–20)*

The expression of Jesus that constantly recurs to the seven churches is, "I know you," a reminder that he knows the secrets of thoughts, words, actions, habits, intentions, and the destiny of all. Thus God is "he who comes" in the future, but also he who offers to come in our present, this very day. Eternity begins today if we invite God into our lives.

It's important to remember that, according to Jesus himself, no one knows the hour of the end times.

> But as for that day and hour no one knows it—not even the angels in heaven—except the Father alone. *(Matthew 24:36)*

To this end, Christ exhorted:

> Therefore stay alert, because you do not know the day or the hour. *(Matthew 25:13)*

Yet he also exhorted us to identify the time in which we now live:

> Learn this parable from the fig tree: Whenever its branch becomes tender and puts out its leaves, you know that summer is near. *(Mark 13:28)*

There are, in fact, multiple, distinctive signs that make our time a propitious period for the fulfillment of the Apocalypse. Several conditions will trigger the last events:

> First the Gospel must be preached to all nations. *(Mark 13:10)*

Apostasy must take root, and the time of the nations, during which Jerusalem was trampled on, must come to an end. Today all these conditions are on the verge of being brought together.

Jesus also announced natural cataclysms:

> There will be great earthquakes, and famines and plagues in various places, and there will be terrifying sights and great signs from heaven. *(Luke 21:11)*

> And there will be signs in the sun and moon and stars, and on the earth nations will be in distress, anxious over the roaring of the sea and the surging waves. *(Luke 21:25)*

It's clear that man has never been as afraid of natural and climactic dangers as in the twenty-first century; whether you believe in global warming, the disturbance of the seasons, throughout the world, is near incontestable—whether temporary or definitive, it's impossible to know.

According to the German philosopher Hegel, "Humanity is always advancing but always by its negativity." Eschatology is effectively certain about one aspect that is quite present in Revelation: the completion of humanity's initial plan to build Babylon and the great global village, allowing men to be united in a world of peace, forming a single people with a single language in the end times. In their ambition to create a human paradise, the Bible implies that men will, in fact, realize a hell on earth, a global totalitarian dictatorship dominated by a second Nimrod, a sort of Pharoah who will demand to be worshipped and will persecute the Church of Jesus Christ and Israel, with these two entities forming a sort of couple.

It's interesting to note that, in the twenty-first century, the age of nations is fading away to the advantage of a small number of geopolitical blocs, held together by treaties and governing under the aegis of transnational authorities.

In a time of globalization, Donald Trump expressed his rejection of "globalism" during his speech before the UN in September 2018. Globalism, a theory much talked about on the web, has some affinities with the "new world order." This expression, used in certain conspiracy-theorist and far-right circles that denounce "the forces that aim to establish a globalist ideology," designates namely Freemasonry and the Trilateral Commission.

Marine Le Pen, for example, wrote in her 2012 book *Pour que vive la France*, "Globalism is an actual ideology, whose main characteristic is its denial of the usefulness of nations, of their adaptation to the 'post-modern' world, and which aims to fashion a new man, a sort of *homo mondialisus*, detached from the land, without any other identity than that of global consumer, relabeled 'citizen of the world' to mask the profoundly mercantile character of this goal. Globalism is an alliance of consumerism and materialism to remove Man from History."[46]

The Bible affirms that our world is a "world of darkness" because it is under the spiritual domination of Satan, "the prince of this world." And authority was indeed granted to him after the fall of Adam and Eve, and Jesus does not contest his power.

> Then the devil led him up to a high place and showed him in a flash all the kingdoms of the world. And he said to him, To you I will grant this whole realm – and the glory that goes along with it, for it has been relinquished to me, and I can give it to anyone I wish. So then, if you will worship me, all this will be yours. *(Luke 4:5–7)*

The second Nimrod, the Antichrist, is he who humbles himself before Satan and will ally with him to obtain the power and glory of the nations to dominate over them on the devil's behalf. Technological tools will be used by the Antichrist to dominate the world, as this famous verse promises:

> Thus no one was allowed to buy or sell things unless he bore the mark of the beast—that is, his name or his number. *(Revelation 13:17)*

Nor is it difficult to see an allusion to television or video surveillance in this passage:

> The second beast was empowered to give life to the image of the first beast so that it could speak, and could cause all those who did not worship the image of the beast to be killed. *(Revelation 13:15)*

Top-secret data from the Snowden affair show that, in June 2012, the "network coverage" of the NSA's system for mass surveillance of the population encompassed nearly every country on every continent.

Never in the history of humanity have technological means permitted such a systematic, coordinated, and intrusive surveillance of people's lives, constituting a notable violation of individual freedoms, thanks to the internet, woven together like a finely meshed cloth. Everyone who uses modern means of communication is creating a digital profile, a virtual identity that follows us everywhere in the world and whose digital footprints are inaccessible and inerasable.

These data represent a threat of unimaginable pressure and surveillance. China, for example, has introduced a massive population control system through facial recognition and video surveillance coupled with artificial intelligence, as documented by the article "China has already begun implementing its citizen evaluation system scheduled for 2020," published in *Le Figaro* on December 27, 2017.

> *Launched in 2014, the project aims to reward good behavior and punish the bad through a points system. Implementation has already commenced: starting on May 1, 2018, Chinese citizens with a bad "social rating" will be denied purchase of train or airplane tickets for a period of up to a year, Beijing announced last Friday. The question of surveillance is a central topic in China. Extra points for purchasing Chinese products, good performance at work, or posting an article boasting about the merits of the national economy on social media; points taken away for dissenting political opinions, suspicious online searches, or jaywalking. Since 2014 China has been developing a citizen evaluation system, scheduled to be implemented in 2020.*
>
> *The country is currently installing the world's most sophisticated video surveillance system. Several hundred million cameras equipped with artificial intelligence are already in place, and according to the Belgian website www.lesoir.be (https://geeko.lesoir.be/ 2019/05/20/la-chine-va-installer-276-milliards-de-cameras-de-surveillance/) a total of close to 2.76 billion cameras are scheduled for installation in China by 2022. Growing rapidly, the facial recognition market surpassed one billion yens (€128 million) in 2016 and should grow to five times that by 2021, according to a study by the firm Analysys. In mid-December, the association Human Rights Watch accused the Chinese authorities of recording the biometric data of the entire population of Xinjiang.[47]*

The article "In China, the great leap forward of facial recognition," written by Elsa Trujillo and published on December 11, 2017, in *Le Figaro*, evokes a similar theme: "*One fall morning, a BBC journalist was walking on the streets of Guiyang, a city in the province of Ghizhou, in China. To test out the city's surveillance system, he obtains the right to conduct an experiment: he asks the local police to take a picture of his face, register it as belonging to a 'suspect' individual, and follow his movements around the city, thanks to the numerous 'smart' cameras installed along its streets. These devices, powered by artificial intelligence, are capable of associating an identity with a known face almost instantaneously. It takes them all of seven minutes to identify the journalist, trigger the alarm, and send out five policemen after him.*"[48]

What would a Stalin or a Hitler do with such a tool? Humanity has never been in so much danger of the rise of totalitarianism as it is today; the technology available would permit mass surveillance and repression at never-before-seen levels.

The dystopia (a utopia that turns into a nightmare) of George Orwell's *1984*—which describes a world after a nuclear war in which a totalitarian regime has been established, quite similar both to Stalinism and certain elements of Nazism, and in which freedom of expression no longer exists, all thought is closely monitored, and huge signs are posted on the streets reminding everyone that "Big Brother Is Watching You"—is not so distant from a possible evolution of the twenty-first century.

The Bible announces a great global crisis. It's quite possible that major disorders such as wars, pandemics, and climate catastrophes lead to globalized economic and political crises, and that humanity calls on an authoritarian strongman (or strongmen) to reestablish order in the chaos, similar to what occurred in 1930s Germany.

The book of Revelation, in fact, announces the worst period of totalitarianism and persecution in the history of humanity. The text even mentions a star that spreads death:

> (Now the name of the star is Wormwood.) So a third of the waters became wormwood, and many people died from these waters because they were poisoned. *(Revelation 8:11)*

This is reminiscent of a nuclear strike that makes the water bitter and unclean; what's more, the Russian word for "wormwood" is *tchernobyl*. A passage in Zechariah describes effects eerily similar to those of an atomic weapon:

> But this will be the nature of the plague with which the LORD will strike all the nations that have fought against Jerusalem: Their flesh will decay while they stand on their feet, their eyes will rot away in their sockets, and their tongues will dissolve in their mouths. *(Zechariah 14:12)*

The Babylon of Genesis was built with identical brick, allowing the endless construction of monuments to the glory of man, just as our world has reduced man to the state of data, numbers, and digital standardization produces dehumanization. Modern man has decided to build the great global village and has constructed a technological world, an artificial paradise.

Today our technical society has largely turned away from the hope of salvation in Christ and the simple faith of the gospel, attempting to save itself by its own technical means. Like:

> ...Tubal-Cain, who heated metal and shaped all kinds of tools made of bronze and iron. *(Genesis 4:22)*

modern man, descended from the line of Cain the cursed and so proud of his technology, believes he has robbed God of knowledge and power.

Transhumanism relies on the progress of medicine, genetics, computer science, robotics, and everything connected to the sciences and artificial intelligence. Its transcendentalism sits in a current of thought dating back to antiquity: the quest for immortality, the pursuit of the Fountain of Youth and the Elixir of Long Life, just as efforts to prevent aging and death represent its most profound expression.

The quest for eternity and immortality through science is exemplified in the death of Lenin, who was embalmed and displayed in a mausoleum on the Red Square in Moscow, seemingly waiting for science to be able to resurrect the venerated totalitarian dictator and founder of the USSR to reign over his people forever.

Faced with the promises of the Apocalypse, there are only two possible ways of positioning ourselves. Either trying to change history or trying to escape it. Well, anyone who lacks the courage to create their own history runs the risk of being controlled by it.

We must remember that, unlike prophecies that are revocable, the announcements of Revelation are irrevocable and definitive. Why try to change history, then, if the latter is already written? In truth, it is a matter of grasping the urgency and seriousness of this revelation and investing all possible resources in saving ourselves and working for the salvation of the men of this generation, in all places; it's less about dodging the disasters of this age than positioning ourselves for the Last Judgment, avoiding the awful second death, and preparing our definitive, eternal state of perdition or salvation. The Apocalypse, therefore, is excellent news, essentially telling us:

> Oh, that today you would listen as he speaks! Do not harden your hearts... *(Hebrews 3:15)*

> ... I take no pleasure in the death of the wicked, but prefer that the wicked change his behavior and live. Turn back, turn back from your evil deeds! Why should you die ...? *(Ezekiel 33:11)*

For those able to interpret it, there could be no greater message of hope for humanity than the one offered by Revelation, for it is the promise of the divine deliverance in which God reemerges to intervene in human history, correct it, and transfigure it.

Reducing this plan of redemption to the salvation of man leads to a quite limited, stunted eschatological vision. The message of Revelation goes much further.

The text announces that the Creator of the world will recreate a completely new universe, in which death, sin, and evil shall be unknown. It is a doxology and a major cosmic upheaval, aiming to manifest the fullness of God's glory!

He will truly make "all things new." It is the promise of paradise regained, of Eden restored to Adam and Eve, of the definitive reconciliation between creatures, of a new-found harmony between creation and the Creator.

The book's final image is one of marriage: the Bible begins, in fact, with a marriage in Eden, and concludes with a marriage at the end of the book of Revelation, the one between the Messiah and his bride, the faithful with whom he joins in an alliance whose joy will know no end, will, literally, be eternal. It promises that long-shattered perfection of the original world will be restored forever and invites everyone to be a part of this heavenly kingdom.

IMAGES

The Creation of Light 18

Adam Contemplating the Sleeping Eve 21

Satan in the Garden of Eden 22

The Fall of the Angels 25

Adam and Eve Cast Out of Eden 27

God Strikes Down the Leviathan 30

Ezekiel Prophesying 35

Daniel in Babylon 43

Daniel in the Lions' Den 45

Daniel Interpreting the Inscription on the Wall of the Banquet Hall 50

Daniel's Vision of the Four Empires 54

Jesus Cures a Mute 62

The Tower of Babel 65

Europe: Many Tongues, One Voice 66

Soviet Plan for the Palace of the Soviets in Moscow 67

The Tower of Babel 67

The Beginning of the Reconstruction of the Temple in Jerusalem 73

The Triumph of Christianity over Paganism 79

The Death of Dirce. 81

Imperium Romanum 88

The UPM, Union for the Mediterranean, founded in 2008 in Paris 89

Sultan Mehmed II Entering Constantinople on May 29, 1453. 92

The Baptism of Christ 95

The 24 Thrones of the Elders and 4 Creatures Performing Acts of Grace. 100

Pharoah's Army Engulfed 104

Vision of the Four Chariots of Zechariah (Ch. 6) 108

The Ascension. 111

Judah Maccabee 118

The Vision of the Valley of Dry Bones 125

The Rapture of the Church. 130

"Yes We Scan" 139

The Fall of Babylon. 144

The Last Judgment 147

The Vision of the Kingdom 153

Waiting for the flight to Greece, Zurich Airport 160

Aerial view of Lake Geneva in Swiss Romandie, Between Puidoux
    and Mont Pelerin 160

Reading Revelation, Above the port of Skala on Patmos. 162

Sunset over one of Patmos's numerous bays 162

Chapels of the island of Patmos 162

Saint John on Patmos. 163

Recess in the wall of the Cave of the Apocalypse on Patmos. 164

City of Chora: the fortified monastery of Saint John the Theologian on Patmos
    in Greece. 165

Manuscript from the library of the monastery of Saint John the Theologian
    on the island of Patmos. 165

Cross inside the chapel of the monastery of Saint John the Theologian in Chora,
    on the island of Patmos. 166

Interior of the chapel of the monastery of Saint John the Theologian in Chora,
    on the island of Patmos. 166

Aeriel view of Kusadasi, Turkey, usual departure port for the Dodecanese
    archipelago and the island of Patmos. 166

Interview with the doyen of the monastery of Saint John the Theologian
    on the island of Patmos. 167

Interview with American Professor Mark Wilson on Patmos 167

Paul in Ephesus 172

View of the agora in the city of Ephesus, where Paul worked 174

The building housed no less than 12,000 scrolls, conserved
    in wooden cupboards set into the walls. 174

Facade of the Library of Celsus in Ephesus. 174

View of the ruins of the city of Ephesus with Basilica of St. John in Selçuk 180

The agora of Smyrna, known as the "Roman agora" 183

The Castle of Smyrna 183

Jean-Marc Thobois with guide Cenk Eronat and Christophe at the
agora of Smyrna 184

Meditation and reading in front of the structures that once housed the
Altar of Zeus in Pergamon. 193

The Asclepeion of Pergamon, dedicated to the god Asclepios 194

Aerial view of the majestic acropolis of Pergamon. 195

Christophe contemplating the countryside of the Bergama region from
the acropolis of Pergamon. 195

Sunset from below the theater of Pergamon 195

Pergamon's Red Basilica, also called the "temple of the Egyptian gods". 197

Pedestal of the altar of Zeus in Pergamon, the presumed location of
the throne of Satan (Revelation 2:13) 199

The Acropolis of Pergamon. 203

The Nazi tribune of the Zeppelinfeld in Nuremberg, inspired by
the Altar of Zeus from Pergamon 206

Interview with archaeologist Akın Ersoy among the ruins of ancient
Thyatira, today's Akhisar, in Turkey. 209

The Death of Jezebel. 211

The City of Thyatira and Modern Akhisar 212

Citadel of Sardis, built by King Meles 217

Sardis with the Palace of Croesus, the church of Panagia, the theater,
the acropolis, the Pactolus River, and Mount Tmolos 218

The Temple of Artemis in Sardis with, in the background, the ruins
of the citadel. 219

Among the ruins of the Temple of Artemis in Sardis. 219

Philadelphia, modern-day Alaşehir. 227

Irène and Jean-Marc Thobois in Philadelphia in front of the ruins
    of the Basilica of Saint John and, in the background, one of
    the numerous mosques of the city of Alaşehir.. 228

Ruins of the Basilica of Saint John in Philadelphia, now called Alaşehir 232

Aerial view of Laodicea over the city basins. 235

Cenk Eronat and Christophe among the columns of Laodicea 236

The Ruins of Laodicea and One of Its Two Theaters 239

View of the city of Istanbul. 244

Sultanahmet Mosque, or the "Blue Mosque," in Istanbul 244

Interior of Sultanahmet Mosque, known as the "Blue Mosque," in Istanbul 244

Interior of the ancient Christian basilica Ayasofya, known as Hagia Sophia,
    in Istanbul. 245

The natural site and tourist attraction of Pamukkale, "cotton palace,"
    near Laodicea, composed of springs that form a tuff waterfall 245

Archaeological site of Hierapolis and view of the pools of Pamukkale. 245

A nineteenth-century Swiss edition of the book of Revelation. 247

The Heavenly Jerusalem 247

BIBLIOGRAPHY

PART ONE:
GENERAL COMMENTARY ON THE END TIMES

Lectures by Jean-Marc Thobois

Between Heaven and Earth

The Two Apocalypses

Messiah Conquering the Serpent

Lum. Rev. 1.8 - Revelation and Prophecies of Daniel

Lum. Rev. 2.8 - The Letters to the Seven Churches of Revelation

Lum. Rev. 3.8 - Celestial Worship in Revelation

Lum. Rev 4.8 - Second Exodus

Lum. Ap. 5.8 - Confrontation with the Powers of Darkness

Lum. Rev. 6.8 - The Rapture of the Church

Lum. Ap. 7.8 - The Millennium

Lum. Rev. 8.8 - The Eternal State

The Four Exiles of Israel

Proph. Zach. 5.5 - The Definitive Restoration of the Kingdom of God

Prophecies of Daniel 1.4 - The Great Statue

Prophecies of Daniel 2.4 - The Four Empires

Prophecies of Daniel 3.4 - The Four Animals

Prophecies of Daniel 4.4 - Abomination and Desolation

The time of the nations - Luke 21

History of two cities - Babylon and Jerusalem

Gog's war - Prophecies for Our Time

Confrontation with the Powers of Darkness

Celestial Worship in Revelation

Have We Reached the Point of No Return - 3.7

Have We Reached the Point of No Return - 5.7

The Unveiling of the Mystery of the Kingdom

The Mysteries of the Two Beasts

From the Millennium to the New Jerusalem

The Return of Jesus in All the Scriptures

The Messianic Birth

Evidence of Borrowing

Pierre Prigent, *Les secrets de l'Apocalypse. Mystique, ésotérisme et apocalypse*, (Éditions du Cerf, Paris, 2002).

The Sign of the End of Time

Flavius Josephus, *The Jewish War*, (Penguin Classics, 1984).

The Great Apostasy

B. J. Oropeza, Ph.D. Professor, Department of Biblical and Religious Studies.

The Antichrist

Alexandre Adler, *Le nouveau rapport de la CIA – Comment sera le monde demain*, preface for éditions (Robert Laffont, 2005).

The Mystery of the Two Beasts

Odon Vallet, *Une autre histoire des religions. Le sacre des pouvoirs* (tome 6), (Paris, Gallimard, 2000),58.

Al-Boukhari, *Les traditions islamiques*, Paris, Éditions Maisonneuse, tome 4, title 86, ch. XVII, 1903, 382-383.

Bat Ye'or, Eurabia. L'axe euro-arabe, Jean-Cyrille Godefroy Éditions.

From Big Data to Big Brother

"National Security Agency," https://fr.wikipedia.org/wiki/National_Security_Agency

"PRISM (Programme de Surveillance)," https://fr.wikipedia.org/wiki/PRISM_(programme_de_surveillance)

"Edward Snowden," https://fr.wikipedia.org/wiki/Edward_Snowden

PART TWO: COMMENTARY ON PATMOS AND THE SEVEN CHURCHES OF REVELATION

Philippe Decorvet, *Reprocher pour rapprocher. L'encouragement du Christ aux sept Églises de l'Apocalypse*, (Éditions Emmaüs, diffuse par Excelsis, 2014).

John Stott, *What Christ Thinks of the Church: Preaching from Revelation 1 to 3*, (Langham Partnership International, 2019).

Additional Books and Texts

Mark Wilson, "Geography of the Island of Patmos," *Lexham Geographic Commentary: on Acts through Revelation* (Lexham Press, 2019), chapter 47.

David A. deSilva, "The Social and Geographical World of Ephesus," *Lexham Geographic Commentary: on Acts through Revelation* (Lexham Press, 2019), chapter 41.

Mark Wilson, "The Social and Geographical World of Philadelphia," *Lexham Geographic Commentary: on Acts through Revelation* (Lexham Press, 2019), chapter 52.

Mark Wilson, "The Social and Geographical World of Thyatira," *Lexham Geographic Commentary: on Acts through Revelation* (Lexham Press, 2019), chapter 50.

Cyndi Parker, "The Social and Geographical World of Laodicea," *Lexham Geographic Commentary: on Acts through Revelation* (Lexham Press, 2019), chapter 53.

Cyndi Parker, "The Social and Geographical World of Pergamum," *Lexham Geographic Commentary: on Acts through Revelation* (Lexham Press, 2019), chapter 49.

David A. deSilva, "The Social and Geographical World of Sardis," *Lexham Geographic Commentary: on Acts through Revelation* (Lexham Press, 2019), chapter 51.

David A. deSilva, "The Social and Geographical World of Smyrna," *Lexham Geographic Commentary: on Acts through Revelation* (Lexham Press, 2019), chapter 48.

Burak Yolaçan, Gözde Şakar, Akın Ersoy, *Smyrna/İzmir Kazı ve Araştırmaları II: Smyrna/Izmir Excavation and Research II*, Antik Smyrna kazısı yayın çalışmaları, II.

Mark Wilson, "Localizing Smyrna in the Apocalypse: John's Visions of the 'First of Asia'." In *Smyrna/Izmir Excavation and Research II*, edited by Akin Ersoy et al. (Istanbul: Ege, 2017).

NOTES

1 Les éditions du Cerf, 24 rue des Tanneries, 75013, Paris.

2 *Antiquities of the Jews*, book I 114–115, chapter IV 2–3.

3 François Blanchetière, *Enquête sur les racines juives du mouvement chrétien (30–135), (éd. Du Cerf, Paris, 2001), 100.*

4 La Tour de Babel (Brueghel), https://fr.wikipedia.org/wiki/La_Tour_de_Babel_(Brueghel).

5 "Apostasy in Christianity," https://en.wikipedia.org/wiki/Apostasy_in_Christianity.

6 Thomas Aquinas, *Summa Theologica* (Benziger Bros. edition, 1947).

7 "Apostasy in Christianity," https://en.wikipedia.org/wiki/Apostasy_in_Christianity.

8 B. J. Oropeza, *Paul and Apostasy (*Mohr Siebeck, 2007), 2–3.

9 David Bercot, *Will the Real Heretics Please Stand Up: A New Look at Today's Evangelical Church in the Light of Early Christianity (*Scroll Publishing Company, 1999), 65.

10 B. J. Oropeza, *Paul and Apostasy (*Mohr Siebeck, 2007), 13.

11 *The Race Set Before Us: A Biblical Theology of Perseverance and Assurance, (*Downers Grove, InterVarsity Press, 2001), 10, note 2.

12 Cardinal Robert Sarah, *The Day is Now Far Spent* (Ignatius Press, 2019).

13 Robert Laffont, *Le nouveau rapport de la CIA* (Robert Laffont, 2009).

14 Paul Valery, *Disillusionment*, 1919.

15 Klaus Schwab and Thierry Malleret, *COVID-19: The Great Reset* (Agentur Schweiz, 2020).

16 Klaus Schwab and Thierry Malleret.

17 Michel Salomon, *L'avenir de la vie* French edition (Seghers, 1981).

18 Bat Ye'or, *Eurabia: The Euro-Arab Axis,* American first edition (Fairleigh Dickinson University Press, 2005).

19 Bat Ye'or, *Eurabia: The Euro-Arab Axis.*

20 Bat Ye'or, *Eurabia: The Euro-Arab Axis.*

21 Bat Ye'or, *Eurabia: The Euro-Arab Axis.*

22 "Index Mondial de Persecution des Chretiens 2019," *Portes Ouvertes*, https://www.portesouvertes.fr/persecution-des-chretiens.

23 Bat Ye'or, *The Dhimmi* (Rutherford: Fairleigh Dickinson University Press, 1985).

24 Ayatollah Khomeini, *Principes politiques, sociaux et religieux,* Paris (Éditions Libres-Hallier, 1979), 22.

25 Surat 5 (112th): 32–33.

26 Odon Vallet, *Une autre histoire des religions. Le sacre des pouvoirs* (tome 6), (Paris, Gallimard, 2000), 58.

27 Al-Boukhari, *Les traditions islamiques,* Paris, Éd. Maisonneuse, tome 4, titre 86, chap. XVII, 1903, 382–383.

28 Fanny Jane Crosby (lyrics) and George Coles Stebbins (music), "Some Day the Silver Cord Will Break," 1891.

29 Glenn Greenwald, Ewen MacAskill, and Laura Poitras, "Edward Snowden: the Whistleblower behind the NSA Surveillance Revelations," *The Guardian,* June 11, 2013, https://www.theguardian.com/world/2013/jun/09/edward-snowden-nsa-whistleblower-surveillance.

30 Timothy B. Lee, "Everything You Need to Know about the NSA's Phone Records Scandal," *The Washington Post,* June 6, 2013, https://www.washingtonpost.com/news/wonk/wp/2013/06/06/everything-you-need-to-know-about-the-nsa-scandal/.

31 Ryan Gallagher, "Operation Auroragold: How the NSA Hacks Cellphone Networks Worldwide," *The Intercept,* December 4, 2014, https://theintercept.com/2014/12/04/nsa-auroragold-hack-cellphones/.

32 Charles C. Luther, "Must I Go, and Empty-Handed?" 1877.

33 Pierre Julien, "Saint Jean et l'épreuve de la coupe empoisonnée au cloître de Notre-Dame-en-Vaux," *Revue d'Histoire de la Pharmacie,* 68, no. 247, 1980, 255–257.

34 Jean-Christian Petitfils, *Jésus,* éd. Fayard, December 2011, 534.

35 *Jean-Christian Petitfils, Jésus, éd.* Fayard, 526.

36 Irenaeus of Lyon, *Against Heresies,* III, 1, 2.

37 "The Maryrdom of Polycarp: Who would have thought the old man had so much courage?" The Word Among Us, https://wau.org/resources/article/the_martyrdom_of_polycarp_1/.

38 "The Maryrdom of Polycarp: Who would have thought the old man had so much courage?" The Word Among Us.

39 Éd. Centurion, Paris, 1988, 42–49.

40 Éditions du Cerf, Paris 2010, Series "Sagesses chrétiennes."

41 J.-P. Charpier, *Comprendre l'Apocalypse,* 100.

42 Paris, Grancher, 1991.

43 Dietrich Bonhoeffer, *The Cost of Discipleship (New York: Macmillan, 1966).*

44 A. Kuen, *Introduction* à *l'Apocalypse,* 58.

45 John Stott, *What Christ Thinks of the Church: Preaching from Revelation 1 to 3* (Langham Partnership International, 2019).

46 Marine Le Pen, *Pour Que Vive La France,* French edition (Grancher, 2012).

47 Elsa Trujillo, "La Chine commence déjà à mettre en place son système de notation des citoyens prévu pour 2020," Le Figaro, December 27, 2017, https://www.

lefigaro.fr/secteur/high-tech/2017/12/27/32001-20171227ARTFIG00197-la-chine-met-en-place-un-systeme-de-notation-de-ses-citoyens-pour-2020.php.

48 Elsa Trujillo, "En Chine, le grand bond en avant de la reconnaissance faciale," Le Figaro, December 11, 2017, https://www.lefigaro.fr/secteur/high-tech/2017/12/11/32001-20171211ARTFIG00240-en-chine-le-grand-bond-en-avant-de-la-reconnaissance-faciale.php.